CW00968341

Whitchurch Divided

Conforming and nonconforming in a Shropshire parish 1526 – 1720

Paul Anderton

Published
by
Whitchurch History and Archaeology Group, Shropshire

Printed by Delmar Press (Colour Printers) Ltd, Wall Lane, Nantwich, Cheshire CW5 5LS

ISBN 978-0-9564059-1-3

Cover : St. Alkmund's parish church, Whitchurch, as it was before the rebuilding in 1713.
Back cover : portrait of Philip Henry and the rear view of the former Presbyterian chapel, Dodington.

CONTENTS

Page

Acknowledgements

This book's origins lie in a long series of meetings held under the aegis of the University of Keele when people interested in Whitchurch history met to research the past in formal programmes of study. I was their tutor and at the beginning knew hardly anything about the town. After eleven years I had shelves full of files of material accumulated to feed the voracious appetite of successive cohorts of class members. Much came from students themselves, and local institutions such as churches, the collections of the Whitchurch History and Archaeology Group, and the county library; a lot was collected from the huge resources available in Shrewsbury, Lichfield and Chester Archive Offices. The National Archives and the British Library were utilised as well. Individuals produced essays and articles, but so far only one attempt has been made to bring together the results of specific investigations into themes I incorporated into annual programmes. This is a second.

My thanks are to all those who came to my classes for their variety of contributions to a common fund of knowledge. For this particular book Joan Barton and Jean North were an inspiration and Maude Gould an indefatigable worker in many vital aspects of research and production. I owe my introduction to Whitchurch to Dr Philip Morgan, who, with his colleague at Keele, Dr Ian Atherton, has always responded to queries with sound advice. My friends in the North Staffordshire Historians' Guild, especially Nigel Coulton and Dr Alun Davies, made their own respective language and medical expertise quickly and generously available. Rose Wheat gave my first draft a thorough going over from which it has benefited enormously and David Hayns could not have been kinder in allowing me access to his historical knowledge and store of Philip Henry material. Dr Anne Tarver kindly provided an index to Consistory Court records and Janet Miller did a splendid job proof reading. Philip Walker is thanked for his photographs, and so too are members of staff at Shrewsbury Archives and at Lichfield Joint Record Office for their patient help over many years. Staff at the Borthwick Institute, Lambeth Palace Library, the Wiltshire & Swindon Record Office and Ian Bolton at Birmingham Central Library are thanked for rapid and helpful responses to numerous queries. I am grateful for permission to publish illustrations to the British Library (page 13), The National Archives (page 95), Sarah Davies at Shropshire Archives (pages 33,47,54,138), Andrew George at Lichfield Joint Record Office (pages 67, 79, 125, 129), Dr Alun Davies (page 126), Cambridge University Press (page 113) and Jonathan Warburton-Lee (page 74). Mr Grant Macgillivray kindly allowed access to the Presbyterian Chapel for Philip Walker to take photographs (page 159). Jonathan Burd is thanked for supplying the index.

Sincere apologies are offered to any helpful person who has not been properly acknowledged. Similarly, I can only apologise to anybody or institution whose rights have been inadvertently and unwittingly infringed in the course of this book's production. Finally, nothing would have been possible without the active support of my wife, Anne, for whose patient tolerance at home and assistance in record offices I am most grateful. For errors of fact, historical misjudgements and infelicities in design I am entirely responsible.

Paul Anderton
September 2011

Prologue

Whitchurch people have a choice between different places when they want to go to church. How has this come about? There is an explanation, a story to tell. There is a history and this book deals with the first stage in that history. It's only one narrow band in the complex fabric of Whitchurch history produced by a process of weaving the results of research into the past into the broad sheet of history. As successive weft threads are interlaced with the warp, even in this one short stretch of the historical cloth, so the contribution of each generation of people becomes clear. Some individuals stand out more clearly than others – they have left a paper trail. Thousands remain obscure.

The purpose of what follows is to collect together what can be discovered about one group of people whose collective activity over two centuries shaped a particular, but most important, part of the multicoloured pattern of Whitchurch's history. Their story answers the question of why there is a choice of church to go to now. It's not a story without grief, animosities, even conflict and personal injury. It's particular to Whitchurch, yet not unique in theme or outline. Like local history in general it's rooted in a certain place, but has a universal value.

In our secular age it may be difficult to imagine Whitchurch society when religious beliefs dominated. For two hundred years after Henry VIII, in the 1520s, first dallied with Anne Boleyn, however, Whitchurch was marked by arguments over how people should act as Christians, especially in their parish church. An agreement to differ and to allow some lawful variation in behaviour was reached for the nation as a whole by 1690. This is the story of how that conflict and the agreement can be traced in one Shropshire parish.

It's impossible to avoid using the word '*church*' despite the problem this presents. It has too many meanings. For some users it's a building, others see a congregation of people. They are not mutually exclusive, but local historians too often dwell only on stones, memorials and chancel reconstructions, giving little attention to those who occupied the pews. There's a third dimension as well: faith. We may only be dealing with Christianity if we delve into Whitchurch history, but we still have to recognise differing ways of expressing faith. It's especially apt, of course, to bring all these together as part of the history of Whitchurch. The very name of the place suggests an origin connected to a religious building – one presumed to strike the traveller from afar as a white sign marking houses ahead and the possibility of refreshment and accommodation.

If in the story of Whitchurch it's the people who matter, then their crucial features are what they believed in, and how they behaved as a result. It's just as true now, of course, as it was in previous ages. Whitchurch people in the distant past had a Christian faith, as supposedly did all their fellow subjects of English monarchs. It's a mistake, though, to assume that there is no distinctive Whitchurch story to tell about how that faith was demonstrated. Kinship groups and blood related families had their residence in Whitchurch in common, but just as important as a bond holding communities together was, and is, religious faith. The most evident sign of how Whitchurch people announced their religion is in church buildings. Curiously, though, what is striking in the town is the absence, with a few significant exceptions, of huge structures, obviously long standing, serving as churches or chapels. Where they exist, it is their histories as *buildings* which generally attract attention because they catch the eye and are of *now*: the people who flowed in through their doors, the variety of their faiths and the stories of how these were acquired are in the *past*. It's a considerable feat of imagination to bring them into the present.

In the history of English communities such as Whitchurch a major characterising feature has been the extent to which people displayed their common belief in regular gatherings in a *parish church*. It is this building which dominates the streetscape of Whitchurch. The assumption is that before Henry VIII's time there wasn't much difference between behaviour in one parish and all others. If there was it's not part of the present investigation to discover this. For immediate purposes, the parish building is the representation in stone, wood and glass of a state-defined religious faith and belief in a Christian god. In so far as, over time, other buildings have been erected in which people have followed rituals not conforming to those practised in the parish church, so the community has expressed its divisions, even tensions, if not necessarily its breakdown. Buildings are only symbols, in other words, of the values and faith of people in Whitchurch, as they are elsewhere.

The proportion of the inhabitants who performed their religious observances, first of all in the Anglican building of St. Alkmund's, and then in later ages all the churches and chapels built in the parish has never been measured properly. Until 1851 there was only one serious attempt to count adherents to a particular religious faith. In 1676 an inquiry was

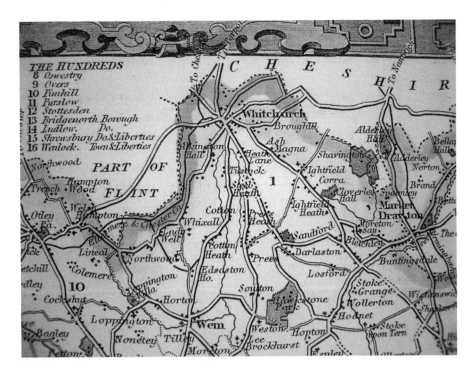

An extract from Moule's map of Shropshire 1830

supposed to discover three facts about every parish – the number in each case of Roman Catholics, conformists to the Anglican church, and thirdly all those not attending the parish church for other reasons. It is much suspect as even a rough guide to that restricted objective. The Religious Census 1851 lies outside the scope of this narrative. In any case, its published results allow little of value to be easily concluded about Whitchurch's religious character. [1]

This narrative, therefore, is about people not buildings. It's about how, in a community defined within the particular administrative parish structure of the Anglican church, tensions grew which led to the construction, ultimately, of a variety of buildings – chapels and churches – to satisfy the needs of groups unable to accept wholesale a state-defined religion. Put simply, it's the story of the inhabitants of a parish who initially displayed their loyalty to the state and nominal religious beliefs by worshipping together, as the law demanded, every Sunday in St. Alkmund's Church. By degrees they separated out into those who continued to conform and those who didn't. Divisions were related to particular residents as well as to influences flowing in from afar. Actions in Whitchurch cannot be divorced from events elsewhere, but explanations of outside forces mustn't be allowed to swamp the local history.

Each north Shropshire community has its own history because each is in its own special location. Whitchurch and Wem differ and may even feel rivalry: Market Drayton and Prees have separate histories too. There is, nevertheless, a lot in common between all English towns and villages when looking at how people thought about life and how to live it, what to believe in, who to emulate, what counted as important and worth admiring, how to win friends and influence people. It is in the context of this shared *cultural* dimension that the individual histories of Whitchurch and Wem, for example, should be seen.

It's important to reiterate that histories of communities are essentially about the *interaction* of people, and not just a select few either. The many and the hitherto unknown must be included. In Whitchurch, for instance, it's not just the Sir John Talbots and Edward Germans who count, but successive generations of long-resident families and the host of short-stay men and women who populated the district over several hundred years. Until 1811 and the second census count of heads there was no reliable figure for the size of population of the parish let alone the town. The physical distribution of urban dwellings and farmsteads mapped in 1761 is an excellent guide to the slow development of a street pattern over the previous three or four hundred years. In 1811 the census recorded 4,900 residents in the parish, much the largest proportion, no doubt, living in town. The rate of population expansion from the 1520s to 1811 has to be a matter of informed guesswork. One rough calculation is based upon a supposed national doubling of the population between the 1670s and 1811, which makes Whitchurch parish about 2,500 when Charles II was on the throne. Another local conclusion drawn from parish register analysis is that the population declined sharply in the mid-seventeenth century from about 3,200 in the mid-1630s. It is anybody's guess as to how far this total varied from the number of people spread around the parish in the 1520s when this story starts. The assumption here is only that the figure was certainly smaller.

Over time, the nature of the cultural environment changed: what people learned in school altered, the ways they entertained themselves shifted, the attitudes they had towards their fellow residents were transformed, new beliefs challenged traditional certainties, and behaviours followed suit. Only some parts of this cultural progression can be followed in any detail in Whitchurch. One obvious starting point, however, is in the one building which, in the sixteenth century, brought all the inhabitants of parish and manor together – the church of St. Alkmund. One person to start off the story is George Constantine, a man with books for sale.

Chapter 1

R*eligious observance, St. Alkmund's Church and the arrival of Protestantism*

It was around September time 1527 that George Constantine rode into Whitchurch. Doubtless, he found that the trackway up from Shrewsbury was in its usual rutted state, hazardous and tiring to travel even on horseback. He must have ridden for he needed a saddlebag for parcels he brought with him. He carried printed books – but they weren't innocent harmless texts. One at least was a potential cultural bombshell. It was the New Testament in English. Merely to possess it was a crime. Yet it seems he was bringing it to friends in his home town.

It's impossible to say what was the immediate reaction of Whitchurch people to George Constantine and the English Bible he was distributing for the translator, William Tyndale. The story of how he came to bring these books into the town, who had the first chance to read them and the circumstances in which they were discussed is clear however. That they would ultimately be profoundly significant in the lives of the congregation regularly gathered in the already ancient building at the top of High Street is also clear.

The tradition of communal worship was established long before the memory of man. Parishioners met within the stone walls of St. Alkmund's Church in the presence of the tombstones of their ancestors. As in ages past, so in the reign of Henry VIII, they were thus confronted by physical reminders of those beliefs which State authorities expected them to hold. In this building people were obliged to worship their God *St.Alkmund's and the social order* publicly, and to listen to explanations of the wondrous mysteries of nature and Divine Providence which puzzled and confused them. The very stones, windows and the arrangement of furniture all expressed messages about the way they were supposed to behave, what they should believe in and what they ought to value most.

George Vernon was the rector of Whitchurch in 1527. He was the agent of a Catholic church organisation headed by the Pope in Rome. He spoke in Latin to his parishioners during services and led them in prayers and supplications in traditional sequences. He quoted from a Bible few others could read; he recited homilies and exhortations admonishing them for bad conduct and urging them to do good. He was clearly of some socially superior position. Pews or other seating methods ranked his congregation, showing which families had servants, substantial landed property and gentry status, and which people were of the lower, yeoman stock. Poorer labouring ranks had benches against the back walls, or simply stood around the edges of the assembly. Everybody knew, literally, their place.

Of course, this doesn't mean that everybody understood what they were told, or why they had to behave in certain ways. It doesn't even mean that there were no other beliefs or interpretations of the signs of nature current in the community. Superstition, magic and witchcraft could well have been just as common in Whitchurch as elsewhere. The absence of evidence for pagan practices and thoughts should not mislead. It is inevitable, however, that it is the official culture which is the easiest to investigate because it was the one for which, for the most part, there are surviving records.

The document which informs us that George Constantine visited Whitchurch in 1527 is the record of a case heard the following year in the Bishop of Lichfield and Coventry's Consistory Court. It reveals that at least one Whitchurch family, if not two, were involved in the potentially heretical act of rejecting belief in child baptism, the veneration of saintly images and the importance of making pilgrimages to holy places. If that is what they were doing it was because they met George Constantine and saw bibles in English as written out by William Tyndale.

Court case at Lichfield

The charges brought in the bishop's court were against Richard Cotton the curate at Atcham, near Shrewsbury. They were that he failed to properly keep the Feast of St. Matthew as a fast day. Instead, he ate two meals, including meat, and preached about this from his pulpit. Moreover, when challenged in the town, he uttered words *"offensive to pious ears"*. In the small print of the case, as it were, it was directly stated that the curate, Richard Cotton, had a brother, Thomas, at whose house in Whitchurch Richard met with others, especially George Constantine, and there discussed Lutheran opinions. It was alleged he read Lutheran books and had declared that *"an infant born and procreated from Christian parents needs no other baptism."*

Richard Cotton and his brother Thomas

Others at the Whitchurch meeting, not easily identified, were two priests (one called Peter came from Cheshire) and Thomas Hancock. One implication from the statements recorded by the bishop's officials was that George Constantine had been a priest who resigned his benefice after his friendship had become known with one called

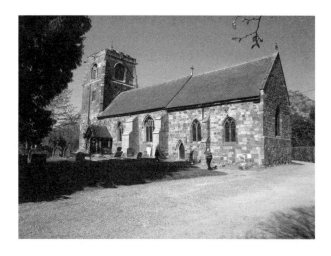

St. Eata's Church, Atcham 2011

'Bylney', a convicted heretic who had abjured his opinions. [2] Richard Cotton denied everything except eating the meat, and specifically denounced Lutheran beliefs. Nevertheless, he was ordered to atone for his error, both in the *act of atonement* cathedral at Lichfield in May 1528 and in his parish church, by parading with a bundle of sticks on his shoulder to advertise himself as a former heretic, and by ceasing to preach. [3]

This case is held by some church historians to be an isolated and relatively insignificant sign that people were discussing the teachings of Martin Luther in north Shropshire scarcely ten years after his famous action of posting ninety-five theses on the church door of Wittenburg castle in October 1517. [4] This dramatic act, by a man damned as a heretic at the time, is the conventional starting point for the Protestant Reformation whose cultural impact on Europe and Britain was profound and long-lasting.

From a Whitchurch point of view, however, what went on in Lichfield cathedral in 1528 was a pointer to a kind of parallel drama at almost the lowest of local levels. After all, the crucial signs of heresy in Henry VIII's kingdom, at this time, were reading the Bible in English and discussing the works of Martin Luther. The case certainly shows that some Whitchurch parishioners were among the earliest English people to listen to, and discuss, the most recent arguments doubting the validity of the old, Catholic, theology. They were imported from the continent and had been proposed by Martin Luther. They were preliminaries to the Protestant conquest of the church in north Shropshire in Elizabethan times, and all this before Henry VIII was seriously entangled with Anne Boleyn. Whitchurch was a long way from Wittenburg, but heard the Protestant faith expounded at a very early, and crucial, stage in its conquest of northern Europe.

The people named in the bishop's court are all important. Thomas Hancock may or may not have lived in Whitchurch: the surname is not found in the town in probate listings before 1561, though it is at Atcham.[5] North Shropshire was, however, Cotton country, and it remains to be seen how the brothers Richard and Thomas were linked to the principal family of that name. The Thomas Cotton who lived in Whitchurch in the 1520s was possibly the second wealthiest man in the parish according to a tax return of 1525. At least, he paid five shillings cash for being assessed as worth £10 in moveable goods. Gryffith Hynton, who paid the most in tax, at ten shillings, was assessed on land alone, this valued at £10. It might be thought that Cotton was more likely to be in trade, with only a small land holding, while Hynton could have been a freeholder working his land for profit. Just a guess. [6]

Richard and Thomas Cotton

It must be this Thomas Cotton whose will was proved in January 1560, and who was eldest son of John Cotton. The probate documents showed Thomas as relatively very wealthy, living and farming at Alkington and possessed of a tannery in Whitchurch. It is the claim that his mother was Katherine, heiress to a Thomas Constantine of Dodington, which makes him highly intriguing. The younger of these Thomases, the Cotton one, will reappear in this story later.[7]

The crucial person named in the case, George Constantine, was in close contact with William Tyndale, then known to be the translator into English of the New Testament part of the Bible. Indeed, George is credited with travelling through Shropshire distributing copies of this dangerous literature on the basis of evidence given in this case. [8] No precise day and month can be found – the state of the roads he obviously followed can only be imagined. The allegations are clear, however, and there can be no doubt about the ultimate impact of the books he carried. In the history of Whitchurch, therefore, a moment pregnant with cultural consequences was reached during his visit.

Constantine's career

A recent account of Constantine's career states that he was born near the Cheshire-Shropshire border and went to a local school before going up to Cambridge University in 1517-18. [9] He was ordained and became vicar

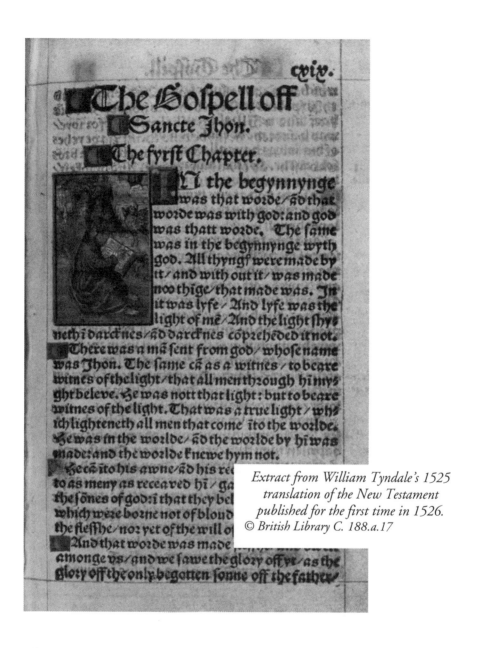

Extract from William Tyndale's 1525 translation of the New Testament published for the first time in 1526.
© British Library C. 188.a.17

of Sedgley in Staffordshire by 1526. It is presumed that it was at Cambridge that he accepted Lutheran ideas and implied that he scarcely set foot in Sedgley for he was recruiting agents in London in 1527 to assist him in the work of selling Tyndale's bibles. Tyndale had moved from London to Germany in 1524 to continue his translation work and organise the printing of copies of his New Testament. Earlier accounts noted that Constantine also went to Germany where he met Tyndale, but this now seems in doubt. It is clear however, that he was involved in smuggling the new bibles into England from 1526 onwards.

Edited transcript the inventory of William Constantine 1544

Li = £1 : s = shillings   d = pence

vi oxen	viLi	a bassen & grydyron & iii broches	iiis viiid
ii steris	xxxs	a chaffurne	iiis
viii kyne	vili	ii pottengles ii cowbardes ii andirons	iiis
vii twynters	xxxvis	a peyre of tonges & iii laduls	vd
xii sponys	xxxvis iiiid		
vi chandlers	iiiis	v stondes	xxiid
a maslyn bassen & a voyder	xvid	a wheting cowmbe & ii turnells	vis
xiiii chargers	viis	a knedyng troghe a brewyng combe	iiis
viii pottyngers & vi cownterfettes	iiiis	vi Coshins iii cheris	vs id
xx stryke of oote malt	xvis	a cupbord & a folding borde bequethyt to	
xxx stryke of barly malt	iiili	Willm Costantine his heyre	xs
xl styrke barly	iiii marks		
xii stryke rye	xvis	vi peyre of flaxen she xvi of canvasse	xxxvis
rye sowen in ye feld	xxiiiis	ii feder beddes ii bolsters	xxs
v pottes & a caldron	xiis	iii mattras vi blankettes	ixs
ii salt salers	xvid	vi coverlettes	xxs
iiii panyes	xiiiis	the hanggyns abowte ye halle	
a fryeng pan	viiid	& ye chambers	iiis ivd
a chafying dish & ii skellettes	iis	iii coffurs & iiii pilloes	xis viiid
ii chandlers & a ewer	xiid	his reparell was gyffyn to poore people	
		all save one gown	vis viiid

[total £34-16-8]

At Richard Cotton's trial Constantine was alleged to be a Lutheran in belief, and clearly he was known to the authorities, though he had not yet suffered arrest.[10] This came in 1531 at the instigation of Sir Thomas More. Contemporary interrogation methods were not for the squeamish and Constantine confessed all. Part of the story he told was relayed by John Foxe in his *Book of Martyrs*.[11] Put simply, Constantine betrayed sailors and merchants who conveyed Lutheran books and New Testaments from the Low Countries to England. He was then allowed to escape and returned to Antwerp.[12] In the history of Whitchurch he had secured his place, however, because, to all intents and purposes, he brought the essential symbol of Protestantism to Whitchurch in his saddlebag. He thus deserves notice in the history of the town.

Constantine's exact birthplace and family connections have not been published, though Thompson Cooper in the older Dictionary of National Biography (original edition) implied a possible origin in Pembrokeshire.[13]

Transcript of the will of William Constantine 1544

In the name of god amen I William Costantyne of Whitchurch of the countie of Salop thelder beyng syk [*in body but*] hole in mynde & beyng in perfyte remembrans make my testament & last Will concerning the dispos[*ition*] of my goods catals And lands in manner and forme foloyng : Furst I bequeth my sowle to Almighty [*God*] my creator and redemer besechying hym that the same may be associat with the celestiall [*company*] of heven and my bodye to be buried in my paresh church and moreover I revoke and disanul all [*other*] testaments and last Wills made by me afore this tyme except the disposicion of certen Lands [*which*] are called the newfelds the okehurst and saint Kotteryns croft Whech lands and pastures I [*gave to my*] sone ylaw Thomas Lee & my daughter Johan for certen yeres { interlined *& surrendurt the same in to a burges [...] for the same*} mencioned in my will by me made & [...] xxth daye of Januarye & in the yere of our lorde god m ccccc xlij which gift and bequest [...] the lands forsaid I ratifye and confirm by this my last Will to the said Thomas Lee & Johan my doghter in manner and forme in the forsaid will by me made specifyed. Item I bequeth to my parish church vjˢ viijᵈ Item I gyve & bequeth to Thomas Lee my sone ylaw & to Johan his wife the contentacion of his mariage money thone half of al my goods catals [..]els and detts that now belong to me forever not accomtyng enye thyng they have hadde afore tyme for enye parte therof. Item my will is that my said sone ylaw shall take freely to his owne use all manner of houshold stuff he has bought or by his procuryng causyd to be bought in to my howse not accomptyng yt for enye parte of the half of my said goods. Item I bequeth to my sonne Phylip iiij marks sterlyng for his childes parte of my goods. Item I bequeth to Alyce Ball iijˡⁱ vjˢ viijᵈ to be paid att hir marriage. Item I constytute & ordene george my sone and Thomas Lee my sone ylaw myne executors to [*be stowe*] thother half of my goods I brought home & my detts paid at their discretion for the we[*?lfare*] of my sowle and to see this my last Will performed in love and peace to theyr power Item I ordene Thomas Coton & John Fygs my overseers of this my last will besechyng them to do their [*?dutyes*] that the same may be accomplyshed accordyng to the effect and tenor herof as my tr[*ust ys yn*] them. In witnes herof I have putt my seale geven att Whitchurch forsaid the ix daye of Januarye & in the yere of our lorde god a thousand fyve hundreth xliij thes beyng witnes Sir William Clerke my gostliefather Richard garrett Thomas Figs William Aston Sir John Lee chaplain & other ones.

In view of Constantine's Whitchurch connection in 1528, however, there now arises the speculation that this George Constantine was a member of the family of that name very well known in Whitchurch town throughout the sixteenth century. [14]

The earliest found to date is William Constantine, assessed in Whitchurch for tax in 1525 at £7. This was the subsidy demanded by Henry VIII consequent upon war with France, and reluctantly accepted by Parliament in 1523. William was liable for goods he owned of various kinds on which he paid at the rate of 6d in the pound as did most of his fellow tax payers. All told, 61 other men in the parish were listed as wealthy enough to

William Tyndale committed acts he knew to be illegal. He was burnt to death in October 1536 after an attempt to strangle him before the flames flared high failed. He knew the penalty for translating the Bible into English, but he did it anyway. There had been earlier English versions of the Bible, and he was far from the first to be burned for heresy. He was near enough 42 years old and had started his principal writing task aged about 29.

Tyndale came from a Gloucester village, went early to Oxford University, took his MA degree and moved to Cambridge. Briefly he was a tutor in a Gloucestershire family, but once engaged on his task of translation in 1523 he was effectively on the run. A short spell in London was followed, after April 1524, by twelve years in Germany and the Netherlands. He died in what is now a suburb of Brussels.

New Testaments in English were being smuggled into England by 1526. Church authorities, backed by the king and the Lord Chancellor, Sir Thomas More, committed huge resources for the next ten years to finding and burning copies, and all the other works by Tyndale and Martin Luther. A vicious war of words, torturings, imprisonments and burnings was conducted with Sir Thomas More at the forefront.

Ironically, the politics of Henry VIII's court and his incessant search for a wife who could produce a son brought Sir Thomas More to the executioner's block, in July 1535, more than a year before Tyndale was betrayed and killed. Within four years Henry VIII found it necessary to authorise the publication of a Bible in English – The Great Bible of 1539. Thereafter, in England, as More prophesied, society was turned inside out.

be charged, and he ranked as third richest – all, it must be said, were very comparable in their tax assessments to merchants in Shrewsbury, although far fewer in number. Another William Constantine, who lived in Dodington, was rated at £4 worth in goods. Inevitably, the possibility is that he was the richer man's son. [15]

It was presumably the first of these Williams whose probate documents were dated 1544. [16] He was noted as William the elder. His inventory, appraised by Thomas Figs and Richard Whitfield, recorded that all but one of his garments were given to the poor, but his will is in too delicate a state to study properly. There was no explicitly Catholic preamble, he giving his soul to *"Almighty god … and redeemer beseeching him that the same may be associate with the celestial company of heaven and my body to be buried in my parish church …".* He named three children, Joan, Philip and George and made Joan's husband, Thomas Lee, and son George executors. The witnesses were Sir William Clarke, Richard Garrett, Thomas Figs, William Aston and Sir John Lee. The inventory makers explicitly stated that two items of furniture were to go to William Constantine the deceased man's heir - that is, George, Philip and Joan had a brother, William.

In 1543 when William Constantine drew up his will he must have assumed that his son George was free to act as executor. Of course, he does not have to be the bible salesman and the George Constantine subtle enough to find employment late in the 1530s as an agent for Thomas Cromwell. But the latest biography of that George Constantine claims that he was again arrested, this time for treason, and sent to the Tower of London in 1539. Then there is a gap in the evidence. He was released at some unknown date and is not identified again until 1545 or thereabouts, now as vicar of Llawhaden in South Wales. [17] If all these clues relate to the same George Constantine, then he had a reason to go home to Whitchurch for at least a short period about 1542. Otherwise, two George Constantines have to be accounted for at the same time.

Lighting the Consistory Court Room of Lichfield Cathedral

A Thomas Constantine of Dodington has already been noted as father of Katherine, the wife of John Cotton, and therefore grandfather of Thomas Cotton (probate 1560). There is no possibility that Katherine had a brother for she was her father's heiress. The elder William Constantine (probate 1544) must have been of her generation, and probably they were cousins.[18] Katherine's son, Thomas Cotton (probate 1560), was of the same generation as William Constantine the younger, and Joan, Philip and George, all children of the aforesaid William the elder. Their close relationship was confirmed by Richard Cotton at his trial who declared that the George Constantine he met in Whitchurch was a kinsman. [19]

It is difficult to escape the conclusion that the visit to Whitchurch by George Constantine in 1527 was to home and family. On his way northwards, towards Shrewsbury, he fell in with one member of his family, Richard Cotton at Atcham, and so influenced him with his new religious interpretations that Richard took him to his brother's house at Whitchurch (was this really at Alkington?) to spread the word there.

It's true that no Constantine resident in Whitchurch was named in the trial of Richard Cotton as meeting with George the bible seller. Thomas Cotton and Thomas Hancock were recorded as doing so. The curate at Atcham did admit though that he shared the meat on St. Matthew's Day with a John Constantine. It may have been an accident that George Constantine went to a place where people had his surname, but were no relations. The marriage of Thomas Cotton to a Constantine, however, and William Constantine's rather anodyne will preamble, plus the fact that he had a son George, do allow for the conclusion that it was this man who was the bible salesman. Further, that he chose to travel through north Shropshire because he expected a welcome from family and friends. The really intriguing question, of course, is whether his religious message was not only heard but had consequences.

The reason for George Constantine moving well beyond that part of England closest to Germany has been thought to be the result of the all-too successful missionary activity of himself and others in the East Anglian region in the mid-1520s. A counter-attack on the itinerant Lutherans by Bishop Tunstall of London made the area too hot for them. Hence Constantine's retreat westward which is only known about through the record of this case heard at Lichfield about meetings in Atcham and Whitchurch. It may be isolated, but it is undeniable that some men in Whitchurch by 1528 were listening to, and perhaps being converted by, a man well recognised for his Protestant fervour, his possession of English versions of the New Testament and his ability to present theological arguments contrary to the teachings of Rome. He didn't stay long, for he was reported in Antwerp by September 1528. [20]

It's not the amount of time he spent around Whitchurch, however, which is crucial. It's the consequences of his meeting with Thomas Cotton and Thomas Hancock which, in the longer term, are significant.

Chapter 2

Whitchurch Free Grammar School

Any link between George Constantine's fleeting association with Whitchurch in 1528 and the building of a school in 1550 is going to be tenuous. It's worth examining, nevertheless.

In the standard list of priests at St. Alkmund's the incumbent in 1528 was George Vernon. He came to the office in 1500 and on his death in 1534 was succeeded by John Talbot. The second was the man who had to respond to the fluctuations in the process of church reformation instituted by Henry VIII after 1534; the first may well have started to lose

George Vernon, rector of Whitchurch

his grip on congregations in the parish church simply by being there for over twenty years, and potentially at least, being a relatively old man when George Constantine came into the area. If Vernon was aware of unofficial and heretical doctrines infecting his parishioners by 1528 he either did nothing about them through church courts - or the evidence has been lost. Evidence exists, however, to suggest that by the mid-1520s Vernon was at odds with some at least of the congregation at St. Alkmund's – and, incidentally, proving him to be not so old after all!

Once again the evidence is provided by testimony given at the Bishop of Coventry and Lichfield's consistory court. The action was initiated by church officials in line with requirements that priests be disciplined for moral failures. Someone in Whitchurch must have given the game away though, because Vernon was cited for having a mistress and siring children on her despite obvious efforts to keep the affair secret. [21] The case was taken in January and

having a mistress

February 1526 and was not to the liking of George Vernon. At first he refused to appear before the court, but changed his mind when excommunicated for his recalcitrance. He was in difficulties even before giving evidence, however, for the writ which announced the action against him had been pinned to his church door, as was normal in these events. His servant, Thomas Austen or Aston, knife in hand, roughly tore down the paper in the presence of the court officer, Richard Glasier, who had posted it there. Austen, or his accomplice Richard Miller (also known as

Woodhouse), was heard to say that it was more fitting for Glasier's ear to be nailed to the door than the notice (or words to that effect). Aston was excommunicated for his contumacy.

George Vernon was noted as MA, and rector of Whitchurch. He had to respond to a series of written questions, or numbered articles, which, unfortunately, have not survived. His answers were often along the lines that he agreed or disagreed with the substance of the article making it difficult to decide just what he was saying. Enough sense can be made of the replies to see that he admitted sexual intercourse with a woman over a period of four years, that they cohabited somewhere out of town, but that he had brought her into Whitchurch to his house, and they had children. He denied rearing the children at the rectory, but admitted paternity and that they were living somewhere near by. He denied much else, and admitted some things contained in the articles – one answer suggesting that Norbury was not a place he frequented. Only his admission that he conducted Mass in a church under an interdict forbidding such a service is clear.

Margaret Bentley   The woman in question was Margaret Bentley. She too appeared before the court, having been excommunicated, and responded to written questions not copied into the record. She confessed to bearing two children fathered by the rector; to eating with him in private but with other people present in both Whitchurch and Leebotwood. This was always during the day and never at night, at John Lee's house at Leebotwood.

It was an open and shut case. Vernon was ordered to pay court costs, fined £3.00 (twenty shillings down and forty shillings later) to go to pious causes and instructed to perform penance at St. Alkmund's at the head of a procession and before his congregation. Part of the

penance   penance seems to have been begging for forgiveness for his misbehaviour and setting up a candle. Thomas Aston had to similarly process around St. Alkmund's, say his Rosary and set up a candle. Margaret Bentley had to suffer her penance on three occasions, the second being a Sunday when she was ordered to

> "*process to the altar in the church at Whitchurch with bare shins and feet carrying a candle in her hand at the time of the procession … as a penitent and on the Sunday following she should similarly do her humble penance at the church of Saint Chad's Salop and she was ordered in the future to absent herself from the company of Sir George which she was willing to deserve if she acted to the contrary.*" [22]

That, at least, seems to be what the Latin means.

An aside from the main narrative, on Margaret Bentley, concerns a probate record for a woman of that name who died in the autumn of 1552. In her will she noted herself as a *"whedowe syke in bodye howelle & p[ar]fytte in myende"* possessed of goods which included *"Twenty angels of howled Gowlde"*. Other than these

who was Margaret Bentley?

intriguing precious items her few household articles of bedclothes and kitchen utensils were scarcely worth more than a couple of pounds, but she was owed eighteen shillings altogether, split between two men and one woman. She had Cotton friends or relatives; one, Raffe [Raufe], owed her money and was an executor, another, John, appraised her inventory, while to William she left *"a greatte Cawfer & xiii S iiii D"* [thirteen shillings and four pence]. She noted a Thomas Cotton as a brother-in-law, who seems to have had two daughters to whom she left a small bequest. Also highly relevant was the statement *"ffyrst I commende my sowelle unto Almyhetye gods hands to all ye Celestyall companye of heaven & my body…"* to be buried in the parish church of Whitchurch. This was the nearest she got to a declaration of faith though one tantalisingly open to various interpretations. [23]

So, was she the woman of the 1526 court case? It's a long shot, and there is no proof, but she invites speculation. There is more speculation if one of the three witnesses to the will (of which only a copy survives) was *"Sir Willyam Adams preyst & curatt of Wytchurch"*. No other evidence has been found of who held the post of rector in 1552, and it is entirely possible that Adams was not rector, but literally the curate to the rector. Either way, the notion that Margaret Bentley was close to a parish priest, of whatever rank, albeit twenty-six years after she (or her namesake) was dragged though the bishop's court for sinful relations with a rector of Whitchurch, attracts attention. The name is noted again in another probate record from the first year of Queen Mary's reign – William Bentley leaving a bequest to his brother's daughter, Margaret Bentley. William did not mention a wife, but he named at least three children. [24] He could not have been the widower of Margaret with the golden angels as she died before him as a widow; William's brother's daughter Margaret must also have been of another generation, but it is possible that she was the daughter of a Margaret, and the latter could have been the wife of William Bentley's brother. The tangles of family history may well be relevant, but without more information this aside on Margaret Bentley stops here.

Returning to George Vernon, he was not necessarily any more guilty of sexual indiscretions than other priests of his day, or cardinals for that matter. Were it not for the incident two years later nothing could be said about reactions among the residents of Whitchurch parish to their rector's wicked life. It does seem legitimate, however, to raise the possibility that Thomas Cotton and at least two others from neighbouring Cheshire were sufficiently disenchanted with the rector of Whitchurch, and what he stood for, to listen to the Lutheran message that George Constantine and Richard Cotton preached. That they were cited in the action against Richard Cotton in the bishop's court also suggests that someone blew the whistle. Vernon had his supporters – or at least he had persons zealous for the ancient faith among his flock who wanted no truck with demands for church reformation.

There is no way of knowing whether Thomas Cotton, with or without help from William Constantine, built up a Bible study group, for example, or whether John Talbot, Vernon's successor as rector, was

John Talbot, rector of Whitchurch

amenable to sections of his congregation learning about Protestant opinions. Talbot's theological preferences did not figure in the account of his career provided by Ernest Clarke when researching the origins of Whitchurch Grammar School. It was not unusual for priests to collect cathedral offices and benefices so that Clarke's conclusion can be accepted that the Dr. John Talbot, sub-dean and then canon of Lincoln Cathedral, was the man of the same name previously at Canterbury College, Cambridge, and the John Talbot instituted to the parish of Glossop in 1494, made rector of St. Lawrence, South Walsham in Norfolk, rector in Rotherfield, Sussex, rector at Cold Overton, Leicestershire, and vicar at Ecclesfield, Yorkshire. His office at Lincoln also brought him two prebendaries. The key question Clarke posed, but could not fully answer, related to the reason why this John Talbot moved out of his cathedral posts in 1535 and concentrated his attention on Whitchurch to which he had been instituted in May 1534. Put simply, Talbot suggested in his resignation statement that he needed to spend more time making sure his flock did not fall into error. At the same time, he noted his own dubious state of health. He was possibly 64 years old.[25]

Then there is the mystery about his aristocratic connections. Thomas Cotton reported that Talbot was a native of Whitchurch.[26] Ernest Clarke speculated that he was an illegitimate member of the Talbot family, Earls of Shrewsbury, whose estates were based upon original holdings at Blakemere in Whitchurch. They were, in fact, the lords of Whitchurch manor. Did this put him in a somewhat equivocal position? The Shrewsbury earls were firmly Catholic then and in several following generations, but that doesn't necessarily apply to John Talbot. He had conformed to Henry VIII's demand that clergy swear allegiance to

The link between the Talbots and Whitchurch is most vividly recalled by viewing the tomb of Sir John Talbot, still a major feature of St. Alkmund's today.

him as head of the church in the place of the Pope in Rome. [27] This could have been simply an act of self-preservation. Did he in his last years move further towards the reformed faith for which Hugh Latimer and Nicholas Ridley were later to die? Did he accept the Six Articles of 1539 which Latimer rejected as too Romish? Who knows?

Nothing can be said at present either about his successor, Alan Charlton, instituted 31 January 1550/51. [28] The living was in the gift of the earls of Shrewsbury – George, the 4th earl, presented John Talbot in 1534 – and Charlton's religious teachings

who followed John Talbot as rector?

might be expected to mirror the earl's theological position. The same can be said, of course, if Charlton was soon replaced by William Adams, already noted as witnessing a will in 1552. Whatever the case, however, a new phenomenon now comes to prominence.

What was consonant with the new religious doctrines and practices very evident in the last years of the reign of Henry VIII was the founding of a 'free' grammar school in Whitchurch in 1550. This was on the basis of a £200 bequest by John Talbot, the rector, whose death followed not long after the accession of Edward VI. One of the crucial features of the

Talbot finances a school

Protestant outlook on Christianity was the need for an educated priesthood and transparency, as we might now say, in the matter of church teachings based upon the Bible. The new boy king was in the care of a regent and it was the tenets of the new faith which attracted support among his councillors and advisers. Henry VIII may not be counted as a Protestant believer, but by his death his church was riven by theological disputes and power struggles brought on by the importation of Lutheran texts. Is it significant that the first twelve governors of the grammar school (feoffees as they were known) were laymen, who, though they had to work with the rector of the day, as *ex officio* one of their number, could presumably outvote him? A place on this governing body was inheritable and thus the school had a degree of independence from the church, albeit its foundation deed laid down the requirement to propagate Christianity as enunciated by the recently created Church of England and to be open to inspection by the bishop.

Whitchurch was far from the only community to be given a grammar school in Tudor times. Wolverhampton in 1512, Manchester in 1515 and Burton on Trent in 1520 are cases in point. Like Loughborough in 1495 they cannot be said to be reflections of a new religious faith. Later schools, at Hawkeshead in the Lake District and Queen Elizabeth (later Heath) Grammar School in Halifax for example, both 1585, may well have been fruits of a state established religion. The significance of John Talbot's ambition to see a grammar school in his native town in 1550 is worth some thought, if only because of the national context in which it was founded.

It is also tempting to see the role of Thomas Cotton as a clue to Protestant

how important was Thomas Cotton ?

leanings among the elite of Whitchurch society because he was given the task by Talbot of bringing the school into existence. Indeed, he is credited with at least partial authorship of the foundation deed. Cotton declared that Talbot aimed at *"the exclusion of vice and the increase of virtue, for the decay of ignorance, and the [provision of the] bread of knowledge"* so far as the young were concerned, for youths were *"incurably wounded with blind ignorance the top and root of all iniquity"*. He regarded *"the chief occasion thereof to be the want and lack of good schools in this realm, and especially about Whitchurch."* [29] Cotton was one of the wealthier businessmen in the parish, perhaps not unaware of ancient religious obligations. He ordered in his will that every poor man, woman and child who attended his funeral should receive one penny.[30]

Thomas Cotton was not among the first feoffees of the Free School, however, but Ralph Cotton was.[31] So was a William Constantine, almost certainly son to the William who died in 1543/4, and brother to George. John Fyges is another intriguing member of the governing board, doubtless a relation to the Thomas Figs noted earlier in association with the older William Constantine.

There is a degree of uncertainty about this series of linked names, assuming for example that the Thomas Cotton of the grammar school deed was the same Thomas Cotton cited in 1525 as a tax payer and in 1528 as a Lutheran sympathiser. In the absence of evidence to the contrary the *a degree of uncertainty* assumption is justified however. There are gaps too after Talbot in the record of rectors: four names have been previously recorded starting with Alan Charlton in 1550, but they do not appear to cover the period from then until 1571, and personal details are totally absent. [32] Two additions are here tentatively offered for the list, one being the William Adams who witnessed Margaret Bentley's will. The other was John Estwycke whose probate inventory was brought to the bishop's court 4 May 1574. [33] He was called a *"Clarke"* in the document, was of Whitchurch and he was worth just over £89 according to those who costed his goods. His library alone was worth £20 and he held leases on land valued at £50. His executors marked his generosity to the local poor by giving them his clothes – linen and woollen cloth with shirts, coats and breeches. It is quite possible that he was another curate, not rector, but he clearly had an impressive library. He has to be accounted for somehow.

It is impossible, given this paucity of information, to understand the relationship of local activity at St. Alkmund's with the fast changing religious allegiances at national level. Edward, king in 1547, and his Protestant *fast changing religious* regents were followed in 1553 by the *allegiances* convinced Catholic, Mary, eldest child of Henry VIII, and wife to Philip of Spain; who, in turn, was succeeded in 1558 by the daughter of Anne Boleyn, and Protestant-by-necessity, Queen Elizabeth. All this in the space of scarcely twelve years. The absence of records might just point to more chaos than order in the religious life of Whitchurch in the second half of the sixteenth century. For the moment, nothing more can be said about clues to the religious character of Whitchurch before the 1630s.

What must be stressed, of course, is that the institution created by John Talbot's bequest has to be recognised as a major contributor to the cultural life of Whitchurch thereafter, even in a sense right up to the present day. It cannot be suggested that the school and its masters in the sixteenth and seventeenth centuries worked against the religious teachings of successive rectors, or were somehow subversive or dangerous to the established social order. Quite the contrary; it was a mainstay of the new orthodoxy as defined during the reign of Queen Elizabeth. Grammar schools became integral components of the lives of lesser gentry and urban elites: purveyors of culture to a critical minority who filled the ranks of local government administrators, preserving the temporal values of ancient Rome (to a lesser extent Greece) through study of Latin, but no longer continuing the medieval tradition of educating priests in the mysteries of Catholic practice. The grammar school in Whitchurch was not an off-duty activity of a chantry priest but the fulfilment of a far-sighted social concern.

Chapter 3

The Anglican Church and parish government

St. Alkmund's was the only building capable of holding any assembly of all the adult men in the parish, if one was ever required. In the sixteenth century this might have been possible. Just how many families and their servants regularly went for services cannot be estimated. It's doubtful if the church was big enough in the seventeenth century for the entire population of the parish at any one time. The only other church building was a small chapel at Tilstock which didn't add much to the total seating capacity provided by the Anglican Church. There was no move under the reformed Tudor Protestant regime to construct new buildings from which to disseminate the teachings of a faith drastically revised from that Henry VIII had defended in the early 1520s. Despite all the changes, the emphasis was on continuity and keeping up the appearance of normality at the local level. Church buildings were the greatest guarantee that life went on as it always had.

Yet everyone was now bound by law to attend church on Sundays. Legally, after 1552, non-attendance at a parish church on Sundays was a civil crime, and by the end of Elizabeth's reign punished with heavy fines. What people did in church was directed by a Book of Prayer approved in Parliament for implementation by a formally appointed clergyman.[34] Uniformity of belief and conformity to the law of the land was thus advertised in stone in every one of the 9,000 or so parishes of which England was composed. The building continued to make the spiritual link between the individual and Divine Power – though its symbolism is best left for theologians to explain. The building also acted as a sign of the power of the State.

bound by law to attend church

The parish church in the seventeenth century was, as in previous ages, a major centre of social, as well as spiritual, life for almost all rural and provincial urban communities. It was the place where news of the world could be most authoritatively discovered. The church door was a notice board, the pulpit the source of official instructions. Going to the parish church expressed acceptance of a common social bond considered to be one of the ties holding the nation together - the bond of religious belief.

Within Whitchurch parish the church building served as an assembly hall for family and communal gatherings to celebrate all kinds of events; it was a shelter and office premises for the work of administrative officials. It was not unknown in some parishes for it to house drinking sessions and commercial trading. Whatever power controlled the use of buildings like St. Alkmund's throughout England could hope to control the hearts and minds of an entire population.

Unfortunately, little has yet been discovered about the nature of religious observance and the people who staffed the offices of Whitchurch parish in the later sixteenth and early seventeenth centuries. The names of successive rectors since John Talbot and before 1606 mean little at present. The extent, if any, of the influence of the earls of Shrewsbury, lords of the manor, on cultural change in Whitchurch before 1598 is quite unknown. Every local historian must be green with envy of all who study Devonshire communities for their access to Eamon Duffy's superb elucidation of how the parish of Morebath and its priest, Christopher Trychay, experienced the transition from Henry VIII's Catholicism to Elizabeth's Protestantism. It is fatally easy to assume that there is some parallel here between a tiny village on the slopes of Exmoor and many other rural communities elsewhere, and thus equate life in Whitchurch with the happenings on the Devon and Somerset border. An alternative window on small town religious practice and its relationship to social order and the minutiae of daily life – albeit somewhat later in date – was provided by David Underdown in his account of Dorchester during the early Stuart period. Again the temptation to import into Whitchurch features of the twenty-year Protestant regime found by Underdown in Dorset's capital town, after the disastrous fire of 1613, must be resisted. Both Duffy and Underdown explored ways into societies of quite different kinds – almost at the extreme and opposite ends of a spectrum, in fact – such that it may be best to assume that neither was in any way typical of English communities in general. It is works such as these, however, which carry us back most convincingly into early modern English community life. It is against these that one might set a picture of Whitchurch if one could be drawn.

Histories of other places can be very revealing about the effects of religious change in Tudor and early Stuart times

Eamon Duffy
The Voices of Morebath: Reformation and Rebellion in an English Village (Yale 2001)

David Underdown
Fire Down from Heaven: Life in an English Town in the Seventeeth Century (1992)

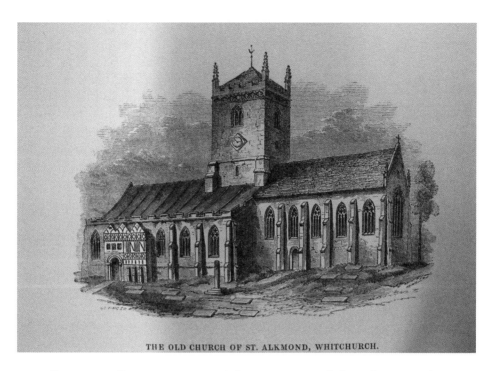

THE OLD CHURCH OF ST. ALKMOND, WHITCHURCH.

Illustration from R.W.Eyton *The Antiquities of Shropshire* 12 vols
1854-60

*There is an assumption that this is the third building on the site and
one which replaced the structure which gave the settlement its name. It
was probably erected in the fourteenth century, but with the tower
added later. Until 1711 this was the religious and social centre of
Whitchurch.*

Of course, the rector of Whitchurch ought to have been a significant figure in the town. There was no resident lord of the manor topping the social hierarchy. After 1598 rectors owed

Rectors of Whitchurch

their appointments to the Egerton family, who that year bought from the Talbots the advowson, or the right to select this spiritual leader. For the man given the post much of its importance lay in the income obtained from working glebe land and the opportunity to collect tithes directly from parishioners. These customary dues on crops and animals were paid annually, but not to vicars or curates who were on fixed salaries from whoever else held the tithe rights. Potentially, rectors were on to a good thing. Just how good in Whitchurch at the start of the seventeenth century is not known, but a listing in October 1701 recorded that tithes were largely paid in kind, not cash. An assiduous rector could gather in, for example, every tenth sheaf of a grain crop and every tenth handful of hemp, plus similar percentages of lambs, geese and pigs. Cash came in from Easter Offerings as so much per head according to age not social status.[35] A non-resident rector had to pay curates to do his job, though how far the rate was negotiable is a nice question.

The first rector to collect an income from the parish appointed by an Egerton – in 1606 - was Thomas Singleton. It is very likely that he hardly ever came to Whitchurch. He was principal of Brasenose College, Oxford, for a start, from 1595 to his death in 1614. Twice he was vice-chancellor of Oxford University, plus holding posts as canon at St. Paul's Cathedral in London and Hereford Cathedral. His career was as an academic and university administrator and he was buried appropriately in Oxford. A suspicion has been expressed that he might have been rather more radical in his views than the established order of his day, but more as a passing phase than a settled theology.[36] Much depends on how the internal politics of the university are interpreted, for the issue on which his potential radicalism rests was that of a response by Oxford theologians to the Millenary Petition presented to James I on his accession in 1603. Singleton did dissent from the majority view on that occasion.[37] Ironically, he was critical of the practice of non-residents holding benefices. It was common for men in his position to collect provincial benefices purely to boost their income. They left the cure of souls in the hands of deputies, often on short-term contracts. In 1612, the curate in Whitchurch was Anthony Buckley, about whom nothing else is known.[38] The effect on Whitchurch of an absentee rector is a matter of guesswork, but the likelihood is that for the first half of the reign of James I Whitchurch had no great spiritual leadership at work.

This might have changed when a successor to Singleton came in 1614, but again it is far from certain. John Rawlinson, aged 38, was another Oxford don and Principal of St. Edmund Hall. He too was a doctor of divinity, possessor of one benefice in Buckinghamshire and another in Essex, and closely associated with Lord Ellesmere (Sir Thomas Egerton). He was chaplain to Ellesmere as Lord Chancellor, an office which made him a central figure in the *John Rawlinson* king's government. [39] Ellesmere was also Chancellor of the University of Oxford and considered somewhat of a Calvinist or radical in matters of church reform. Rawlinson was certainly a committed opponent of Catholicism when he tried unsuccessfully to become President of St. John's College in 1611 with Ellesmere's blessing. It was Ellesmere, of course, who gave him the rectorship of Whitchurch to add to another rectorship at Selsey, in Sussex, he acquired in 1613. By 1619 he was enjoying royal favour as a chaplain to James I.

Rawlinson has been described as "a fluent, florid, and edifying preacher" who made sure his sermons were published and gained suitable rewards. Oxford was his power base and he built a new house on High Street there in the 1620s quite possibly in the hope this would strengthen his suitability to become Bishop of Oxford. In this he failed. Was he just a bit too anti- the Catholic colouring of the Anglican church which Charles I revered? [40]

The principal clues suggesting that Rawlinson was more active in the care of his Whitchurch parish than any of his other benefices are, first, that he was buried at St. Alkmund's and, second, he left substantial bequests for the benefit of the poor. The principal one was a direction, registered in the manor court, that specific copyhold lands left to Richard Alport were to be charged with £12 per annum for the benefit of poor residents in the parish. The churchwardens were given the responsibility of administering this. [41]

The third clue is, of course, the name of Richard Alport. He was Rawlinson's son-in-law, married to Joyce the only surviving child of Rawlinson. Joyce must have spent time in Whitchurch to become acquainted with Alport – or her father did. The Alports lived at Overton Hall and profited from land and industrial investments. Richard's father died in 1625 having put his property in trust for his younger son, Richard, who reached the age of eighteen early in January 1631. On the 23 January he married Joyce Rawlinson in St. Alkmund's. Three days later the Court Baron met and registered the land deal whereby John Rawlinson surrendered several pieces of land in Whitchurch to Richard Alport with the charge for the benefit of the poor laid on. [42] On the 29 January John Rawlinson drew up his will, witnessed by his very new son-in-law, Richard

Alport, and on 3 February he died. On the 10th he was buried. This rush to complete deals invites speculation. [43]

Rawlinson made Catherine, his wife, sole executrix. [44] Among his smaller bequests he left

"to my Curate Mr Arthur Dudley Marlozate in folio upon the New Testament a Latin Concordance, one Volume of St Jerom's works and Origens works in Two Volumes in Folio My best Cloth gowne faced with velvet and another Clothe gowne faced with Budge and my Turky Grogrun Cassock".

Arthur Dudley had been his curate in Whitchurch since 1616. [45] To Joyce there was another gift suggestive of residence in Whitchurch.

"to my daughter Joyce all my Plate goods and oud utensils in my Parsonage house at Whitchurch as Bedds and Beddinge Brasse Pewter and the lyke except one Truncke one waynescotte .... which I give & bequeath to Catherine my wife ..."

Rawlinson had at least furnished the old rectory with stuff he considered valuable and presumably well known to his wife and daughter. Was this because he paid lengthy, if not regular, visits?

Finally, with respect to Whitchurch, Rawlinson left £20 in cash to the poor of the parish to be distributed by the curate and churchwardens - £8 immediately to those in greatest need and the other £12 to *"six score of the most needie poor of that parish by forty shillings at a tyme the first Sunday in every month for the space of six months next after my decease"* at a rate of four pence each! He could have felt this kind of last minute philanthropy was necessary for all sorts of reasons – one thing it indicates to a modern mind is that he knew very well that there were a lot of poor people deserving a dole: 120 every month to be precise.

It's possible to see into the life of Whitchurch parish from Rawlinson's

Churchwardens' accounts

time onwards in a quite new way. From 1619 a series of financial accounts and lists of inhabitants become available, not because they necessarily started at that point, but because they have not been lost in the way previous records disappeared. Churchwardens and their fellow parish officials, the Overseers of the Poor, reported annually on their year's work. The substantial pile of paper they left behind provides clues to concerns and practical problems inherent in the relationship between church and people.

For the most part the records are reports of routine activities. Not often is there a glimpse of some untoward incident such as the hint of catastrophe in 1619 when a man was killed by a team of horses on the parsonage land.

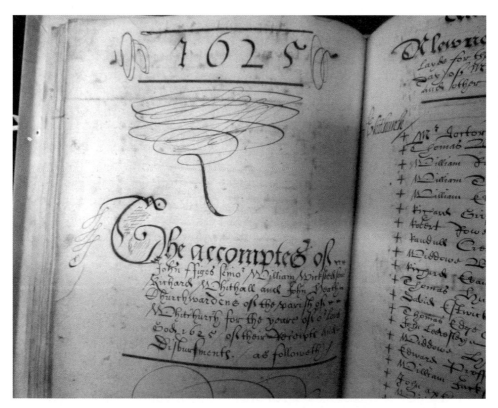

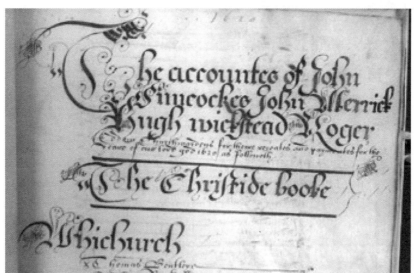

Sample pages from churchwardens' accounts in the 1620s.
Shropshire Archives P303mf 268,267

A fine of £12 was levied on the orders of the Lord Chancellor to be spent on *"the good of the towne of Whitchurch"*. This was quite a sum given that the income for the year available to the churchwardens from normal sources was £22-9-4.[46]

The rector came from outside the community; churchwardens were selected annually, from among resident property holders, by their neighbours. They had two linked principal duties – to manage the parish stock of goods and money, and keep the church building in good repair. They could raise an income from charges on parishioners as well as take care of bequests in cash and kind. By the time of James I churchwardens were accruing more responsibilities under Parliamentary legislation and had to work alongside other parish officers, chiefly the Overseers of the Poor and the Surveyors of Highways. Together these men formed the administrative heart of the community.

The first men named as churchwardens, for 1619, were Peter Morehall, William Ranshall, John Symcocke and John Mericke. [47] It was their successors in 1622 who had the bigger task to deal with, however, for they managed the casting and hanging of new bells in the church tower. There would appear to have been four bells, one taken down for recasting at Wellington. It cost 1/6d to remove it from the church and load it on a cart. Re-hanging it with some repairs to the ironwork cost 3/4d. Transport back from Wellington organised by Richard Lovell and Daniel Kempster cost 15/-. Kempster also provided five new bell ropes for 16/-.

The accounts were written out in such a sequence that it would seem that putting up the new bell had a knock-on effect, for the third bell was then found faulty. William Clibery, the bell founder from Wellington, was consulted and more repairs were done to the iron frame. Another opinion was sought from a William Church, the result being that this bell was also taken off for recasting at Wellington. After this was restored to the tower more alterations were required and the fourth bell had to be repositioned. From other sums spent it would seem that there was damage to the floor that had to be put right as a result of all this structural work. Interestingly, the churchwardens took out insurance against a bell falling for they made Clibery give in a bond to reimburse them if any fell within a year and a day.

All this was in addition to normal repairs on the lychgate door, for instance, and the weathercock pole which let in rain through the roof. Their income came to £27-17-3 but despite the bells they still had £3-6-6 in hand at the end of the year.

Men holding the office of churchwarden during
the period 1619 –40 inclusive

Ball, Thomas	Morehall, George x 2
Benyon, John	Morehall, John
Brindley, Robert	Morehall, Peter
Brooke, Thomas	Morhall, Robert
Chetwood, Roger	Penkston, William
Constantyne, William	Ranshall, Thomas
Eddowe, Roger x 3	Ranshall, William
fflewellin, Thomas	Rycrofte, Laurence x 2
Figes, John senr gent	Shenton, Randull
Figges, John junr	Stokes, Nathaniel
Hawkes, Robert	Symcocke, John
Heath, John	Symcockes, Nathaniel
Hochkis, John	Trym, John
Hopkin, George	Tushingham, George
Hotchkis, John junr	Welch, Raph junr
Hughes, John	Welch Raphe senr
Hughes, William	Whithall, Richard
Jackson, Robert	Wickstead, William junr
Lea, William	Wickstead, William senr
Merricke, John x 2	Wicksted, Hugh
Merricke, William	Wicksted, William senr

Four were chosen every year, and each served for two successive years,
retiring in pairs
x 2 = number of times appointed to the office

Any praise for the careful management of the churchwardens in 1622 has
to be qualified with the memorandum entered in their records in April
1623 when their accounts were audited.

*"That at a public meeting of the whole Parish, April 29 1623 it was by
a generall voice concluded that the general summes then levyed upon
several men for the raising of this maine lewne should be no precedent,
or presindies, to any man for any lewne hereafter to be raised but, before
any other lewne shall be layed in time to come, there shall be a generall
meeting of the whole parish, to consider of every particular mans estate,
not according to what it hath been, but according to what shall be
thought meete and reasonable, and conscionable at the time, when the
next lewne should be layde."*

This was witnessed by John Rawlinson, though whether on a visit or now in residence cannot be determined.

One aspect of the relationship between the church and the inhabitants of the parish is clear from this episode. The ancient right of the churchwardens to levy a lewne, or rate, on all property holders to cover the cost of running the community's spiritual and leisure centre was a potential source of conflict. It wasn't simply the justification for expenditure on some individual project which was at issue, but also the monetary valuation of properties on the basis of which rates were set. Obviously, in Whitchurch by 1622 there were those who thought they

Township	No. of lewne payers 1622	Township	Number of lewne payers 1622
Whitchurch	72	Dodington	44
Green End	24	Alkington	17
Pepper St	16	Edgley	5
St Marie's St	15	Burghall	18
Total in urban settlement	**127**	New Woodhouses	21
This count is more accurately a count of the number of rateable properties as some entries include reference to sons, for example, or some other person sharing in the payment.		Old Woodhouses	11
		Ash Magna	14
		Ash Parva	13
		Tilstock	26
		Hollihurst & Chinnell	5
It understates the number of properties in the urban area because some in Dodington must have been along the street of that name. Those in Blackoe do not come within the urban settlement.		Worsewall & Bradley Green	13
		Hinton	6
		Black Park	3
Total overall	**323**	**Total**	**196**

were over rated – that their properties were not worth as much as previously reckoned. Was this a sign of an economic depression, perhaps, as well as of a system bound by ancient custom and practice?

Another way the churchwardens raised cash was through payments made for seats in church. They carefully recorded all the names of those required to pay, what they paid and in which section of the building they were located. In 1623 there were five groups of people divided between those paying at the old charge or rent, those at a new rent, some in north seats, others in south seats and a few in the gallery. [48] The implications of what the difference was between new and old rents are not obvious now, nor the reason why the rents were revised or when. It is also far from clear how these payments relate to specific seats. It is tempting to think in terms of north and south aisles either side of a central block with the new and old rents applying only to the seats in the middle. There was a small gallery, though just how this was located cannot now be established.

Other sources of income for the churchwardens came from the 'Christide Book' and fees for burials inside the church. Those listed by name and amount in the Christide Book were clearly contributing to the general fund for church maintenance but the account's title suggests that this was collected at Christmas. It could refer, however, to what in other parishes was part of the income of the clergyman known as Easter Dues. This cash collection was not recorded later in the century and may have fallen into disuse in the days of the republic. A small number of burials inside the church continued to take place throughout the seventeenth century following the five noted in 1619. [49]

Some reorganisation of Whitchurch parish government may have taken place in 1625. The churchwardens chose to include in their records a list of "*Vestrie men*" chosen by the whole parish, six to represent Whitchurch, four from Dodington, two *Vestrie men* from Hinton heading the list, with all the other townships similarly dealt with. This might be seen as a reform in the name of efficiency, replacing a meeting of the whole set of parish ratepayers which it could be clumsy to organise. On the other hand, it might have been a reaction by a self-selected minority to the decisions taken at full parish assemblies thought inimical to the interests of the relatively wealthy few. It didn't stop the churchwardens and Overseer of the Poor continuing to keep separate accounts or alter the duties of the wardens with respect to the church and the morals of parishioners.

The death of John Rawlinson in 1631 did not mark some major change in the character of religious activity in Whitchurch if he had, indeed, taken up residence there and played an active part in parish life. However, if he had been but an occasional visitor and left the cure of souls to his deputies, as his predecessor had done, then the change of personality at the rectory was of some importance. For the next century Whitchurch was to have the benefit of permanently resident rectors. It was also to experience far more tempestuous times than had been the case for the previous century. Despite all that Henry VIII, King Edward and Queens Mary and Elizabeth had wrought upon their realm in the way of the outward and visible display of religious beliefs at least the land had remained peaceful. All that was to change precisely because of what their Stuart successor monarchs took to be their inheritance from their Tudor predecessors.

Chapter 4

The Anglican Church personified: Thomas Fowler and the descent into Civil War

In 1631, Thomas Fowler got the job of rector of Whitchurch at the direction of the then Lord of the Manor, Alice, widow of that Sir Thomas Egerton who had bought the manor and rights in the first place. He was the second son of Walter Fowler of Pendeford, near Wolverhampton, whose manor had been acquired from the sale of properties at the dissolution of St. Thomas' Priory, near Stafford. Thomas was about twenty-nine years of age when he came into his benefice.

He was an Oxford graduate, from Trinity College, who went up around the age of fifteen and had his MA conferred in 1625. It has been suggested that he came to the notice of his patroness by virtue of becoming tutor to her son, Viscount Brackley. [50] He took up his post just as the Church leadership nationally was coming to be personified by William Laud, soon to be Archbishop of Canterbury. He was intent upon removing, or at least neutralising, a strong Puritan movement within the clergy and many congregations.

Without diverging too far from the main thread of narrative it is appropriate to note that the monolithic appearance of the Church of England was deceptive by the time James I came to the throne in 1603. Theological dispute amongst Church of England clergy was now a *theological disputes* growing feature of their activities, with those ultimately labelled Puritan most succinctly described as zealous for further movement away from the Catholic inheritance. Symbolic acts such as kneeling at the mention of Christ and making the sign of the cross on the baptism of babies figured high on their list of objectionable practices. Preaching was an essential task, but only if based upon sound learning such as that acquired at university. Eye-catching, colourful clerical clothing and stone statues, redolent with Roman Catholic meaning, were superstitious obstacles to the true faith. As opposition grew to established traditions and ancient roles preserved from medieval religious observance so it was easy to label the minority with a pejorative name – 'Puritan' carried overtones of fundamentalist zealotry, self-denial and humourlessness, still familiar to us, and deliberately chosen for this reason. The ranks of the Establishment never had a label, but for convenience sake can be called Anglican to ease the flow of narrative. Archbishop Laud led an Anglican counter-movement to the dissemination of Puritan thinking, and was appointed by Charles I for the express purpose of re-balancing the Church of England, if not removing Puritanism altogether. A key moment was the move by Charles to extend this policy to Scotland, a Puritan society *par-excellence*. From 1637 religious debate turned into a political power struggle and armed conflict.

One small measure of the depth of divisions within the Church of England was provided in 1635 by the minister at St Chad's, Shrewsbury. In a pamphlet he published that year he wrote

> *"Know, good reader, that this towne of Shrewsbury, the place of my birth and residence, is generally troubled with a sect of men and women, with whom I have had much intercourse of conversement; not by way of intimate familiarity approving their wayes, but of vexation and trouble of minde, that I could not, in thirteen yeares of painefull ministry among them, reclaime them from their wandering fancies, and reduce them to obedience of supreme Majestie."* [51]

If Shrewsbury was infected with Puritanism, could Whitchurch be far behind?

Thomas Fowler had personal and parish concerns to occupy his mind apart from potential theological challenges from his congregation. The

the state of the parsonage and chancel of the church

first of four children was baptised on 1 October 1631. There was no intention, apparently, to expand his horizons beyond Whitchurch. He also wanted to make his home more comfortable, an ambition he combined with anxieties about the state of the fabric of his church buildings. He must have carried on an argument with the widow of his predecessor, Catherine Rawlinson, for some time, ending up taking her to the Court of Arches in London. Here he complained in 1639 that she, as executrix of her husband's estate, was responsible for paying for repairs to the parsonage and the chancel of the church. This was the time-honoured duty of the rector, and something John Rawlinson had seriously neglected. Fowler sent in detailed estimates of what the charges of plasterers, carpenters and masons would be to deal with his domestic buildings and the chancel. He claimed to know that Rawlinson left quite enough money in his estate to pay the bills. Unfortunately, the supplementary documents don't survive, and it is not clear what judgement the court came to. [52]

Fowler, as an Anglican, would have been more and more aware of tensions within the church nationally as the 1630s wore on, but what his reactions were, and whether he found groups of his parishioners inclined to Puritanism is unknown. Some must have been aware of the state of things in Shrewsbury, at least. When the explosion came in the form of a civil war, there is no doubt about Thomas Fowler's attachment to the King's cause and the Anglican position. Too much ought not to be read into his letter of support for the king written to *"my honoured friend Francis Ottley, Esq."* on 19 August 1642, for this was still a time when every man claimed that his actions were in the best interests of the king. [53] But when troops in the forces opposing Charles I came into town in May 1643, Fowler fled. His services for the king thereafter were given in Shrewsbury, as that town was garrisoned by royalists.

Civil Wars 1642-51

It is presumed that he was captured there along with many others and taken prisoner to Nantwich. In May 1645 a Dr Fowler, at Nantwich, had the chance to go free by giving his parole to Sir William Brereton, the Parliamentary army commander, that he would arrange an exchange with a Puritan minister held by the king's troops in Dublin. The County Committee for Shropshire, opponents of Charles I, told Brereton that they had no interest in Dr Fowler's future, and Brereton was free to deal with him as he thought fit. It is possible that Thomas Fowler did succeed in his objective, though he was only allowed a month to go to Ireland to find his exchange partner. [54]

In 1646 the first civil war was ended when Charles I surrendered himself to an army from Scotland. Fowler's opposition to the victorious Puritan authorities, conveniently labelled Parliament for simplicity's sake, included not signing the religious declaration called the Solemn League and Covenant. This refusal was followed by the sequestration of his property, on Parliamentary orders, for his delinquency *"in going into Shrewsbury when a garrison for the King."* After fighting had long ceased and the king executed, Fowler began making his peace with the new, republican and fiercely Puritanical, regime. He bought his estates back in April 1649 at a cost of £130. 00. [55] It has been correctly supposed that Thomas Fowler did not return to duties in Whitchurch, but took refuge at Little Gaddesden in Hertfordshire, at the centre of the Earl of Bridgewater's estates. At all events, a memorial inscription in Little Gaddesden church reported the burial of Thomas Fowler, teacher of theology and rector of Whitchurch in the County of Shropshire who died

Fowler's death

27 February 1652. The memorial was erected by two sons, John and Thomas. [56]

Meantime, the state of religious observance in Whitchurch and the cultural climate thereby implied presents intriguing possibilities. In the following fifty years or so, numerous Whitchurch parishioners showed a

effects of war on Whitchurch

strong tendency to support alternative forms of religious worship to those of the Anglican Church, though it is not possible to trace this before 1643. Interestingly though, the historian of the Free School, Ernest Clarke, commented on the preponderance of ex-Free School pupils who turned up in the ranks of Charles I's opponents in contrast to those who followed the King. [57] Whatever the implications of this, by the 1670s, as will emerge from this narrative, a determined group of parishioners defied state imposition of that form of public religious observance required by the Established Church. They suffered persecution for their beliefs. For the local historian the puzzle is to find when such a view came to the fore, who first sowed the message, how many accepted it and which were the leading families involved? One obvious starting point is the time when the traditional religious authority was absent from the parish.

From May 1643 Whitchurch had no resident clergyman, so far as is known. Troops commanded by Sir William Brereton, Parliament's principal military leader in Cheshire and north Staffordshire, did not stay long in the town after clearing out the royalist forces. Any ministers embedded in their ranks presumably went with them. Thereafter, for three years, civil war swirled around Whitchurch, seriously affecting the local economy no doubt, frightening the population as rumours and counter-rumours of royalist and then Parliamentarian forces threatening to occupy the town ran rife. Long after the event, it is possible to see that this was a bitter, viciously fought, immensely destructive conflict. The social and psychological consequences are the subject of guesswork. It was ostensibly a power struggle of great political magnitude: it is easy to forget it was also about religious belief and the freedom to express in public what was privately held incontrovertible. So what went on in St. Alkmund's?

Direct information about how the parish was affected by military action is scarce, mainly because it was not the focus of anybody's attention. Rather it was a place troops moved through as rival commanders orchestrated their regiments to relieve or enforce various sieges. Cholmondeley Hall, Beeston Castle, Shrewsbury and Chester were the key sites. Wem, Middlewich and Nantwich briefly held the centre stage, but putting a permanent garrison in Whitchurch was not a major objective by either side. It is highly likely that this slow churning of small armies moving about north Shropshire and west Cheshire left Whitchurch somewhat isolated, subject only to brief occupations alternately by the king's men and the troops of Sir William Brereton. Interestingly, one historian of the Egerton estates, Eric Hopkins, found that there was good evidence of damage to property and loss of rents in the Ellesmere part of the Earl of Bridgewater's lands in Shropshire, but a distinct lack of such evidence for Whitchurch. The absence of paperwork hinders research, but Hopkins speculated that no rents from north Shropshire ever reached the earl while fighting continued, although these lands provided almost half his normal annual income. [58]

The marauding soldier, hung about with looted food pictured by a contemporary satirist

Town residents had a foretaste of trouble very early on, for within a month of Charles I calling for an army to assemble in August 1642 he was passing up High Street around midday on 23 September bound for Chester. He wanted recruits and cash, and some of his officers were not too careful how they acquired essential supplies. Shropshire was generally reckoned to be favourable territory for the king, but Sir William Brereton gathered strong support for the Parliamentary cause in Cheshire. Around Christmas 1642 a temporary royalist garrison lodged in Whitchurch and soon after fought skirmishes with Brereton's men coming out of his headquarters in Nantwich. Brereton's attack, made in May 1643, which drove out Thomas Fowler, was designed to cut easy access for royalists from Shrewsbury to their compatriots holding Chester. During the next eighteen months and more this pattern of activity was repeated more than once.

A clearer picture of just how this worked out can be discovered for several weeks in the spring of 1645. The voluminous correspondence files of Sir William Brereton for this period reveal how the king's desperate attempts to relieve the siege

military action Spring 1645

of his garrison at Chester included sending the two princes, Maurice and Rupert, to lead about 7,000 troops, joining forces on Fenns Moss on 17 March and intending to march through Whitchurch. [59] They had some success in the next two or three days, but were beaten back into Whitchurch by Thursday 20 March. Brereton had been reinforced by a contingent from a Scottish army, under General Leslie, and they moved in as the king's regiments left Whitchurch. After three days they left to return to Yorkshire. A few days later Brereton's other support group, a cavalry troop from Yorkshire led by Sir William Constable, settled in Whitchurch. They countered a threat by Charles I, now leading an army up from the south, again heading for Chester. The Yorkshire men were a thoroughly disgruntled lot, not yet paid the five shillings a week they had been promised for venturing into Cheshire. Their officers reported them as verging on deserting. Fortunately for Whitchurch they soon disappeared. Their presence had been enough, however, to compel the bulk of Charles's army to take a more easterly route than really desirable. Even so Sir William Vaughan quartered a royal regiment in Whitchurch on 20 April 1645. [60] Such a rapid turnover of soldiers wanting beds, drink and horse fodder presented townsfolk with severe problems.

This flurry of military activity is the only one to show up in the records of the churchwardens. Every year there were repairs necessary to the fabric of the building, and it was not unusual for windows to be replaced. A little more was spent perhaps between April 1645 and April 1646 than in previous years, but the conclusive proof of disorderly troops in town were the three entries of payments amounting to three shillings and a penny to at least two men for cleaning the church on three separate occasions *"after souldiers"*. [61] Just which side was most to blame cannot be judged.

Divine services on Sunday in St. Alkmund's church were an integral

Of God,   Of Man,   Of the Divell.

feature of life's routines for every parishioner. War obviously upset things. The questions are, how ruinously and with what consequences? Who organised public worship and in what form? There was no resident rector. Who took his place?

Chapter 5

Religious revolution: the arrival of Thomas Porter

It is well recognised that Fowler's eventual successor at St. Alkmund's was Thomas Porter, and that he was a stalwart of the expanding Presbyterian movement in England, from which sectarian Dissent was ultimately formed. The nature of his religious message was, in its day, revolutionary. The same was true of the manner in which he came to his role as minister at Whitchurch.

Porter, a Northamptonshire man by birth, had served as vicar in Hanmer, Flintshire, throughout the 1630s. This was the parish in which his father was born, and where Sir Thomas Hanmer held the advowson. By 1642 Porter had an appointment as a Lecturer in Chester immediately prior to military action in England starting against the King. [62] This type of preaching post was a Puritan-inspired move intended to repair weaknesses in parish spiritual care where clergy failed to do their duties properly. It ran counter to the spirit of Archbishop William Laud's Anglican policies issued from London. Porter had been a sizar (financially poor student working as a servant) at Christ's College, Cambridge, from 1616. He got his MA there and was ordained in 1623. He possibly brought Puritan convictions with him to Hanmer and there developed an unfulfilled missionary zeal. Why else move to a city job in Chester?

It was presumably opportunities opened up by war which allowed Porter to move to a London parish by 1645, at St. Catherine Cree. This took him close to the heart of the military regime being constructed in the nation's capital. He joined a Presbyterian 'Classis'   *moved to London* or association of ministers designed to be the model of church organisation for future implementation nationwide. This, and his lectureship at St. Lawrence Jury, confirmed him as one of those most active promoters of reforms in religious observance formulated by an assembly of divines at Westminster and similar to, but not an exact copy of, those advocated by Scottish forces. [63] When the fighting ceased in 1646, however, it was a variety of Independent sects which were in the ascendant. Porter left London before the main struggle for control took place between his Presbyterian colleagues and the Independents. Essentially, they were divided by the issue of whether any form of national church organisation should be retained. Conspicuous among the targets for removal by reformers were bishops as spiritual leaders and church administrators. Presbyterians such as Porter were against dismantling the structure of the church completely.

But when did he move to Whitchurch, at whose invitation and approval, and by what means? Did he cause dissension, or was he brought in to entrench it? Just as importantly, what differences were there between Porter's religious message and that of the Church as established and headed by Charles I and William Laud?

It is almost certain that Porter went to Whitchurch in 1646. One presumption has been that he was directed there by the Parliamentary Committee for Plundered Ministers, but the

How Porter came to Whitchurch

local historian T. C. Duggan in his *History of the Parish Church* went further and positively stated that Porter was appointed by Oliver Cromwell acting as the patron.[64] There is no reason to suppose that Cromwell was in any position to act as patron in 1646. Equally, there is no evidence that the first Earl of Bridgewater moved to replace Thomas Fowler. There is substantial evidence that Thomas Porter claimed to be the 'Minister of the Gospel' at Whitchurch before February 1649/50 as he had one of his sermons delivered in that post, titled *'Spiritual Salt'*, printed that month. [65]

Porter was a leading figure in the 'Classical Presbytery in Bradford North', and his sermon was preached on the occasion of the appointment of five new ministers. Probably the first step in the move from London to Whitchurch came just after June 1644 when the House of Commons passed an Ordnance giving its controlling Committee in Shropshire, based then at Wem, powers to replace clergymen *"ill affected to Parliament"* with *"learned, able, godly, and fit persons"*. Thomas Fowler was thus a target for removal. Two years later the Commons ordered that Presbyteries be established in every county. In effect, this neutralised bishops and threatened to replace the parish as the unit of church organisation. A pamphlet published in April 1647 gave details of the creation of a Shropshire Classical Presbytery for which Thomas Porter, minister at Whitchurch, was eligible along with John Hotchkys (or Hotchkis) and Joshua Witter also of Whitchurch. [66] John Hotchkis was a draper in Dodington and, a little later, Witter was noted as having a house in High Street. [67] William Cotton of Bellaport and Daniel Benyon of Ash were among others similarly named .[68]

The exact date of Porter taking on himself the duties of a Presbyterian minister in the parish of Whitchurch may be fixed by entries in the churchwardens' accounts, first of all in January 1645/6.

> *"Jan ye 20th spent in goeing to Shrewsbury to the Committee being these two of us out two days and two nights in concerning means for a mynister spent upon ourselves and horses 10s."* [69]

Other notes around the same time refer to Mr Benyon being absent from his *"cure"* as though he was temporarily acting as a minister, perhaps alternating with a Mr Harding. [70] The Committee, of course, was that set up by order of Parliament to administer Shropshire. It presumably moved its headquarters from Wem to Shrewsbury after the county capital was captured by a Parliamentary force early in 1645.

The course of proceedings which this evidence suggests corresponds to that found, for example, in Cheshire parishes. In the absence of the Anglican rector, a few parishioners, including *local men involved* Daniel Benyon, John Hotchkis and Joshua Witter, looked around to find a way of implementing the wishes of the House of Commons to have godly men acting as ministers. They were

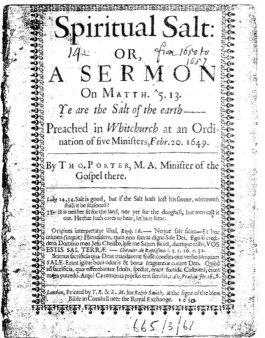

Shropshire Archives 665/3/61

predisposed to have one who was a Presbyterian rather than an Independent or Baptist in beliefs. They filled the vacuum as best they could until Thomas Porter from a London living was suggested to them by the County Committee. Perhaps his name as a former vicar of Hanmer was already familiar to them: possibly Porter was looking to return as near as may be to his former home, and contacted Benyon and friends privately. Whatever the case, it seems more than likely that Porter came to Whitchurch early in 1646 by arrangement with local men, and that he was thus welcomed by a group of Puritans, possibly long-time critics of Thomas Fowler. Here, clearly was a significant consequence of civil war and a reliable indication that no ordained clergyman had been officiating at St. Alkmund's for many months. It might even be said that the levers of power within the parish had passed into new hands.

The churchwardens who must have been the official actors in this transfer of power – if such it was – were John Merricke, Samuel Symcockes, Thomas Ball and Thomas Welsh. Like their colleagues from 1619 onwards they kept impeccable records of their income and expenditure, listing all lewne payers and renters of seats, as was the well-established custom. Apart from the entries already quoted from their book of accounts, it is not possible to see that there was a civil war all around them, that men's beliefs were subject to vehement debate, and everywhere was disorder, death and destruction. Curiously, none of the wardens who went off to Shrewsbury to find a new minister show up in subsequent records of Presbyterian activity. They filled the office, but it seems effective power lay elsewhere.

Power struggles in London continued to interest Porter. He signed, as *"pastor of Whitchurch"*, a document published in 1648, most simply known as the *Testimony*. This was drawn up in Shropshire to support the fierce criticisms London Presbyterian ministers made of a variety of Independent sects apparently proliferating uncontrollably. [71] To men of Porter's mind the world was being turned upside down and chaos loomed.

Porter's part in organising a Presbyterian Classis for the Bradford Hundred (ie a religious organisation for a civil district of administration) was one thing. Another matter, of at least equal importance to him, as to other ministers of the reforming faith, was to get into a benefice with the approval, or at least connivance, of the traditional patron. This way Porter could pick up the house, glebe lands and income of a parish clergyman with which to support himself and his family. It was this financial aspect of church organisation which, ironically, preserved the traditional Anglican (indeed Catholic) structure otherwise disliked by Puritan reformers. The evidence of Adam Martindale's tribulations in Cheshire at this same time proves to just what lengths incoming Presbyterians, and their local Anglican opponents, would go in struggles over possession of benefices. [72] Key factors in success were a vacancy, preferably through the death of the Anglican incumbent, and the neutrality of the patron.

In the case of Whitchurch, Fowler was absent, but not dead until 1652, and the first Earl of Bridgewater was an equivocal patron beset by financial problems within his family. [73] The earl died in 1649 with his estates intact, but leaving a twenty-seven year old son much suspected of conspiring against the newly born republic. This second earl, John Egerton, inherited large debts from his father, and was taken prisoner in April 1651 for his alleged political activities. Peers, by definition, were royal creations and must have had severe doubts about their future. Bridgewater bought his freedom by finding bail bonds worth £20,000 and promising to do nothing *"prejudicial to the present government"*. [74] It was in this context that Oliver Cromwell wrote to Lord Bridgewater in May 1654 on the subject of the presentation to the rectorship of

Cromwell's letter

Whitchurch. He explained that he did not wish to interfere with the rights of the Earl in this matter, but he was nevertheless in favour of appointing Thomas Porter.

> *"And although I can find it in my heart to incline you to Mr Porter yet it is with this cleernesse, That I shall leave your Lordship most free to exercise your own Libertie; assuring your Lordship that if you shall intend the reall good of the people in your choyce, a person answering that will be equally acceptable to me, as Mr Porter, wherefore leaving the business wholly to your Lordship's dispose, I rest your very loving Freind. Oliver P."* [75]

Lord Bridgewater drafted a reply in June, though it cannot be shown that this was ever sent. Bridgewater claimed that he had already made an appointment, a Dr Bernard, and could not undo this. Otherwise, he said, he would have been happy to select a person approved by His Highness. No one had made objection to Bernard. The earl went on to say that Mr Porter's carriage towards him in this matter had been such that he could not with any consideration for his honour have given him the post. Indeed, the earl thought that there never would be any peace among the inhabitants so long as Porter remained. Finally, Lord Bridgewater apologised for not meeting Cromwell personally on the matter, but pressure of business left by his father made it unsafe for him to appear in public. [76] The gist of this reached Cromwell, for in a declaration he made in August 1654 he withdrew an order made by him in a difference between Dr Bernard and Mr Porter. He stated that he had since learned of the Earl of Bridgewater's rights, which he did not wish to prejudice. [77]

At the very least, it would seem that around 1652-3 the Earl of Bridgewater sought to fill the vacancy at Whitchurch left by Thomas Fowler's retreat to Little Gaddesden, and/or subsequent death. He chose a Dr Bernard who possibly never entered the parish because there already was, on site, a pretender to the benefice. Thomas Porter, fighting to stave off Bernard's claim by right of the Earl of Bridgewater, appealed to the Lord Protector for assistance. Cromwell issued an order in his favour, and then cancelled it, after making some effort to persuade Bridgewater to look for a Calvinistic minister similar to Porter.

Obviously, Porter achieved the rectorship *de facto* if not *de jure* because in 1655 a survey, or Inquisition, of Shropshire parishes ordered by the Lord Protector, Oliver Cromwell, confirmed that Porter was in this post and receiving the income due to the rector. [78] The Earl of Bridgewater probably still felt it best to do nothing to upset Cromwell. There nevertheless remains an intriguing question as to how far Porter thrust himself upon Whitchurch when a local vacuum existed, or whether some residents actively invited him to come up from London knowing of his Presbyterian reputation.

AN INQUISITION INDENTED taken at Salop the   day of Januarie in the year of our Lord God 1655 by vertue of a Commission from His Highness the Lord Protector of the Commonwealth of England Scotland and Ireland and the Dominio[ns] thereunto belongeinge, directed unto Creswell Tayleur, Robt Corbet, Edward Cresset [and others] for the unitinge of p[ar]ishes etc by ye oathes of Tho[m]as Brayne Samuell Smith [and 17 others]THE HUNDRED OF BRADFORD NORTHWHITTCHURCH we find personage or Rectorie, the Earle of Bridgwater patron, Mr Thomas Porter A Constant and Able preacher of ye word of God Minister and p[re]sent Incumbent there, he doeth officiate in his owne p[er]s[o]n The personage house And Gleabe thereunto belonginge is worth £10 p[er] annu[m] And all the Tythes belonginge to the said Rectorie in this Countie are worth p[er] annu[m] £260 And the Township of Worsenall w[i]thin the County palatine of Chester. And yet a Member of the said Rectorie is worth p[er] ann[um] £14 the whole Tythes And Gleabe worth p[er] annu[m] £284. There is an Antient Chappell w[i]thin the Towne of Tilstock which Towne is A Member and belongeinge to the Rectorie of Whittchurch. There is noe certaine meanes belongeinge to the said Chappell. Mr Thomas Porter the younger sonne unto Mr Thomas Porter Rector of Whittchurch A verie hopefull Scholler A Constant painfull preacher of ye Gospell doeth officiate there, And is paid his salorie by Mr Thomas Porter his father ye Rector of Whittchurch But to what value we knowe not, which Chappell we humblie conceive fit to be Continued.

IGHTFIELD is a Rectorie .... Mr Robert Bynney p[ar]son and p[re]sent incumbent there an Able painfull and constant preacher ....

An extract from a document found in 1932 in deeds relating to the Mackworth family, one Humphrey Mackworth, a Colonel in the Parliamentary forces in the 1640s, who died in 1654, being Governor of the town. His son, also Humphrey, became Town Clerk of Shrewsbury. See Transactions of Shropshire Archaeological Society Vol XLVII Part I (1933)

Chapter 6

Thomas Porter at work in Whitchurch 1646 – 60

It is clear that, despite his reservations, the Earl of Bridgewater was not an insuperable obstacle to Porter's acquisition of the parish perquisites, but the unwelcome minister did prove to be a powerful influence on the neighbourhood, as Bridgewater feared.

Presbyterian ideas on the practices of Christianity were not the only brand circulating, but they spread far and wide, rapidly and with success. John Aubrey, the Wiltshire antiquarian, later in the century, was only one of several who thought there was some link between reforming ideas in religion and ways of earning a living. He considered dissent from religious authority more likely in *dissent spreads* dairying country than in arable or sheep districts. Dairymen had more time to read than shepherds. [79] Some historians have portrayed shoemakers as too literate for their own good. The experience of Porter's contemporary, Richard Baxter, was that weavers were especially adept at reading or talking on religious subjects amongst themselves while at work. [80] Baxter was a Shropshire-born Dissenting divine who, as a lad about 1630, saw his father buy Dr Sibb's *Bruised Reed* from an itinerant chapman at the door of his house in Eaton Constantine. Young Richard found this well-known volume of Puritan sermons powerfully persuasive. A contemporary, though anonymous, seventeenth century writer is quoted to explain how it was that Puritanism spread effectively

> "*by means of the City of London, the nest and seminary of the seditious faction, and by reason of its universal trade throughout the kingdom with its commodities conveying and deriving this civil contagion to all our cities, and corporations, and thereby poisoning whole counties.*" [81]

Manchester in the 1640s was said by another writer to be "*as the very London of those parts, the liver that sends blood into all the counties thereabouts.*"

Richard Heywood, a merchant of Bolton, reported that

> "*when he was abroad his design and practice was to hear the best preachers; he travelled to London once or twice every year and he constantly heard old Mr Edmund Calamy at Aldemanbury ... and such like. His practice at London was to furnish himself with the best*

books, the most plain, practical, experimental treatises in divinity, such as Calvin, Luther in English, Mr Perkins, Dr Preston, Dr Sibbs, wherein he took much pleasure in reading." [82]

Among numerous other examples, Chester horse fairs are quoted as means whereby traders linked different manufacturing areas with each other, and their markets, and thus acted as probable conduits for subversive religious literature. They supplied animals to the Lancashire and Yorkshire weaving districts. If this view has any validity then Whitchurch's commercial connections with Chester and its situation in good dairy country, sheltering numerous shoemakers and leather tanning trades, make it even more likely that Puritan literature was available in the town and taking effect before Porter arrived. [83] The result of his short stay was to root Protestant dissent deep in the parish.

Evidence that controversy and disharmony arose in Whitchurch parish over Porter's arrival and religious issues is scattered, difficult to access and tantalising. In the family papers of the Egertons, earls of Bridgewater, now held in the Huntington Library in California, there is a petition dated 6 January 1653. This named eight people complaining of Porter's behaviour towards a Mr Bowry, minister at Marbury. These parishioners wanted Porter removed and Dr Bernard installed as the lawful parson. Four other documents in January and February supported this or pressed other charges against Porter, one being that he uttered seditious words against the government. [84]

disharmony in Whitchurch

Of all local official positions and appointments, other than that of rector, the one most likely to be controversial for religious reasons was that of schoolmaster. All the Free School records for the Commonwealth period have disappeared, and it is not possible to be sure that the mastership, for example, was subject to dispute. In any case, inclinations towards Puritanism may have been reinforced by masters prior to the civil war period, when such views were not necessarily considered inconsistent with the existence of the Church as then Established. [85] Once the Anglican Church was abolished in 1649 there may well have been parishioners anxious to prevent new masters being appointed who might entrench anti-Establishment opinions more strongly. For example, a potential parish registrar in October 1653, George Whittingham, was noted by the magistrates at Quarter Sessions as controversial because he was an alehouse keeper and disordered, a man supposed to be disaffected to the State (ie the Republic), and brought forward to represent a particular *'interest'*. [86] This would not have been an unusual accusation to make against a member of an opposite sect. It is just possible that Whittingham was also intended to be the school master as well, and that these charges were totally unfounded. Clearly the accusations were made by an *'interest'* in conflict with that which Whittingham supported, indicating a split of sorts in the parish. [87] The incident cannot be easily discounted because Whitchurch affairs rarely went up to the magistrates for resolution in Quarter Sessions, and must be considered tips of icebergs when they did.

The extent to which the Free School was influenced by opponents of an established Anglican Church may be registered by the presence among the feoffees *grammar school men* of the school by 1660 of four men with distinctly anti-establishment records. Rowland Whitehall helped Parliament raise money for troops in 1650; Daniel Benyon and John Hotchkis [88] have already been mentioned as Presbyterians; while Luke Lloyd of Hanmer in Flintshire had been a Captain in the Parliamentary army. [89] It is not certain that this influence disappeared with the restoration of the Anglican Church in 1660. Two Masters came and went rapidly before Samuel Edwards took the job in 1665, and he was much favoured by Philip Henry, the most celebrated of the Whitchurch Dissenters. Perhaps the most telling example was Edward Lawrence, admitted into the Presbyterian ministry in 1648, and a product of Whitchurch Grammar School and Magdalene College, Cambridge. By definition he must have been given his scholastic grounding well before civil wars troubled the nation. [90] He will appear again later.

If controversy within the parish during the 1650s is difficult to trace this isn't the case outside. In January 1649 Charles I was executed and shortly afterwards the Church of England was to all intents and purposes abolished. Thus bishops and the Prayer Book by which religious observance had been regulated no longer operated. Rivalry between sects to establish a *sectarian rivalries* hold over the minds of people in general in the resulting vacuum was reflected in public disputations over theological issues and practices of public worship. Another of the pamphlets bearing Thomas Porter's name reported in much detail an argument over the validity of baptising infants, as opposed to waiting until they became adults. This disputation was conducted at Ellesmere when hundreds if not thousands were said to attend, and where Porter defended traditional child baptism against Mr Henry Haggar. The origin was a sermon on the same subject Porter had given earlier and which upset the local Anabaptists to the point where they challenged him to a public debate. Porter, apparently, raised much laughter and some hisses, by making figures of fun out of his opponents. This was blamed on a claque which, it was alleged, Porter brought with him for this very purpose! He denied it, of course, and accused his critics of inviting derision by their foolish antics. Just what the people of Ellesmere generally made of this cannot be discovered, but according to the report there was standing room only, and the event continued for five hours.[91]

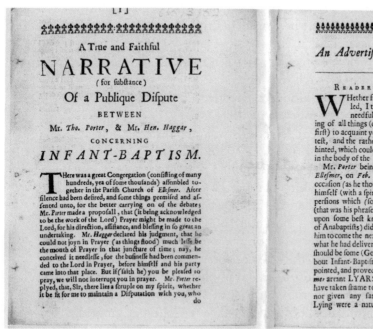

LIJ

A True and Faithful

NARRATIVE

(for fubftance)

Of a Publique Difpute

BETWEEN

Mr. Tho. Porter, & Mr. Hen. Haggar,

CONCERNING

INFANT-BAPTISM.

There was a great Congregation (confifting of many hundreds, yea of fome thoufands) affembled together in the Parifh Church of Ellefmer. After filence had been defired, and fome things premifed and affented unto, for the better carrying on of the debate; Mr. Porter made a propofall, that (it being acknowledged to be the work of the Lord) Prayer might be made to the Lord, for his direction, affiftance, and bleffing in fo great an undertaking. Mr. Haggar declared his judgment, that he could not joyn in Prayer (as things ftood) much leffe be the mouth of Prayer in that juncture of time; nay, he conceived it needleffe, for the bufineffe had been commended to the Lord in Prayer, before himfelf and his party came into that place. But if (faith he) you be pleafed to pray, we will not interrupt you in prayer. Mr. Porter replyed, that, Sir, there lies a fcruple on my fpirit, whether it be fit for me to maintain a Difputation with you, who do

665/3/52

An Advertifement to the Readers.

READERS,

Hether friends or foes, ftaggering or fetled, I though it not only expedient, but needfull (having had perfect underftanding of all things (concerning the debate) from the firft) to acquaint you with the occafion of this Conteft, and the rather that fome things here may be hinted, which could not be fo conveniently fet down in the body of the Narrative.

Mr. Porter being called to Preach the Gofpel in Ellefmer, on Feb. 13. 1655. did in his Sermon take occafion (as he thought he was bound) to vindicate himfelf (with a fpirit of meekneffe) from fome afperfions which (fome of the rebaptized judgement (that was his phrafe) had caft upon him. Whereupon fome beft known for diftinction by the name of Anabaptifts) did write a Letter to him, defiring him to come the next monthly Lecture to make good what he had delivered, and that then and there, there fhould be fome (God willing) to difpute with him about Infant-Baptifm. Mr. Porter came the day appointed, and proved four of the Anabaptifts in Ellef-[Nath. Gil.] mer arrant LYARS (though I cannot learn that they [Jo. Capp.] have taken fhame to themfelves for their fin of Lying, [Jo. Edw.] nor given any fatisfaction to Mr. Porter. As if [Mа. Edw] Lying were a natural ingredient into Anabaptifm A 2 (as

Extracts from the pamphlet reporting the disputation at Ellesmere
"There was a great Congregation (consisting of many hundreds, yea of some thousands) assembled together in the Parish Church at Ellesmer…"
Shropshire Archives 665/3/52

Porter's attitudes to baptism were signs that he advocated a view of Christian faith and its practice in daily life not too far different from that of the Anglican Church represented by Thomas Fowler. Porter was a long way from being as revolutionary in his theology as were the members of the Society of Friends founded by George Fox, for example, popularly called Quakers. Porter rejected Baptists and the free-thinkers, roughly identified as Independents. Presbyterians like Porter, essentially, looked for a more effective way of obtaining obedience to high moral standards than that provided by a bishop-led, parish-rooted church organisation. They challenged the top-down flow of directives and appointments of the Church of Elizabeth I. Hence their use of congregations of the like-minded, or classes, each choosing its own minister, with laymen acting as a kind of executive committee. Unfortunately, this implied a direct threat to the maintenance of the wider social order and property ownership. In practice, they intended no such thing, although there were cultural implications of their theology, stressing the importance of literacy and schooling, for example, which could be construed as disturbing.

In Whitchurch the best sign that Porter stood for continuity in parish practice, whatever the revolutionary consequences of his theology, was the accounts register of the churchwardens. These officers were appointed every Easter time as traditionally required, kept their records as neatly and efficiently as ever, probably now subject to a tighter annual audit. The evidence for this is the list of men who signed off the accounts each year in the later 1650s. Prominent among them were John Hotchkis, Joseph Wittar and Daniel Benyon. Income came from the standard sources of lewnes (the tax on property) and for seats in church: expenditures scarcely varied, including money spent on the bells. Business, in fact, was much as usual.

Thomas Porter seems to have enjoyed a favourable reputation among contemporaries locally, but not necessarily with central authorities. Shortly after the *Porter's reputation* king's execution the Commonwealth government sought to isolate critics by enforcing the taking of an oath – the Engagement – and arresting for questioning those refusing. Porter was so detained. [92] On the other hand, he was praised as *"He by his great prudence so managed the Ministers on that side of the county where a Presbytery was settled that he found no need for compulsory laws".* [93] Richard Baxter noted him as *"an ancient, grave Divine of great integrity, blamelessness and Diligence"* and *"so excellent a Preacher".* [94] A recent historian, after reading his sermon printed in 1650, concludes that it was "a pleasing address, not overlong and not without humour. It was on the text 'Ye are the salt of the earth, but if the salt lose his savour wherewith shall it be salted' (Matthew v. 13)". [95]

The Presbyterian 'classis', or meeting of ministers, had amongst its responsibilities that of authorising new ministers. Their work included the expansion of the Presbyterian movement into areas not previously touched. Thomas *other Presbyterian* Porter served as the President of the 4th Salop *ministers* Classis in September 1657 when the application for a ministership by a young man called Philip Henry was approved. [96] He was only one of a number of preachers and teachers selected by the 4th Classis during the 1650s, and there is little reason to suppose that he was considered any more significant at that time than any of his colleagues. His journals or memoires composed in tiny books survived, however, and made him a unique figure in the history of

Whitchurch. More particularly he left evidence of many of the experiences of dissenters after the Restoration of monarchy and the collapse of the republic in 1660.

Thomas Porter was undoubtedly at the centre of an active Presbyterian movement while at Whitchurch. His son, Thomas, *("a very hopefull Scholar. A Constant painfull preacher of the Gospell"* [97]) took services at the chapel at Tilstock, and was among the ministers ordained by the Classis. At the ceremony for this, in 1656, a sermon was delivered printed under the title *"Authoritative Separation of Men to the Work of Christ, a Ministerial Privilege".* [98] A Mr Bruce took over the Marbury district of Whitchurch parish when its rector died in December 1647. He was a Scot considered, as a Presbyterian, to be a *"lively affectionate preacher"* and one with small financial means. [99] Philip Henry's first post was at Worthenbury in 1657 where he had the Puleston family as his support. Robert Fogg worked in Bangor-on-Dee as a Presbyterian , and at Malpas the minister was George Mainwaring. Not far away, at Hanmer, Richard Steel officiated and came to be a noted friend of Philip Henry. Outside the Shropshire group, Porter's circle came to include the minister at Swynnerton, in Staffordshire, Joseph Sond or Sound. He was called to witness Thomas' will made in August 1666 at Wycherly.

Something may be said about Porter's private life. He and his wife Mary had three sons, Thomas, Samuel and Jabez (named after his grandfather) who was buried as an infant in 1653. Mary was buried in Whitchurch in September 1657. As he left property at Dudleston and Baschurch, as well as at Moulton in the county of his birth, Northamptonshire, he presumably did not entirely rely on income from the rectorship of Whitchurch. [100] The effort he put into obtaining the post argues that he either had great awareness of its symbolic value as legitimising his role in the community, or it was a source of income too good to spurn – or, of course, both. It may be unfair to judge his liking for a comfortable material standard of living from the lengthy list of goods his second wife left at her death and to point up the absence of any charitable bequest in his will. His personality remains enigmatic, more's the pity.

Presbyterianism, however, was the order of the day in Whitchurch only as long as the republic lasted. The arrival of Charles II in London at the end

Porter withdraws of May 1660 signalled a revival of the former Anglican Church. Bishops came back, clergymen forced out of their livings during troubled times returned to reclaim them, and Thomas Porter was faced once more by that same Dr Nicholas Bernard appointed by the Earl of Bridgewater some eight years previously. The near contemporary historian of these times, Edmund Calamy, recording the fate of Presbyterian clergy in a work called *The Nonconformists' Memorial,* implied that Porter quickly retreated from Whitchurch to allow Bernard to take over. [101] His last sermon at St. Alkmund's was on 28 August, and Bernard began in December 1660. [102] Calamy thought Bernard a *"worthy moderate man"* and perhaps inferred that Porter hoped his own mission would continue under his learned replacement. Of Porter, Calamy thought highly. At Hanmer

> *"his ministry was blessed with wonderful acceptance and success: both in that and neighbouring parishes; and a great harvest of souls was gathered in to Christ .. ... He removed to Whitchurch, where he continued to be an instrument of much good. By his great prudence he so managed the ministers on that side of the county, where a Presbytery was settled, that he found no need of compulsory laws."*

One of Porter's strengths for Calamy was his preaching excellence, which also drew approval from the principal Presbyterian of his day, Richard Baxter.

Porter found immediate refuge in the household of Robert Clive of Styche whose wife, Mary, could have been his benefactor. In fact, it is entirely possible that the move out of Whitchurch was not due simply to the reappearance of Dr. Bernard. On 26 March   *last years* 1660 Thomas Porter married Susanna Clive, Robert's sister. [103] At that stage the revival of monarchical government and the Anglican church hegemony was all rumour, not fact. There is no knowing whether Porter had the foresight to prepare for ejection from Whitchurch by marrying a propertied woman, or whether he took his bride there with every intention of remaining, or, indeed, whether he planned to retire whatever the national situation. After all, he must have been 60 years old.

He is not known to have been able to practise his oratorical skills and pastoral care thereafter except occasionally, as in Shrewsbury where he preached twice in that town at St. Chad's. In July 1661 Porter, was back in Whitchurch preaching at a marriage, and in November joined other ejected ministers at an Exercise in Wem. He may well have settled for a time in Shrewsbury for he was buried there in June 1667. [104] Philip Henry noted at the time that he died

> *"in a good old age; a man much honoured by God with success in his ministry, there being many who call him Father – Hee was exercis'd long with payn upon his bed & ye multitude of his bones with strong payn, so unsearchable are they Judgements of lord ... His dying counsel to the lords people was, to stick to Christ & not let him goe, tide life, tide death."* [105]

Despite Thomas Porter's own strength of faith his last years may have been clouded by the weakening of his son Thomas's resolution. He conformed to the new regime in 1663 and was ordained by the Bishop of Chester to take up a post at Bunbury. [106] He was not alone in finding such an accommodation possible.

Porter's legacy was in the beliefs and value systems of Whitchurch people. He rooted a variety of the Christian faith in the town which was to have long lasting consequences. It was not so much the numerical strength of the congregations which met in the years after his removal, but rather the perpetuation of a tradition of nonconformity which thereafter had a continuous history to the present day. The Anglican Church reasserted its legal authority after 1662 and the town has ever since been taken to be firmly in the hands of successive aristocratically appointed rectors. In practice, Whitchurch was a microcosmic reflection of the nation as a whole: it did not entirely lose the habit of refusing to accept the dominant credo of an Established Church acquired in the mid-seventeenth century.

Chapter 7

*A*nglican Clergy restored and a congregation forced underground : Matthew Fowler and Philip Henry in contention

Until 1660 St. Alkmund's was the place where Whitchurch people did their public religious duty. Thereafter its symbolic representation of the unifying bond of religious belief was broken. Dr Bernard, and after his death in October 1661 his successor, Richard Heylin, reintroduced acts of Christian worship as laid down in statutes going back to Queen Elizabeth's time. The reason for the break was the collapse of the Commonwealth and the Lord Protectorship of the Cromwells and the restoration of a monarchy and the Anglican Church. It might not be going too far to say that, for royalists, it was revenge time. A new Parliament called by Charles II in 1662 was the agent, despite promises the king made before his return, at Breda in the Netherlands, which had given Presbyterians at least the hope that they could achieve some accommodation with the new regime.

In Whitchurch, the Anglican model of religious observance had been publicly rejected for at least fourteen years by a significant minority of local inhabitants. Many of Porter's congregation refused to conform to the new regime so that, in effect, two congregations existed where, in principle, there had formerly *two congregations* been one. The rector who faced the dissenters for longest was Matthew Fowler. He had to implement the new, deliberately oppressive, regulations enshrined in Acts of Parliament from 1662 onwards. The intention was to eradicate all forms of Protestant nonconformity. Catholics had been oppressed for a century and denied the ability to worship openly. Now it was the turn of a multitude of Protestant inspired sects to suffer the lash of persecution.

Inevitably, the minority, subject to severe legislative attack, hid their activities. Their meetings and ways of mutual support are still largely hidden from view, being scarcely recorded outside Quarter Session and Consistory Court papers dealing with discoveries of illegal services. This is the reason why the diaries of Philip Henry, briefly mentioned earlier, are so useful. It's true they were the work of a man committed to one side of an intellectual argument, and a victim of social and economic persecution. He never had ministerial status in Whitchurch such as Thomas Porter had enjoyed, but he did exercise that office in a parish close by. He was often in town, was intimate with many of its residents and sat through services in St. Alkmund's so far as his conscience allowed. Henry's account of life as it was lived, day by day, during a very special episode in the history of Whitchurch, is made vivid by a cool recording of thoughts and actions. There is a window here on a world hidden at the time.

The biography of Philip Henry is well known.[107] He was not local by birth and education, but came into the district as a

Philip Henry twenty-two year old private tutor to a lawyer's family, the Pulestons, at Worthenbury. He was of a gentry family himself, an Oxford graduate, but not an ordained clergyman. It has already been noted that he was subsequently accepted as a minister in the 4th Salop Classis sharing in the work of spreading the Presbyterian message in north Shropshire, as it happened just at the time when the republican government was in its final stage. Worthenbury, in Flintshire and a few miles west of Whitchurch, was his base and his source of income. His experience thereafter was publicly summarised by his son, Matthew, in a book brought out in 1698. The significance of this homage to his father was re-inforced nearly two hundred years later by the publication of a collection of Philip Henry's diaries and letters. This allowed the dissenting minister to be seen almost every day during the period when not conforming to the rites of the Anglican church made criminals out of a section of Whitchurch society. It is the uniqueness of this evidence from the 'inside' of a nonconforming congregation that elevates Philip Henry to the forefront of the history of religious worship in later seventeenth-century north Shropshire.

It was the new Prayer Book of 1662, unacceptable to many Presbyterians, which drove men such as Porter and Philip Henry to find alternative

new Prayer Book 1662 sources of income and to organising services outside the law. The book was incorporated in an Act of Parliament and using it was a test of religious loyalty. By inference, it was also a test of political allegiance. Both Porter and Henry lost hope of obtaining benefices by refusing to use it. A series of other Acts of Parliament, such as the 1664 Conventicle Act (due to expire after four years) and the 1665 Five Mile Act, gave powers to magistrates to arrest, imprison and fine nonconforming ministers and their congregations for holding conventicles, or meetings for religious worship without the use of the Prayer Book. Discovery of these meetings depended exclusively on information sent to a magistrate by somebody keen to persecute dissenters out of religious conviction, personal antipathy or desire for the reward money. Inevitably, interest in pursuing dissenters varied from place to place and time to time. Philip Henry's record of arrests and imprisonment was not unusual, but it is revealing about the state of affairs in Whitchurch and district. Alongside some other evidence it points to continuous, though fluctuating, friction in the area between the minority faithful to the discredited Puritanism of the 1650s and the Anglican segment of society.

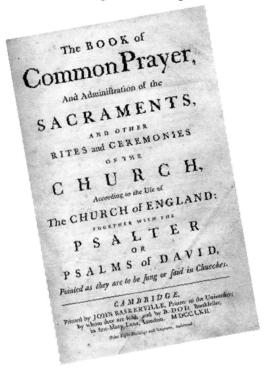

An early, though somewhat confusing, sign was Philip Henry's arrest on 10 October 1663 on suspicion of being implicated in a plot against Charles II. He had moved to Broad Oak, close to Whitchurch and in Malpas parish, but still in Flintshire, after ejection from Worthenbury in October 1661 for refusing to use the new Prayer Book. He aimed to keep a low profile. As a man married for three years, with a child and in financial difficulties, he could not afford to fall foul of the law. *"Things are low with me in the world; but threepence left"*, he wrote, *"My hope is yet in the lord that in due time he will supply me."* [108] Part of his problem was that he didn't get on particularly well with his father-in-law on whom he depended for access to a small-holding in Broad Oak. Apparently, what he thought was a dowry in fact cost him £800. [109]

Henry arrested and in financial difficulties

The supposed plot was scarcely more than a few scattered, much misled and mis-informed republicans and dissenters who gathered under arms in Yorkshire and Westmorland but never assembled as a force. They melted away just as quickly, or allowed themselves to be caught from sheer folly. This 'northern rebellion' was taken as an excuse by Charles II's government for a wide-spread round-up of numerous known nonconformists, including many from the north midlands, in part to justify persecuting local leaders of the republican era hitherto untouched. Henry was swept up with another thirteen and taken to a gaol in Hanmer for four days as but a small fish, briefly inconvenienced, in this over-enthusiastic trawl. [110] The motivation for this sprang more from central government requirements than north Shropshire antipathies. Twenty-four of the twenty-six condemned to death as a consequence in a royal court in London were less fortunate: they were executed. Little wonder Philip wrote in his diary *"Tis the first time I was ever a prisoner but perhaps may never be the last."* [111]

Those imprisoned with Philip Henry do not appear to have come from Whitchurch, but in his diary for April 1663 Henry not only noted the

Matthew Fowler arrives April 1663

first appearance of Dr Matthew Fowler in St. Alkmund's but also that *"Mr Thomas threatned … at Tilstock by Dr Fowler, if hee should bee remov'd twill bee ill not with that place only but with the neighbourhood also: therefore spare lord".* [112] Henry had a lot of respect for Zechariah Thomas, although he had been appointed by Dr Bernard to replace Thomas Porter's son. [113] Fowler succeeded, for Thomas was indeed compelled to leave the curacy at Tilstock, a chapel of ease in Whitchurch parish, in May. [114] On the other hand, Henry's first reaction to Fowler was not inimical. On 10 April Henry confided to his diary, *"Dr. Matthew Fowler came to bee Preacher at Whitch. in the stead of Dr. Heylin, likt better than he was if it hold."* [115]

In September 1665 Henry was again under arrest. The charge was attendance at a conventicle in Hanmer. There, it was claimed, he conducted the service of the Lord's Supper. Again, he spent only a few days in gaol, but was released upon a recognisance of £20 for good behaviour for which Allen Sheret and Thomas Davies stood surety. Among the others, Richard Steel was detained as a *"dangerous and disaffected person"*. [116] The Conventicle Act justifying this was passed in 1664 and made illegal any meeting for purposes of religious observance unless using the Revised Prayer Book. Somebody must have spied on him and the others present, and informed the magistrates. Steel was a particular friend of Philip Henry who recorded on 24 December that *"hee was pronounct in Hanmer excommunicate."* [117] Earlier in the year three of the others arrested with Henry in September had already been excommunicated in Hanmer. [118]

One of the figures who appears crucial in this affair, and in others of a

Sir Thomas Hanmer

similar kind, was Sir Thomas Hanmer of Bettisfield, justice of the peace and deputy lieutenant of the county. The parish of Hanmer was, of course, that in which Thomas Porter had served as an ordained clergyman in the 1630s. Henry's friend, Richard Steel, then took over. How this was linked with the leanings Sir Thomas is thought, initially, to have had towards the Parliamentary cause is not clear. After he lost his property as punishment for supporting Charles I, and a skirmish in and around Hanmer church, Sir Thomas apparently hardened his religious affiliation to the Anglican establishment. [119] Long before the restoration of monarchy Sir Thomas had returned to Bettisfield and is generally thought to have concentrated on his estate and his passion for gardening. The return of the king, presumably, released him to become more active in local administration and politics. So long as Henry resided at Broad Oak he was subject to Sir Thomas Hanmer's predilections rather than Matthew Fowler's. [120]

In 1666 Henry had to answer at an archdeacon's visitation to Malpas for not attending church to take communion. He sent his wife to pay the fees and obtain *Mrs Henry pays fees* his discharge. Presumably the Mr Tanat and Mr Bromley who laid the charge were fellow parishioners. A Thomas Tanat lived at Broxton Hall in the 1660s and paid hearth tax for eight hearths. He called himself a gentleman in his will and died leaving personal goods to the value of £262. [121]

To prevent false accusation under the Five Mile Act that he was living in a prohibited area (ie within five miles of the parish in which he had officiated as a minister) Henry measured the distance from Worthenbury to Broad Oak with extreme care. In March 1667 he moved with his family to Dodington, in *Henry moves into* Whitchurch town, just after he established that he *Whitchurch* was about sixty or so yards on the right side of the law! By doing this he was liable to be jumping from the frying pan into the fire, for he now came within the purview of the rector of Whitchurch, Matthew Fowler. In details of this kind the lifestyle of a persecuted minority is laid bare.

Not that the Henry family stayed long. By the end of July they were back at Broad Oak. Mrs Henry was expecting another child, the harvest needed careful management and there was fear that they would all catch small pox which was rampant in the town. With harvest in and child born the Henry family returned to Whitchurch town before Christmas. They stayed for the winter, but after May 1668 Philip Henry always resided in Broad Oak. He habitually attended the chapel close to Broad Oak at Whitewell as well as St. Alkmund's where he heard Fowler preach. This practice continued, but technically Henry was not a parishioner in Whitchurch for more than about eleven months.

Clearly, in and around Whitchurch Henry had sufficient support and encouragement to arrange, or to join, gatherings of like-minded people for collective worship as Thomas Porter had taught them. Inevitably, meetings were in the homes or barns of believers and no record was kept of their frequency and numbers attending, still less of names or financial accounts. Only when Henry was arrested did such events come to public notice: only if reported for his own private purposes in his diary can we learn of other activities.

One exceptional occurrence brings out a few names of associates and brilliantly illustrates tensions in the community. In October 1670 the curate at St. Alkmund's, Benjamin Taylor, recorded an excommunication in the parish register. This unusual, but increasingly widely adopted, action was entered formally in Latin, itself indicative of the tone suffusing Anglican practices at the time. In effect, it threw seven people out of the parish church for refusing to take communion there. Four men were named as John Beard, 'Randulphus' or Ralph Eddowes, Robert Bennion and John Robinson, and three females were Elizabeth Yardley, Sarah the wife of Ralph Eddows and Anna the wife of Thomas Chetwood. There is no other information as to what triggered this startling denunciation, or why it was the curate and not the rector who made the entry. The implication of the charge was that these people had contumaciously and contemptuously refused to go up to the altar rails to take the bread and wine, quite possibly for some long time and in a very public manner. [122]

dissenters

excommunicated

Taking communion was the ultimate test of religious loyalty, not attendance at Anglican services as such. Once Thomas Porter left the pulpit and Richard Heylin was responsible for leading the parish in worship there was no bar on dissenters joining the congregation, and many no doubt did so. Philip Henry was certainly one for he frequently made comments about the text of the rector's sermons in his diaries.

Extract from Whitchurch parish register

Joh'es Beard, Radulphus Eddowes, Robt Bennion, Sara uxor sp'd'cti Ralphi Eddows, Elizabetha Yardley, Joh'es Robinson, et Anna uxor Thomas Chetwood, p'ochi de Whitchurch, palam et publice in Eccl'a p'cali de Whitchurch sp'dct' denunciat'et declarat' fuere, esse et fuisse excommunicati, propter eorum manifest' contumacia' et contemptu', pr imprimis autem quia p'ticipes sacrae co'minionis non fuere. Ita.testor, Ben: Taylor Curat.

John Beard, Ralph Eddowes, Robert Bennion, Sara, wife of the above-named Ralph Eddows, Elizabeth Yardley, John Robinson and Ann, wife of Thomas Chetwood of the parish of Whitchurch above-named, were openly and publicly in the parish church of Whitchurch denounced and pronounced as being and having been excommunicated because of their manifest contumacy and contempt (*of court*), particularly since they have not partaken of Holy Communion. Such is my testimony. Ben. Taylor, Curate.

Original Latin as provided by Rev. G. Vane in *Transactions Shropshire Archaeological and Natural History Society* vol. XII (1900) page 295
Translation supplied by Nigel Coulton
Radulphus Latin = Ralph English

There is no doubt that Philip Henry and his fellow dissenters from the Anglican church were in a minority in north Shropshire. No later than August 1662 all ministers who refused to use the new Book of Common Prayer had been thrown out of their parish posts. It is a safe assumption, therefore, that as it was illegal for people to attend any services the ejected men organised, the majority of Whitchurch inhabitants continued to sit in St. Alkmund's on Sundays for services conducted according to Anglican rules. It has already been noted that Dr Bernard was officially rector of Whitchurch before the end of 1660 and that he died in the following year. The Earl of Bridgewater, a noted Anglican, replaced him with Richard Heylin. Neither of these two rectors are easy to place theologically and their impact on the parish is unknown. It is quite likely that neither took up permanent residence and both left their flock in the hands of curates. In June 1662 a Joshua Lee of Whitchurch made his will as a clerk, which ought to mean that he was a clergyman there. He was certainly unusual, leaving £25 worth of books according to an inventory of his personal possessions. Unfortunately he has not been traced in the standard records of Anglican clergy so his possible role as a curate is in doubt. [123]

Perhaps fear held the Presbyterians in check during the months when the focus of attention was on ejecting nonconforming clergy. Certainly, Philip Henry admitted to his diary that he was in a dilemma in April 1663, not knowing whether to go to the all-important Easter communion or not. He would not kneel to accept the bread and wine, but he felt unable to condemn those who did. Fowler had only just arrived and was a bit of an unknown quantity. [124]

The nice question concerns the extent to which it was Matthew Fowler's arrival in Whitchurch which gave a boost to anti-nonconformist forces in his parish. The report of him preaching first in April 1663 has already been linked to his success in removing a dissent-minded curate at Tilstock, Mr Thomas. It might be expected that more urgent action would follow this. After all, in a sense he had form. He was the younger brother of Thomas Fowler, the devoted follower of Charles I, with a career in the 1650s much disturbed by a republican government promoting Presbyterianism. His biographer puts him in High Ercall in 1645-6 as the vicar there, appointed by Lord Newport. [125] He is presumed to have experienced the military campaign by which Lord Newport's royalist troops lost their fight with a Parliamentary besieging force. He disappears from view after this, possibly going abroad for a time, though returning before 1653 to marry Letitia, or Lettice, Wald, a Devon girl. He surfaces again in London in 1661 petitioning the King to instruct the University of Oxford to award him the degree of Doctor of Divinity. His grounds for this were that he had been denied the opportunity to obtain this honour by the hostile regime dominant at the time he was eligible. Shortly after, he obtained a parish in Hammersmith, replacing a Mr Doolittle, well known for his Presbyterianism. [126] He didn't stay long for, according to his biographer, in January 1664 he was instituted as the rector of Hinstock, near to Market Drayton. Three years later, in February 1667, he added the rectorship at Whitchurch to his responsibilities, although he had been preaching there since 1663 according to Philip Henry. [127] Indeed, he almost certainly came in the first instance as a locum for Dr Heylin in Spring 1663, becoming formally a curate in 1664. Certainly he made himself very active in parish business from early 1663, taking oaths, for example, for probate purposes from May 1663. [128] It may be reasonable to suppose that this preferment at the hands of the second Earl of Bridgewater gave him great satisfaction in the light of his brother's long incumbency in the parish. Matthew Fowler remained in post until his death in December 1683. He personified the Anglican

Matthew Fowler's career

supremacy established in law by the 1662 legislation, and carried with him all the marks suffered by Anglican opposition to republican Presbyterianism in the 1650s.

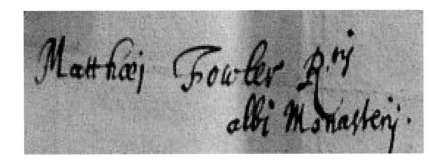

Matthew Fowler could not directly touch Philip Henry, resident in a Flintshire township and the parish of Malpas. The striking thing about Henry's diaries is that he did not note any particular acts by Fowler directed at dissenters in Whitchurch until 1670. Henry recorded events in Hanmer and Chester, for example, *a new Conventicle Act* involving other people, but had almost nothing to say about Whitchurch. In his mind, things changed in 1670 because new legislation could be implemented from May that year. The rule was re-imposed that no more than five people could join a family for religious worship unless the Prayer Book was fully in use. [129] The penalties for a preacher and a house owner were £20 each, and for those over sixteen years of age five shillings on first offence. Only one magistrate was required to hear a charge and order distraint of goods if fines were not paid, and magistrates and constables were equally liable to prosecution if they failed to enforce the law. [130]

So, just what was happening in October 1670 when seven parishioners were singled out for excommunication? Something touched a nerve in the curate, Benjamin Taylor, for there is a possibility that Matthew Fowler was not the instigator. Philip Henry suggested that the Bishop, John Hackett, of Coventry and Lichfield did not support the action and recorded that one of his court officials, Sir Walter Littleton, soon absolved the alleged offenders from the penalties laid upon them. [131] Unfortunately, no further evidence bearing on the case has come to light, so Philip Henry's diaries are vital documents. [132]

According to Henry there were two key people. One was Ralph Eddowes and the other Edward Lawrence. The train of events began, Henry implied at an earlier meeting (assumed to be a service of worship) held in

A portrait of Philip Henry

Ralph Eddowes' house in May 1670 about which he wrote
  "Mr Lawrence in trouble at Whitchurch, for meeting this day at Ralph
  Eddowes upon pretence yt Sarah Eddowes com'n from Chester was
  none of her father's family." [133]

In other words, within twelve days of the 1670 Act to Prevent and
Suppress Seditious Conventicles, renewing the 1664 legislation, coming
into force, someone reported Ralph Eddowes for holding an illegal
meeting. An unknown magistrate immediately imposed penalties and
presumably had a refusal to pay. This was duly noted by Henry the
following week when he wrote that a distraint order was carried out on the
goods of Ralph Eddowes to the tune of £20-5-0 with the consequence
that *"the town and country full of noise aboyt it. Also many elsewhere in*
trouble on ye like occasion". [134] This was the fine specified in the Act for
refusal to pay, and confirmation that it was the legal requirement of the
new law which motivated the action was also given by Henry.
  "May 31ʳ : Distress made upon their goods: Ralph Eddowes - £20-5-0,
  Mr Lawrence £10, John Bird [recte Beard] & Thomas Kettle [recte.
  Kelley] £5 each, Elis Yardly five shillings, by Constables and
  Churchwardens."[135]
  [The corrections to the transcription were made by Rev. Geoffrey F. Nuttall
  presumably after consulting the original manuscripts. [136]]

It's hardly surprising that this set the tongues wagging in the
neighbourhood. What better way could there be of throwing into relief
the divisions of faith in the parish?

Philip Henry then seems to have almost deliberately run the risk of similar
treatment himself, for he went on June 1 with his wife to Ash, *"where mett*

occasionally divers other Friends, noys'd to bee a Conventical, churchwardens & other officers came to search, but ye company was gone before." [137] The Benyon family were long established in Ash, though the elder Daniel Benyon of Great Ash had died the previous year. [138]

This was not the end of the matter. According to Henry, the target was really Mr Lawrence not Ralph Eddowes. [139] Edward Lawrence was well-known in dissenting circles and to the authorities. He was born at Moston, Hawkstone, Shropshire and was   *Edward Lawrence* Whitchurch Grammar School educated. He was named in a Return of 1669 under the Conventicle Act as one of eleven *'teachers'* who met in his house every Sunday and led a congregation of about 80 people, mostly women. Four of the teachers certainly were formerly beneficed clergy and Ralph Eddowes was also named as among the others. It would appear, therefore, that the man who was most responsible in Whitchurch parish for keeping alive the Presbyterian principles laid out by Thomas Porter was Edward Lawrence. Not that he had officiated locally as a minister during the republic. His post had been at Baschurch, a village south-west of Wem in Shropshire. [140] He did not move back to Whitchurch immediately after ejection around 1662, for he found shelter with a Baschurch family. In 1666, however, it has been claimed that he brought his family to Tilstock to escape the tentacles of the Five Mile Act. [141]

The 'noise' that disturbed Philip Henry in May presumably recurred in October 1670 when Ralph Eddowes and his colleagues were excommunicated. Henry's account amplified that written by the curate.
"October 2   Ralph Eddow, John Beard with others excommunicated at Whitch. Dr Fowler protesting hee did it unwillingly yet by his own procurement. They did not presently depart ye congregation, whereupon hee sayd, unless they did, hee would be gone, & so went forth his Desk."

The clue to the meaning of this event was given by Henry a week later.
"October 8   Mr Lawrence, Ralph Eddow &, having su'd the Justices for recovery of their goods taken from them in June last, they endeavour their excommunication to prevent proceedings at law, the former hitherto escapes, not without special providence; the lord bee seen in that affayr & putt a good issue to it … Amongst other discourse Dr Hacket the present B[ishop] told Mr Lawrence that these proceedings of Dr Fowler would do no good but hurt in his parish, that hee was 29 years minister at St. Andrews in Holborn yet never presented one neither Papist nor Puritan in all that time."

The meaning may be here, but is not exactly clear. Whitchurch parish officials had taken goods away from those fined for non-attendance at communion, but what did Henry convey by saying that *"they endeavour their excommunication to prevent proceedings at law"*? It almost looks as though they asked to be banned from church, according to this ancient practice, in self-defence. On the other hand, there seems little doubt that Lawrence went to see

Bishop Hackett

Bishop Hackett who gave no support whatsoever to Matthew Fowler whom he blamed for deliberately stirring things up for no good reason. Interestingly, Hackett, although promoted by Charles II in 1661 to the bench of bishops on the basis, probably, of his previous service as a royal chaplain, was well known for his Calvinistic theological position. The implication here is that, once told by Fowler about the meeting at Ralph Eddowes' house in May, the unknown magistrates were compelled to take action – as indeed the constable was when the distraint order was issued – but Fowler had not consulted his bishop. Confirmation of Hackett's sympathies followed, as Henry again reported on a decision made by a diocesan Consistory Court official

> *"November 13   Ralph Eddow & absolved by Sir Walter Littleton chancellor, Dr Fowler refus'd to publish their absolutions, nevertheless they came to Church. The wound is wide there between the Pastor and people, lord heal & help, & let contentions cease. Their absolution is but till Hilary Term next."* [142]

Philip Henry was in no doubt in 1670 that Matthew Fowler was at least partly responsible for a faction fight within

case at the Assizes

Whitchurch parish. The ramifications of this reached the Assize Court in Shrewsbury in January 1671. There Ralph Eddowes and Edward Lawrence brought their claim against the magistrates to have their distrained goods returned, and in recounting the story of this Philip Henry made the central issue clear. Members of the Eddowes family did not count for purposes of declaring a meeting illegal – it was the number and ages of strangers which was crucial. The reference to Sarah Eddowes coming from Chester in Henry's earlier diary entry must be to a daughter, as in Henry's words, *"ye question was whether Mr Eddow's daughter was one of the family"*. The reply to this was that she most decidedly was of the family, a fact made clear *"by ye oath of several witnesses that shee came home intending to stay"*. In addition, John Beard's son was at the meeting, but a lad of only about twelve or fourteen years old. He was not to be punished, but the judge had to decide the question of whether he counted numerically, so presumably increasing the number of strangers above five. Eddowes and Lawrence claimed he should be discounted and the meeting was thus not an illegal one. It was a Mr Thomas *"late of Shrewsbury being on the Jury [who] stood it out on the Plaintiff's behalf against [all the] rest all night alledging hee was fully satisfied the girl was of the Family, saying hee would dye rather than yield"*. The judge then referred the matter to two legal advisers with the result that Eddowes and Lawrence won their case, but Mr Thomas, for his pains, was fined £10 for *"words spoken to one of the Jurors"*. [143]

Some group or individual in Whitchurch parish, not necessarily Fowler alone, was intent upon crushing nonconformist worship and had Edward Lawrence in view as the major influence keeping Presbyterianism alive. Success was achieved in the sense that Lawrence did leave the parish the following year, in May 1671, but may not have had to suffer the extreme penalty of the law. He moved his family (he had ten children [144]) to London where he *Lawrence driven out* continued to be an active dissenting minister until his death in 1695. Somewhat enigmatically Henry noted for a second time that God intervened on behalf of Lawrence

> *"November 1 Ralph Eddow, John Beard, Robert Benyon & others lately excommunicated at Whitch. Mr Lawrence, a[gains]t whom especially the design was, by special providence escap'd. Within a few days after B[isho]p Hacket dy'd."* [145]

Shortly after, Henry made another entry in his diary

> *"December ? Sir Walter Littleton, chancellor of Lichfield, dy'd about this time, within a few weekes after the Bishop."*

It looks very much as though Lawrence was aided by Bishop Hackett in some secret way, and was fortunate to get this help just before Hackett and his chancellor, Littleton, both died. A narrow escape, indeed.

Several dramatic scenes might be conjured from Philip Henry's simple record of events. One inside St. Alkmund's might be imagined of the seven individuals sitting in church and ostentatiously refusing to go up to the chancel to take communion, with Fowler in his pulpit demanding they should either do so, or leave, the alternative being his own withdrawal. Equally, the day at the assizes seems to have been a long one if Mr Thomas really did keep the court in session well into, if not over, night. His vehement speeches to fellow jurors proved effective but costly. All is testimony to the strength of feeling in and around Whitchurch on the matter of how best God might be worshipped.

This clash of wills in the parish in 1670-71 was scarcely over when an action by the king altered the circumstances in which people expressed their religious allegiance. On 15 March 1672 Charles II issued a Declaration of Indulgence, being persuaded by his advisers of the wisdom of relieving all his subjects of the penalties liable to be paid for non-attendance at Anglican churches. Catholics could say mass without fear in private chapels and Protestant dissenters could hold services in licensed

1672 Declaration of Indulgence

premises. Charles was embarking at the time on an ambitious policy of war against the leading European Protestant power, Holland, actually declared on 17 March. For this, he had almost no money and few financiers prepared to make loans. In January the king had similarly declared a moratorium on repayment of loans and the interest thereon, to the great shock of city merchants. [146] The Indulgence was intended to remove a major grievance bedevilling domestic politics, but it was founded on dodgy legal grounds. It was the prerogative of the king to make war on foreigners without consulting Parliament: lifting statutory penalties comprehensively was contentious. Moreover, it was politically inflammatory.

Philip Henry knew this immediately he heard. His reaction, as he wrote, was to consider it

"a thing diversely resented, as men's Interest leades them, the Conformists generally displeas'd at it, the Presbyterians glad, the Independents very glad, the Papists triumph." [147]

It worried him that a proliferation of meeting houses would weaken parish government and continue to divide the forces opposed to Catholicism rather than strengthen them against their common enemy. Papists, he thought, *"fish best in troubled waters."* Personally, he was still torn between turning conformist, going Independent or just continuing silently to suffer waiting for God to supply a different solution. His own was to simply allow Presbyterians access to Anglican pulpits as a means of debating away prejudices and animosities. [148]

In fact, Henry got a licence to hold meetings in Malpas parish on 7 May,

Henry licensed

"unsought and unexpected, precur'd by Mr Steel, sent in a post letter to Mr Yates who had publisht it before I knew, else my intention was to have said nothing, a while." [149] The effect, in practice, was to allow him freedom to tour the neighbourhood preaching for just one year. In March 1673, Charles revoked his declaration under intense pressure of war, cash shortages, anger in the House of Commons and conflicts among his government ministers. Philip Henry noted that

"the broad seal is taken off from it again at Parliament's desire. Out of ye mouth of ye most high proceedeth not evil & good?" ... Reports affrighten as if an after reckoning must come for ye use of past liberty, the will of the lord bee done. Amen!." [150]

What this year of licensed freedom did, of course, was reveal who the dissenters were and where they met. Or rather, who the ministers were who obtained a licence to preach and the houses they could use. The size of their congregations remains a mystery. Apart, that is from the estimate of 80 already noted of those at Edward Lawrence's house every Sunday in 1669. Three houses and three preachers, in addition to Philip Henry, at Broad Oak, were named. Thomas Yates, John Smith and Robert Benion had buildings registered in their names, the latter at Alkington. Richard Sadler, Thomas Yates and John Malden were the preachers. [151]

There is still little evidence other than Philip Henry's journals to show what followed the brief spell of freedom dissenters enjoyed, and the extent of Anglican reaction to the number of followers gathered around the four licensed ministers. What cannot be doubted is that in the Whitchurch community there were several families devoted enough to the teachings of Thomas Porter and his like to stand aside from conventional public worship. Dissent was never destined to supplant the Established Church as defined by the 1662 Prayer Book. That it survived the worst of a period of persecution into a relatively freer age is owed to the determination of people like the Eddowes, the Chetwoods, the Yardleys and the Benions banned, albeit temporarily, from St. Alkmund's in 1670. Their individual stories deserve some examination, as does the further experience of Philip Henry in the years of the renewed persecution of Protestant dissenters.

Whitewell Chapel as Philip Henry knew it from a picture by Marianne Congreve reproduced in H.D.Roberts, Matthew Henry and his Chapel (1901)

... J heard of yᵉ burning of mʳ delawns house
near Lothbury in London, in yᵉ flames whereof
perisht himⁱ. wife children & servants, to
the number of 10. or. 12. twas a brick house
the firt began in yᵉ lowtst roomes, twas on
Dec. 25. at night –

9. J read yᵉ K. Declaration of Dec. 26. wherein
hee promises to mantayn yᵉ Act of Oblivion,
to govern by law not by sword, to procure
liberty from yᵉ Parl. for tender consciences,
to take off sanguinary lawes agt Papists –

10. Will. Griffith came to live with us for
this year following, J am to give him 4ᵗ
wages, Lord make him a blessing to us.

11. J went to Tilstock, mʳ Thomas preacht
about living by Faith under Afflictions,
J had fainted unless J had beleived.

14. J sett yᵉ short at Widow meaKing Tentin.
to bee repayrd & yᵉ loft to bee layd to
Thomas Proos for. 17ˢ –besides nayles. 4.

15. Private day at Ash, Lord hear prayers
pardon sin & lett yᵗ family fare yᵉ better.
16. an end made w. John Benyon, hee is to
hold yᵉ losse of yᵉ two Crofts by cliffs for
6ˢ this next year till Christmas.

18. mʳ Bridge preacht at chapel. Cant. 5. 8.
two sermons which cost him little, Lord
if thou hast Jnterest in him, it is it, hee
hath gifts but if repentance on his part &
mercy on Gods part prevent not, they will
quickly wither & come to nothing.

An extract from Philip Henry's diary for January 1663,
noting a house fire in London, a declaration by the king
promising to get Parliament to lift penalties from Catholics
and sermons by Mr Bridge, a man of feeble talents.

Chapter 8

Dissenting families and their interconnections

One starting point in a search for the principal members of the dissenting congregation of Whitchurch is the 1670 list of those excommunicated. There can be no hope that all those who attended the secret services organised by Edward Lawrence, or Philip Henry for that matter, can be identified. If the report that the 80 habitually gathered around Lawrence were mostly female was accurate, this suggests the task will be even harder. It does not follow that all members of a family in which the head is thought to be a dissenter will, in practice, be of like mind. Equally, not all husbands need follow their wives to a dissenters' meeting. As the period of persecution lengthened so the pressure to conform became greater. Younger generations, not able to recall the era of Puritan struggle and freedom in the 1640s and 1650s, would not necessarily keep the faith of their parents all their lives. Only a sample has been studied, but it does at least highlight the interconnectedness of a group of families. Some of them retained their loyalty to the teachings of Thomas Porter and Edward Lawrence long enough to ensure the survival of Presbyterianism in Whitchurch beyond the age of persecution.

Ralph Eddowes has already been seen to be a significant nonconformist. His family had several branches in the later seventeenth *Ralph Eddowes* century in part stemming from Thomas Eddoes, a shopkeeper specialising in fabrics and small iron wares.[152] Evidently the family was of some prominence socially. In April 1663 probate was granted to Ralph ('Raph') Eddowes to handle the affairs of his deceased brother, Randle or Randulph Eddowes, an ironmonger. (In his will he called himself Randulph, but his appraisers preferred Randle).[153] By the will of Randle a seat in St. Alkmund's church passed to Ralph, which was not an unknown bequest among middle ranking people in the seventeenth century. Possession of a pew was a sure sign of social eminence. One of the appraisers of Randle's goods for probate purposes was Joseph Wittar, which may point to a link with that dissenting group in the town in 1647 responsible for setting up the Presbyterian classis already described.[154] Randle cannot, of course, have been caught at a conventicle in 1670.

Ralph Eddowes, excommunicated in 1670, was younger than Randle, and married to Sarah, daughter of John Hotchkis, draper and resident of Dodington (c1580 to 10 January 1666).[155] This man was another of those in the group previously noted in 1647 who created the Presbyterian classis. Ralph's steadfastness during the difficult episode of the excommunication and subsequent court hearings was testimony to his faith. Although counted as a teacher among the dissenters he had not held any ministerial position and he was not driven out of town in 1671, unlike his ally, Edward Lawrence. Ralph's importance was underlined, in fact, when he was named as an 'abettor' in the registration of nonconformist meeting houses in 1672. [156]

In a manorial survey in 1667 Ralph Eddowes was noted as occupier of a barn and land on the Bridgewater estate, at Bargates, as a copyholder or possibly as a tenant-at-will. [157] He could well have had a freehold house as well. There was a family connection between Ralph and Philip Henry, for at least on one occasion Philip noted him as a cousin. [158] The evidence of parish registers is that he and his wife had three surviving children, John (baptised 1656), Samuel (baptised 1658) and possibly a much older daughter, Martha, who married the curate of Marbury, Joshua Hanmer, in 1662/3. [159] Sarah, Ralph's wife died in May 1698 and he died 31 January 1704. [160] Not all of these details are confirmed by the pedigree published by James Hall in his *History of Nantwich*. [161]

Much more significant in the élite section of Whitchurch society was John

John Eddowes Eddowes (variously Eddow and Eddows) who, in 1659, was understeward for the Earl of Bridgewater.[162] He it was who drew up the 1667 manorial rent roll for the earl which is, for this period, the nearest thing surviving to a register of property occupiers for the parish. John had a house and land at *'Danmoor'* in Dodington township.[163] In the Poll Tax register 1662 he was identified as a gentleman paying £1.00 for himself and six pence for his wife, plus a shilling each for Marie and Robert, both assumed to be his children. [164] There is no suggestion that he was among the dissenting congregation fostered by Edward Lawrence, but he must have been a close relation of Ralph. Families divided by religious affiliations invite speculation. Ralph had another brother, William, who also can be traced through parish records, but he too seems to have kept clear of religious controversy. There has been a suggestion that William, Ralph and Randle Eddowes jointly financed the building of a gallery in St. Alkmund's in 1651, which, if it were the case, might just point to brothers recognising that their minister, Thomas Porter, was attracting larger crowds than any Thomas Fowler brought in. [165] Was this an act of collective support for the reformed church Porter advocated? How were these brothers related to John the earl's steward?

John Eddowes quite possibly had a greater role within the Egerton estate than that of steward at Whitchurch manor. In 1672 and the following year he was in correspondence with the Earl of Bridgewater about the marriage settlement of the earl's son, Lord Brackley. Shropshire rents were to be included in the sources of income for the young man. In December 1679 Eddowes had a problem finding money for the earl's Christmas gifts. By that date he might well have moved to Hertfordshire to the earl's chief estate at Ashridge.[166] Among the manor court records for Whitchurch from 1684 to 1686 there are references to John Eddowes and his wife Mary, for example, surrendering possession of the George Inn in High Street and then the Old Swan. [167] That is to say, they passed the tenancies of these Bridgewater estate properties to new people without in any sense meaning that they personally acted as managers of either inn. They had sub-tenants for this purpose. On the other hand, it might look as though these transactions were part of a clear-out of their possessions in Whitchurch consequent on retirement to the headquarters of the Bridgewater estate. In 1684 and 1688 John Eddowes the elder was reported to be of Gaddesden (that is Little Gaddesden) in Hertfordshire but still dealing with property in Whitchurch. He transferred a house and cottages with pasture land to Ralph Eddowes and set up arrangements for the ultimate occupation of Terrick House to pass to Ralph's heirs. John died before 19 February 1718 for a deed for Terrick House of that date noted him as deceased. [168]

As John Eddowes appears, during the whole of the reign of Charles II, to have held on to his position as steward for the Earl of Bridgewater – an active Anglican – and his relatives were leaders among the dissenting community there is ground for speculation in various directions. No members of the Egerton family, Lords of the Manor, were resident in Whitchurch parish, or anywhere near. The parish's social leaders were the rector, Matthew Fowler, and John Eddowes who was, in effect, the land agent for the earl. The domestic circumstances of the latter are unknown, but the rector had glebe land to work, cottages to let, fee income for church duties and tithes to fund his lifestyle. He lived in a house with seven bedrooms and eight fireplaces, and drove around the countryside in a coach. It would be no surprise to find Fowler and John Eddowes on the same side of a cultural divide such as that of religious observance. Eddowes, nevertheless, might well have felt that family ties were also strong when it came to enforcing the law. Action against dissenters was only taken when somebody denounced them before the magistrates. If John Eddowes frowned upon this kind of behaviour as mischief making and unnecessarily disruptive of parish harmony, it is possible to see this as the reason why Edward Lawrence and his colleagues succeeded in maintaining their congregations.

John Beard's role among the excommunicated group and in the parish is uncertain. He was named in the 1669 Conventicle Act Return but is not known to have held any benefice although considered a teacher. In 1672, Beard was registered as an 'abettor' under the terms of the Declaration of *John Beard* Indulgence. [169] It is perhaps apt to report that a Mary Beard, widow, appeared in the 1667 manorial rent roll as having a burgage in Newtown and two fields and a barn near Chester Lane. [170] More to the point is the John Beard of Tilstock who died in 1699. In his will he left money to *"Samuell Larrance minister"* as well as to William Benyon. One of the dissenting ministers who continued the local Presbyterian tradition was Samuel Lawrence who was active in the Nantwich area. [171] Philip Henry knew John Beard earlier, for in 1663 Henry was moved by Beard's misfortune in having to bury two children in one week dying of smallpox. [172]

John Robinson may or may not have been some relation of the Elizabeth Robinson named in the 1667 rent roll as having a house in Newtown and *John Robinson* a meadow near Castle Well. Much more likely he was related to Thomas Robinson who had a house at *'Chaundle'* in Dodington in 1667. This Thomas, a fellmonger or cleaner of animal skins, living in Dodington, made his will in November 1681 naming his brother John, together with Thomas Yates the younger, as supporters of his wife in her task as his executrix. John also was one of the appraisers of Thomas's goods for probate purposes. [173] These included £25-15-0 in leather and £25 in debts owing to him. Possibly, John was also in some branch of the leather trade but did not have property in Dodington or Whitchurch townships.

Thomas Chetwood did not hold property in these townships in 1667 either, though he was one of three appraisers of a butcher's goods and *the Chetwoods* chattels (John Lovell) in January 1666. [174] He was probably the Thomas Chetwood, yeoman, of Dodington who died in 1697. He called himself a tanner in his will but he didn't leave evidence of his trade among his personal possessions nor mention any wife. [175] He referred to his late brother John who, just as an aside, could have been the one with a house on Pool Dam and a garden in Newtown in 1667. He and his son, also John, quarrelled with a neighbour, Sarah Horton, over the possession of a pew in St. Alkmund's. Their behaviour neatly illuminates the significance Whitchurch families attached to exactly where they sat in the parish church. The younger John was brought up before the bishop's court in 1676 for physically assaulting Sarah Horton in church the previous January. Such was the force of John's blows that *"Sara Horton's hatt was throwne down from off her head, and she the sayd Sarah was forced to shreeke and cry out in the church."* [176]

There were no Yardleys in Whitchurch or Dodington townships in the list made by John Eddowes when he surveyed rents in 1667. However, Philip Henry stood surety for his friend, Robert Bickley, in April 1666, when Bickley *Elizabeth Yardley* borrowed £30 on a short-term loan from Elizabeth Yardley. This financial transaction does not have to imply that Bickley was a nonconformist, but it does identify Elizabeth Yardley, at that time, as a woman of independent means. Her will written in June 1676, as a spinster, suggests more. [177] She was undoubtedly a central figure in Lawrence's congregation in the 1660s, and possibly during Thomas Porter's time also. Although she had personal goods worth only £63-6-2 in her probate inventory, £45 of that was in money owing to her by special bonds. Moreover, she listed numerous cash bequests naming, among others, two Eddowes and Ann Chetwood, plus twenty shillings each to Philip Henry, John Malden and Edward Lawrence. The last three were all dissenting ministers ejected after Charles II returned. The men who made the inventory were Ralph Eddowes and John Beard. She herself had been a beneficiary under the will of Elizabeth Hotchkis in 1674 for whom John Beard had acted as an appraiser of goods for probate purposes. Dissenters had a good friend in Elizabeth Yardley. Her loans might have kept more than Robert Bickley afloat.

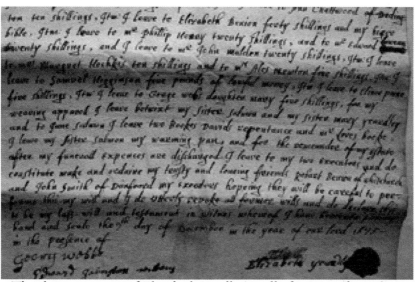

The closing passages of Elizabeth Yardley's will of 9 December 1675

Thomas Kelley was not listed by John Eddowes in the 1667 Survey, and left no papers on death in the diocese of Lichfield, but he was among the *'abettors'* of nonconformist ministers in 1672. [178] Incidentally, a Thomas Kettle had a field in Whitchurch in the 1667 Survey. [179] It is tempting to assume that if the man had been a Kettle not a Kelley then he might have been the Thomas Keittell (sic) whose probate inventory was made in April 1672.[180] He was a corvisor, or shoemaker of the superior kind, actually worth only eight shillings and eleven pence once his debts of £21-15-5 had been subtracted from the value of the stock of footwear in his shop. His clothes and all other *"necessaries"* were worth only five shillings! But this is to speculate too far.

the Benyon family   Robert Bennion (variously Benyon and Benion), on the other hand, had a name very much associated with religious dissent. He was almost certainly a relative of Daniel Bennion with a house on Pool Dam in 1667. It looks as though Robert lived at Alkington, for in 1672 his house there was licensed for religious services. A William Bennion was also named in 1672 as living at Prees in a house licensed for dissenting services.[181] In neither case were they listed as the preachers given leave to officiate by the royal Declaration of Indulgence.

A key relationship would be that which Robert and William (and the Daniel with a Pool Dam house) had with the Daniel Benyon of Great Ash

Daniel Benyon of Great Ash   who was one of the 1647 group initiating a Presbyterian reform in the parish. It must have been this man who had been noted a year earlier almost acting as a minister to a dissenting congregation. He died in October 1669 worth some £234 in personal estate according to his probate inventory. Philip Henry recorded his funeral, for this involved burial in the same grave as that already occupied by one of Henry's children. The child's coffin had to be lifted out and put back on top![182] Daniel was a gentleman and clearly worked his farm successfully for he had on death in November cattle to the value of £72 and corn and hay listed at £63-10-0. In contemporary inventories cows, heifers and beasts were valued at anything between £2 and £4 which would have made Daniel Benyon the owner of one of the largest herds in the district. He had a son, Daniel, and four unmarried daughters.[183] This meant that Robert Bennion was, at the closest, a nephew of Daniel of Great Ash. It's a moot point as to whether or not he was the Robert Bennion, a yeoman of Alkington, who died in 1690 leaving £24 worth of personal possessions.[184]

To Philip Henry this Daniel was *"uncle Benyon of Ash"*. The link came through Henry's wife, Katherine, the daughter of Daniel Matthews. Her marriage to Philip in April 1660 also brought him into close contact with others who were of the dissenting mind set, most obviously the Hotchkis family. In turn, their relations became Henry's concern so that several cousins were noted in his diaries – as Ralph Eddowes already named – although the exact blood tie with Katherine Henry is far from certain. Uncle Benyon, or Daniel, was brother to Katherine Henry's mother, she being Sarah Benyon and daughter of John Benyon, presumed to be of Ash.[185] This Daniel Benyon of Great Ash obviously had some interest in land at Broad Oak which brought him into a brief conflict with Daniel Matthews in February - March 1661.[186] This was shortly before Philip Henry was forced out of Worthenbury and found refuge in his father-in-law's property at Broad Oak. Uncle Benyon's son, another Daniel – "*cousin Daniel*" to Philip Henry - was sent shortly after his mother died to Mr Lewis's school in Wrexham.[187] It must have been this "*cousin Daniel*" that had Philip Henry's good wishes when going off to Oxford in April 1665.[188] In which case, of course, the question arises as to what a dissenter's son did to gain admittance to the university? Two years later, in June 1667, Philip Henry and Uncle Benyon travelled to Boreatton, close to Stanwardine-in-the-Fields, near Baschurch in Shropshire, to buy law books for cousin Daniel.[189] For whatever reason, Oriel College did not suit and Daniel turned in 1666 to Gray's Inn instead.[190]

From all this it seems quite likely that the Daniel Benyon with property on Pool Dam in 1667 was the same Daniel who was of Great Ash who died in October 1669. In which case Robert and William Bennion were probably his nephews, with William the one to whom Philip Henry was looking for a loan of £100 in September 1663.[191]

One complication about Philip Henry's references to '*uncle Benyon*' is that there were two men who qualified for this familial status. Daniel and Sarah (Katherine Henry's mother) had a brother Joshua.[192] He was not named as such by Philip Henry in his diary, nor were there references to an '*uncle*' Benyon after 1669. The daughters of Daniel of Ash did not figure much either in Philip Henry's diaries, though cousin Mary was reported to have returned to Ash from London, in June 1670, ill with consumption. There is also the distinct possibility that a separate family of Benyons lived at Broad Oak, or near Iscoyd. At least one other Benyon spent time in Whitchurch itself. In 1657, at Easter Quarter Sessions, one Mary Capper of Milton Green, Cheshire, appeared before the Shropshire magistrates alleging that she had been delivered of a bastard boy child fathered on her by George Benyon, a feltmaker from Whitchurch. In desperation she had taken the child to the doorstep of Benyon's shop in Whitchurch and left it there. The magistrates could not find either of the parents, both presumed to have left the district.[193] In the later eighteenth century, there were Bennions in Broad Oak though the links between these individual instances have not yet been made.[194]

Robert Bennion was not left alone after the excommunication incident and the affair at the assize. Indeed, it appears to be a measure of Matthew Fowler's antagonism towards dissenters in general, and the Benyons in particular, that he brought an action at Quarter Sessions in April 1673

Robert Bennion at Quarter Sessions
against Benyon. Philip Henry would seem to have taken some pleasure in writing in his diary for 19 April

"*Robert Benyon troubled at Quart.Sess. by Dr. F. procuremt, touching accounts for highw. 7 or 8 y[ears] since – the accounts found & found true to his credit & his Adversaries shame, their spight tow him is much bec[ause] His house a licenst house, but if so & his ends therein bee right they cannot hurt him.*"[195]

Fowler must have judged that if he couldn't close a conventicle directly he might ruin a dissenter individually by checking up on his financial accounts as parish surveyor of highways, even after seven years elapsed since leaving office. Is this the measure of the man?

The most well-known member of the family for his dissenting career was Dr Samuel Benion. In a sermon preached at his funeral in March 1707-8

Dr Samuel Benion
Matthew Henry spoke of his birth in 1673 at Whixall in the parish of Prees. He was the eldest surviving son of William Benion and his wife, the daughter of Richard Sadler. In the 1650s Sadler had been a minister in Ludlow, ejected in 1662. It clearly follows that Samuel was brought up within a dissenting family and his home was for a time the meeting place used for services. He finished off his education from 1691 in the household of Philip Henry at Broad Oak. In practice, he was a teaching assistant to Henry in a school he ran in his house. It is quite possible that he was a great-nephew of the elder Daniel Benyon of Great Ash and nephew of Robert Bennion of Alkington. He comes back into the story in the 1690s.

the Hotchkis family
An omission from the 1670 list of dissenters suffering persecution is that of the Hotchkis family. This could well be because they did not stay the course. One John Hotchkis, according to Philip Henry, died, aged 91, in January 1666

"*who got to heaven, as few doe without a blot, Being askt if hee were willing to dye, hee answered yes, what else? Being askt w[hat] he thought of present th[ings] & whether his Friends might safely venture to suffer rather than conform, hee ans[wered] yea by all meanes for the cause is Gods. His last word, being askt how he did was, well.*"[196]

Despite all, Dr Fowler took the funeral service for this convinced Puritan.

This must be the man whose will was proved for probate at Lichfield in March 1666. It's a nice question whether he was the *"old Mr Hotchkis"* Philip Henry saw on 2 December 1663, and most likely, therefore, to have been the John Hotchkis noticed among the Presbyterian group of 1647. [197] Difficulties arise because Henry only ever identified a Hotchkis as *'old'* on two occasions. Normally he wrote about *'uncle Hotchkis'* – that is to say, an uncle in his wife's family. It seems, however, that John, dying in January 1666, was not called uncle, for the aforementioned will left something of a problem for Philip Henry's *"Uncle Hotchkis & cosin Raph Eddow"*. They fell out over a *'legacy left in old Mr Hotchis will.'* [198] Strictly speaking, to be this worried uncle to Philip Henry's wife, Katherine, he has to be the John Hotchkis married to Alice Benyon, sister to Katherine Henry's mother. As it was Thomas Hotchkis, brother of *'uncle Hotchkis'* who came to help Philip Henry sort out the family quarrel (not entirely successfully) the logic is that both were uncles to Katherine and sons of *'old Mr Hotchkis'*. [199] The logic also is that this Thomas was the rector of Stanton Fitzwarren in Wiltshire from 1638, of whom more later. [200]

The list of those to whom John Hotchkis (*old Mr Hotchkis*), draper, left bequests in his will in 1666, however, is quite clear. He had sons John, Thomas (the clergyman, though not so identified in the will), Joshua and Samuel. [201] None of their wives were mentioned, but one of their four sisters was Sarah, married to Ralph Eddowes. Despite the reference by Philip Henry to Ralph Eddowes as *'cousin'*, like his four brothers-in-law he was, strictly speaking, an uncle to Katherine Henry.

Uncle John Hotchkis, or John the younger for present purposes, succeeded his father as a draper in Dodington. He died in 1681 worth in household goods and debts owed to him some £285. [202] No shop stock was listed in his inventory. He had sons Thomas, Daniel, Richard, Joshua and Samuel, and daughters Margaret, Sarah, and Alice. [203] The last two were married. He also had a daughter-in-law, Jane Hotchkis. John's wife, Alice, was named as one of his beneficiaries and his sole executrix. There were no clues as to this family belonging to the dissenting community.

In the event, one of the papers filed with John's will shows that his wife did not take up her responsibilities. Instead, his daughter-in-law, Jane, a widow, and Daniel Hotchkis took over the duties of administering the will. Philip Henry noted the sad and quick end to life of John, but also recorded a tribute to him, his father and his son, all three being Johns and all three trading as drapers, eminent in their business. Clearly, Jane was the youngest John's widow. The absence of any reference by Philip Henry to the religious affiliations of this family appears to confirm their conformity.

There is just the possibility that Elizabeth Hotchkis, sister to John the younger, whose will was proved in April 1675, was in the nonconforming congregation. She was a relatively rich woman as there was £127 owing to her in special debts, and in total her personal estate was valued at £236-16-8. It included a *'chattell lease'* worth £80.

Elizabeth Hotchkis

As already noted, John Beard was one of the appraisers and she left a bequest to Elizabeth Yardley. She remembered Ralph Eddowes, her brother-in-law, and two Eddowes cousins, Sarah and Joshua.

two Thomases

There was more than one Thomas Hotchkis, however. Philip Henry normally referred to *'cousin'* Thomas, who ought not to be the Thomas, brother of John the younger, and rector of Stanton. Properly speaking, Philip Henry ought to have called him uncle. Thomas, the cousin, seems to have lived in London – visiting Henry in March 1662, and then giving a home to his sister, Sarah Hotchkis, who moved to London in April. In May, Philip Henry wrote that he had seen *"cosin Thomas Hotchkis a Conformist upon this principle – that whatever our magistrate commands which the word doth not forbid 'tis our duty to obey: which I confess is not clear to mee in the th. of God."*[204] It was presumably this Thomas who survived the plague as noted by Henry in January 1666.

The other Thomas, the rector at Stanton Fitzwarren in Wiltshire, fathered seven children on his wife, Grace, all baptised at Stanton. One of these, Jane, in September 1670, became the second wife of Thomas Yates the builder of Dearnford Hall. [205] Thomas began his clerical career as curate at Easton-in-Gordano, Somerset, in 1635, having attended Corpus Christi College, Cambridge, and acquired an MA in 1634. [206] He seems to have been a man of very flexible theology, but also something of a controversialist. He died in post in 1693, having bent one way in the 1650s to the demands of the Commonwealth regime, and quite the opposite way in 1662 to escape ejection by accepting the use of the new Prayer Book. In 1654/5 he published *An Exercitation Concerning the Nature of Forgiveness of Sin* ... which had a preface by Richard Baxter one of the most prominent Presbyterians of his day. Presumably this was to the liking of his father, John, in Whitchurch, but not to others. William Robertson, a University of Edinburgh man, published a rejoinder, *An Admonitory Epistle* ... In the 1670s Thomas Hotchkis had at least two other works printed which were part of a disputation with a long time Independent controversialist, Dr. John Owen. Thomas was indefatigable in writing out his sermons in neat tiny script in an exercise book surviving in Wiltshire and Swindon Archives. [207] Perhaps it was his influence on his siblings and their children which deflected them from the path *'old'* John

Hotchkis had followed in the 1640s. None of this prevented Philip Henry keeping in touch. At the end of May 1665 Henry went for a quick visit to London, and returned via Oxford and Stanton, *"where pr. pub. & June 21 found all well at home."* [208] Henry was taking risks. He found the plague increasing in London to his horror, and if he preached publicly in Thomas Hotchkis's parish he put them both in danger. Not that he stopped long for he was back at Broad Oak by 21 June.

Joshua Hotchkis was Ralph Eddowes brother-in-law – hence the brother of uncle John Hotchkis (so far as Philip Henry is concerned) and brother to Sarah married to Ralph Eddowes. [209] He was the one Hotchkis male to stay in Whitchurch, it seems. At least, he was the one with whom Philip Henry shared the journey to London in May 1665. [210] Presumably they both went to Stanton for the reverend Thomas was Joshua's brother. Margaret Hotchkis lived in and around Broad Oak, it would appear, to judge from the closeness of her relationship with Philip Henry. In July 1669 they had to share a horse riding back to Broad Oak when both accidentally fell off, luckily without serious injury! [211] By these means were the dissenting families tied together.

The significant new name appearing in 1672 when dissenters came out into the open was Thomas Yates. As in many other families there

Thomas Yates

was a tradition of naming sons after fathers. This habit gives historians headaches. One Thomas Yates was baptised in 1634, the son of a mercer in the town, also called Thomas who died in 1682. [212] The younger of these Thomases is the one credited with building Dearnford Hall in Alkington township around 1690. He is sometimes referred to, confusingly, as 'the elder', and he died in 1709. In his will he left a house and land in Heath Lane and another house and land in Whixall, apart, presumably, from Dearnford Hall which was not mentioned in his will. [213] David Benyon and Grace Benion were witnesses. His son Thomas, the third in this line, was given the two properties with a charge on them in favour of the children of Samuel Yates his brother.

In the 1667 survey of Bridgewater property a Thomas Yates had a house in Backhouse Street (later St. Mary's Street) and four houses in Dodington, but it is not clear to which Thomas these entries apply. The house in Backhouse Street was recorded in a land transfer in the manor court in the 1630s when Thomas Yates was called a gentleman. This must have been the father of the second Thomas. [214] It is not clear which, if any, of these five houses was the one licensed for worship in 1672, and equally uncertain as to whether the minister, Thomas Yates, was the father or the son.

There are other mysteries about who did what if, for example, the claim is accepted that Thomas Yates gave a copy of Foxe's *Book of Martyrs,* fixed to a stand, for public reading in St. Alkmund's. This, in 1667, was about four years after the arrival of Matthew Fowler as a preacher and in the year of his formal institution as rector. Which Thomas was this, and what significance, if any, did it have *vis-a-vis* the theological stance of the new rector? [215] One of the two was also the Mr Yates who pre-empted the publication of Philip Henry's preaching license in May 1672 . Whichever Yates it was must have been the one whose house Henry preached in on 8 August – *"I preacht ye 1ˢᵗ lecture at Mr Yates house in Whitchurch."* [216]

**Thomas Yates'
will 1708**

A charity collection made in January 1687/8 on behalf of refugee French Protestants, fleeing persecution under Louis XIV, undoubtedly had a contribution from the second Thomas of £1-5-0 which was greatly in excess of any other sums recorded by the churchwardens except those of the then rector, his curate and their wives who totalled £6-11-6 between them. [217] This was not just generosity but a statement of social position and obligation. Whitchurch dissenters came from a social range which started at the top of local society but is not measurable at its lower end.

Both the Thomases personified this, and the likelihood is that it was the father who first took up the principles advocated by Thomas Porter. The younger one was of school age during Porter's tenure in Whitchurch and though it's true that he could have caught the Presbyterian faith in opposition to his parents, it doesn't seem likely. There is no evidence of a family split of any kind, and the more pertinent question, therefore, is what delayed the older Thomas from making positive declarations of religious outlook before 1672. He did not figure in Henry's diaries in the 1660s.

Curiously, the younger Yates did attract Henry's sympathy in an earlier year. For some reason, in June 1667, Henry confided to his diary, *"Yong Mr Yates childless, his wife also not like to live, marry'd since wee, hath had 4 children, and now they are not."* [218] In fact, Thomas's wife, Martha, from a Chester family, died in October. Three years later Thomas Yates remarried, to Jane Hotchkis, daughter of the Reverend Thomas Hotchkis already noted as brother to John who died in 1681. They had two sons

Richard Gough, in about 1700, writing about his parish of Myddle within the estates of the Earl of Bridgewater during his lifetime, noted the appointment by Parliamentary order of Mr Joshua Richardson as minister in 1646.

"He was an able and laborious minister … his wife being a prudent women … the Right Hon. John Earle of Bridgewater (knowng Mr Richardson was well beloved in his parish,) by a certaine kind of state amnesty permitted him to continue minister on the same termes and conditions that hee was put in by the parliament …

"After the Restauration of King Charles the Second, when the Act for conformity came out, Mr. Richardson refusing to subscribe the declaration incerted in the act concerning the solemn League and Covenant, lost his place; and with him fell the minister of Hadnall's Ease. I had so much intimate acquaintance with Mr. Richardson, that hee would willingly have conformed to the discipline and constitution of the Church of England, but hee tould mee hee could not with a safe conscience subscribe to the declaration against the Covenant. Hee received the tythes due before Bartholomew-tide, according to the act of parliament, at which time all the rye and the wheate was gott in, and some oates. Hee removed to Broughton, where hee lived one yeare with his brother, Captain Richardson, and afterwards went to a farme called Ditches, near Wem, but when the act of Parliament came forth that noe outed Minister should live within five miles of the place where hee had formerly officiated, hee removed to Alkinton, neare Whitchurch (the place from whence his father came, when hee had purchased his lands in Broughton, of Mr. Ottey). Here Mr. Richardson lived a private, peaceable, and pyouse life; exercising himselfe in religious duties, and instructing and teaching his owne and some of his relations children in good literature.

Hee dyed at Alkinton, and was buried at Whitchurch. Dr. Fowler preached his funerall sermon, and there gave him a deserved comendation. Hee bequeathed a certaine number of Bibles, and of those bookes of Mr. Baxter entitled, 'A Call to the Unconverted,' to bee given to certaine poore people in the parishe of Myddle, after his decease, which legacy was faithfully performed by his prudent widdow and executrix."

Richard Gough, *The History of Myddle*, edited by David Hey (Penguin 1981) pages 42-43.

who outlived their father, both mentioned in his will in 1709, and three daughters and another son, John, who died in infancy. [219]

It has been said that Thomas Yates the second changed from the trade of mercer some time after his father died in 1682 and joined George Paine in a timber business. Whatever the case, Thomas Yates found the money to move out of town and build a house in Alkington township called Dearnford Hall.[220] Here was conclusive proof of the prosperity and status of the Yates family, and, for the moment, the point where Thomas can be left to come back into the narrative later.

One feature of this inquiry into the lives of those named as dissenters in the 1660s and 1670s is that, for the most part, they did not meet in Whitchurch town itself. True, Philip Henry briefly lived in Dodington which is assumed to mean a house on the street now so named. There's no proof that he held meetings there. The exact location of Edward Lawrence's home is not known, but it has been claimed to have been in Tilstock township. The principal guide to places where services were held is the list of those houses licensed in 1672. These were at Prees (that is Whixall) where Richard Sadler, grandfather of Samuel Benion, was the minister; Alkington in the house of Robert Benion, and the house of Thomas Yates somewhere unstated, in Whitchurch. John Malden acted as minister in Yates's house, whereas Thomas Yates officiated at Benion's home in Alkington. [221] Other places where conventicles were held included Hodnet, Hanmer and Broad Oak. Whatever happened in the urban settlement was disguised by this distribution of licensed premises in 1672. Incidentally, though, it might suggest why the excommunications took place in 1670. It's possible that using the home of Ralph Eddowes, quite likely in High Street, for a religious service was a new development. What roused Benjamin Taylor, the curate, was an incursion into town of a despised sect, too close to St. Alkmund's for comfort. Just a thought.

location of meeting houses

In total it has already been stated that in 1669 the dissenting congregation was thought to number about 80. The fact that in the famous Compton Survey 1676 the number was reduced to 30 may not be too significant. [222] Matthew Fowler put this figure in the Return Questionnaire as required by the bishop and blithely claimed that he had 2,000 communicants in his parish. As he said he had 12 Catholics it would seem, to modern statistically sensitive eyes at least, that he plucked some rounded figures out of the air. It was not in his interests to advertise a large dissenting section of the local populace.

how many dissenters?

Chapter 9

Matthew Fowler political agent and national political crises 1678 - 1684

The persecution of religious dissent after 1662 is not fairly represented if the focus is entirely upon Presbyterians, Baptists, Independents and Quakers. The fate of those holding firm to the even older Christian tradition of Roman Catholicism was just as critical. They, of course, had suffered financial persecution and political ostracism for over a century. Their numbers had dwindled to a small resolute core. The pity is that Matthew Fowler didn't name the twelve papists he thought he had in his parish in 1676. [223] At present they remain undiscovered.

The difference from pre-Civil War days was that England had in Charles II a crypto-Catholic king. This may not have been immediately obvious but as his reign unfolded an even brighter prospect opened up for Catholics. A full blown, quite open Catholic monarch in Charles' only legitimate heir, his brother James, was on the cards. Charles had a son, also a James, created Duke of Monmouth, but he was always denied legitimacy by his father. In the political struggle for supremacy at court, and among Parliamentary politicians, what could be more natural than the adoption by Protestants of Monmouth as their figurehead and potential monarch?

rivalries in the royal court

The crisis was a long time coming but was probably inevitable after Parliament insisted on passing the Test Act in 1673. This made taking communion in an Anglican service a condition of holding any government, military or local administrative office. James, Duke of York, held the senior job in the Admiralty which he was compelled to give up when he refused to comply. He would not hide his religious allegiance to the Pope. Fear of a Catholic revival had become ingrained in English politics during the period of Stuart rule. One of the fixed points in an annual calendar of popular demonstrations was November 5th with celebrations in the streets of the collapse of the 1605 Gunpowder Plot. Any disaster was liable to be explained as a Catholic ploy to win control – even the fire of London could be laid at their door. Sir Peter Leicester of Tabley Hall, in 1677, read a history-cum propaganda lecture to the

Cheshire Grand Jury at a Quarter Sessions meeting in Knutsford and rehearsed the charges against Catholics. He recalled the *"Gunpowder Traison"* and preparations then for rebellion while *"at this present how many Jesuiticall Pamphlets are dayley scattered among the People to ensnare weaker Judgements, and draw them on to raise a new Rebellion."* [224]

In 1678 stories started circulating in London of a new Popish Plot. Charles was to be killed and James crowned king. The

Popish Plot central figure was a mysterious self-publicist, Titus Oates, who alleged he knew the details. He spun a tissue of lies, entangling such innocent victims as Samuel Pepys and causing trials for treason in 1680 of leading Catholic aristocrats. Executions of the supposed guilty fed public antagonism towards a Catholic population miniscule in size.

A parallel development was the emergence of a group of courtiers encouraging the Duke of Monmouth to test out support for his claim on the throne. Among the key issues which arose from this was, on the one hand, the role of Protestant dissent and, on the other, the election of members to a House of Commons when Charles next cared to call a Parliament. Dissenters such as Philip Henry in Flintshire and Adam Martindale in Cheshire were not at all keen on paying, as the price of their own relief from persecution, the granting of freedom to Catholics to worship openly. Their best hope was to persuade those who organised the selection of candidates at Parliamentary elections to put up men keen to rigorously enforce the law against Catholics while voting for the lifting of those same laws from the backs of Protestant nonconformists. Determined Anglicans simply wanted all to be driven by the law into worshipping in parish churches. For them, however, the greatest danger was clearly the Catholic preferences of Charles and James.

In this political climate in England around 1680 the birth pangs of two British political parties are found. Their

birth pangs of political parties mutual enmity was expressed in the insulting terms each applied to the other. 'Whigs' were the king's critics, 'Tories' were his friends. The effects of this verbal conflict were felt in north Shropshire. In November 1678 Philip Henry had heard of Titus Oates and his stories of a Popish Plot. He also knew of *"one Harcourt a priest taken about Stoke"*, who was interrogated by the justices at Whitchurch and committed to the gaol at Shrewsbury. [225] In July 1679 two priests were hanged, drawn and quartered after trials at the assize, one in Denbigh and the other in Chester. They were not the only ones. [226] In 1680 Henry noted that Lord Stafford was executed on Tower

Hill. William Howard, Viscount Stafford, was among the most prominent of the Catholic men who suffered death on the false accusations of Oates and his mendacious followers. [227] Henry was well informed about Parliamentary affairs too, and he took a close interest in the contests for seats in the House of Commons Charles II called to meet in Oxford in March 1681. He not only recorded the names of the locally successful candidates, but succinctly reported the fate of Parliament itself. *"March 21 they met at Oxford, March 28 they were sent home again dissolv'd."* [228]

The dangers to Protestant dissenters in the climate of fear surrounding the royal court were exemplified in north Shropshire and surrounding districts also. Most evidently, in the case of Philip Henry, there was the consequence of a meeting at which Henry did the preaching in June 1681 at the house of Thomas Millington at Weston, beyond Prees. There were apparently 143 *Philip Henry fined* people present when two justices entered and took all their names. Millingon, Edward Bury and William Benion of Whixall were among those heavily fined afterwards, but none was more viciously punished than Philip Henry. He refused to pay his fine of £40 and so his goods at Broad Oak were distrained in a fashion he described in his diary in exact and full detail.

> *"This day Mr Pemerton & Jo.y. came again with the same warrant as before & distraind upon the Coles, the Hay, the Muck-Cart, and wheels, the great Slead, & Field of Barley."*

He did little to stop the high constable and the teams of men and carts – he carefully wrote down all their names – who came over several days to remove the essential husbandry equipment and crops on which he depended for his living. The value of some items struck him especially. Watching hay being removed when it was known to be scarce in the district was widow Payne. She said she had given 30s for about the same quantity a few days before. It took five men to shift it, paid 12 pence each as wages. The first load of coal to go he thought worth 13s 4d. Pemerton, the high constable, had to press labourers he found on the roadside to get the job done, though there were neighbours of Henry among the gangs taking barley and coals. It was the job of the parish constable to arrange for the sale of such confiscated property and Henry noted who bought some of it. A maltster over at Orton had a parcel of barley, for example. Throughout this potentially life threatening, week-long theft of his property Henry was sustained by his simple faith that as he was doing God's work. God would make things come right for him in the end.

This wasn't the end though. In September he was presented at Flint Assizes, along with numerous others (some possibly Catholic) for other offences. In his case it was holding a conventicle at Broad Oak: fellow sufferers, Lady Broughton and her daughter, had not been to church for twelve months. [229]

There is no doubt that Matthew Fowler equally kept abreast of contemporary events in London and in the four counties he could reach within half a day's travel. He and his wife Letitia *Fowler's letters* had suffered a personal blow in 1678 which reduced their contacts with the great world outside Shropshire. [230] Their twenty-four year old son, also called Matthew, their only child, a student of medicine, died in Paris. A few neatly written surviving letters, relating only to one episode it's true, nevertheless suggest that Fowler was a diligent correspondent, well informed, with possibly a wide circle of acquaintances. The focus of attention was James, Duke of Monmouth, the son of Lucy Walter, to whom, the young man claimed, King Charles had been formally married at the time of his birth. His potential challenge to James, Duke of York, the king's brother, was made startlingly clear when moves were made in Parliament in 1679-81 to declare the Duke of York ineligible to wear the crown by reason of his religious faith. For quite some time, the Earl of Shaftesbury, who led the Whig campaign to exclude James from the line of succession, was coy in the extreme as to who the throne should pass to. Popular opinion jumped to the obvious conclusion that it had to be Monmouth. This was enough to fire up a man with a military reputation of some worth, a plausible personality, a known allegiance to Protestantism, and a sense of grievance at the denial of his legitimacy.

One route to success was to win sufficient support in the provinces, among urban merchants and county gentry, to guarantee a favourable majority in a future House of Commons. Every politician was aware of how Charles I had been removed from the throne. No one wanted another war. The obvious way to forestall civil disobedience was to organise a party in Parliament so overwhelmingly of one opinion that no king could veto its proposed legislation. For the moment, it was not at all understood that Charles had no intention of holding another Parliament. Indeed, in 1681 the king stripped Monmouth of the court and state offices he held for publicly congratulating the Earl of Shaftesbury in November on escaping a charge of treason tried before a Middlesex jury. James, Duke of York, was shortly thereafter restored to royal favour after a period of exile. Monmouth's reaction was to refuse to recognise this and to go out into the provinces on what was only a little less than a royal progress. He had already almost invented the whistle stop tours beloved of twentieth century politicians. In the spring of 1680 he visited the strongly dissenting counties of the West Country to foment popular demonstrations in his favour. One report claimed that 20,000 turned out in Exeter to greet him. He even touched for the King's Evil! [231] In 1682 he repeated the trick with an excursion north to Chester via Staffordshire, almost solely to cultivate provincial opinion in anticipation of Parliamentary elections.

The king had a reputation for the easy life, but he appointed officials who knew their business. It was the job of the Secretary of State for Home Affairs to discover *the King's spymaster* what the king's enemies were doing and to have spies in place to keep him up to date. In the present circumstance he was obliged to garner every scrap of intelligence about Monmouth's movements, friends and conversations, correspondence, meetings and private as well as public pronouncements. Sir Leoline Jenkins became Secretary of State in April 1680, replacing Sir Henry Coventry. Ronald Hutton, in his biography of Charles II, reports him as "solemn, industrious, devoted to the episcopal Church of England, and of marginal political importance." He had some reputation as a safe pair of hands and as a diplomatist, but none as a speaker. Some thought him merely the office drudge. Jenkins was one of those on the Privy Council, however, who was most evidently a James, Duke of York, supporter and he made it his business to keep the closest eye on Monmouth's activities. [232] It was in connection with his search for information on Monmouth that Jenkins came into contact with the Rector of Whitchurch, Matthew Fowler.

Nine letters contain the essence of Matthew Fowler's last employment in royal service. He would not appear *Fowler the spy* to have engaged himself in this kind of role previously, for his first letter was not to Sir Leoline Jenkins direct, but to a certain Dr Bell, vicar of the London parish of St. Sepulchre's. Fowler addressed Bell as 'brother', but this need not necessarily mean anything other than friend. It's more to the point that Bell was known by Fowler to have Court connexions and could pass on the provincial news Fowler provided to the relevant people of influence near the king. Fowler clearly thought of Bell as someone who knew his capabilities and would recognise that Fowler was not inclined to panic. *"I think you believe me at 65 to be no vain fellow nor apt to be afraid, where no cause of fear is."* [233]

Fowler was a worried man. He had lived through a politically dangerous period like this before. Monmouth's appeal for popular support looked likely to succeed in Cheshire. It was important that this was reported to royal officials. On July 26 he wrote
> *"I am very apprehensive of danger by his coming, for the lower parts of Staffordshire, Cheshire and Lancashire are very rotten and full of potent*

*Whigs and malcontents. .... In Cheshire these are the Earl of
Macclesfield and his son, Brandon, Col. Whitley, Sir Robert Cotton,
Thomas Mainwaring, Mr Booth, Lord Delamer's eldest son; and
generally, except for a few persons,the whole country is disloyal."* [234]

Fowler made no comment at this point, interestingly, about the state of
Shropshire. He had, however, gathered his news from discussions on the
bowling green, quite possibly in Whitchurch.

> *"I was yesterday among a knot of loyal gentlemen, it being our bowling
> day, where the discourse was that the Duke of Monmouth intended to
> come into Staffordshire and Cheshire and to be at Wallasey horse race.
> ... I remember that, when Oliver usurped the dominion, the loyal
> gentry used to meet at horse races and cock matches, under colour
> whereof they drove on some design, which made Oliver forbid all such
> meetings. ...
> Our Whigs are of late much given to such kind of sports ."* [235]

It takes one to know one, and Fowler had certainly understood what his
fellow royalists were doing in the 1650s. Shaftesbury's Whigs could be
assumed to have adopted the weapons forged by their enemies.

The letter got through to its intended recipient and Sir Leoline Jenkins
replied to Dr Bell asking that Fowler write more often. Indeed, he wrote
direct to Fowler on the same lines. And he was not the only agent Jenkins
contacted. Walter Chetwynd, for example, of Ingestre in Staffordshire,
was another. On 16 August Matthew Fowler indicated the constraints
under which he worked. *"I am aged and stir little abroad,"* he wrote. *"I can
only impart the intelligence I receive from others".* It wasn't his fault, he said,
if his reports proved false. Nevertheless, he had heard of the Duke's
itinerary and the gentlemen in Staffordshire expected to receive him; that
he intended to visit Dunham Massey, and his objective was Wallasey races
early in September. Races on the Wirral peninsula were not new, but were
"the most famous of all these parts, and to which there is usually great resort."

Fowler now added his first remarks about Shropshire. *"The loyal gentry of
Salop are far more than the
disaffected... yet Shrewsbury is full of
faction and conventicles are publicly
kept without any opposition of the magistrates".*

Shrewsbury full of faction

It wasn't perhaps as bad as Chester – *"full of disloyal rotten-hearted people"*
– but both places had castles which Fowler thought ought to be made
secure for the king. He gave every impression of fearing insurrection and
betrayed a mind alert to military considerations. [236] This must have
impressed Secretary Jenkins who copied to Fowler his letter to Walter
Chetwynd contracting him to be one of the agents of *"secret service"*

Two extracts from Matthew Fowler's first letter to Dr. Bell written on 26 July 1682 by which he sought to relay to the king's government his fears about insurrection in Cheshire
The National Archives SP29/419/246

who could "*employ a discreet and trusty person … to go to that meeting* [races at Wallasey] *and to observe narrowly what passes…. I shall reimburse your charges on such a messenger very punctually … I have commission to bear their charges, if you should employ two or three … I desire to hear from you frequently.* "[237]

Fowler could well have relished his task. On 11 September he told Jenkins of his plans. "*Though I live 24 miles from Wallasey, I shall readily pursue your directions, so far as a sickly old man of 65 can. I have a nephew of good parts and equal discretion. Him I have sent with the best instructions I can give him.*" As to the Duke, he had arrived at Nantwich from Trentham the previous Saturday with about 120 horsemen, all armed and well mounted. For the last two miles into town a gaping rabble lined the hedgerows to greet him. Half way along this multitude the Duke exchanged his coach for a horse supplied by the Earl of Macclesfield. Once in the streets his vanguard roused the "*beasts of the people*" to roar and shout in approval. Only the cry of "*Vive le Roy*" was missing! The duke stopped just long enough to have dinner at the Crown before leaving for Chester. [238]

Philip Henry at Broad Oak knew of all this, but was much less affected. "*Sept 9. D of Monm[outh]. past through Nantw[ich] tow[ards] Chest[er] - some applauding others vilifying - studia in contraria vulgus.*" [239] The lower, or vulgar, orders were always liable to be emotionally unstable.

Chester riots   In Chester riot was the mood of the moment. Matthew Anderton, a customs officer, wrote to Sir Philip Egerton that crowds shouted "*A Monmouth. A Monmouth*", lit bonfires in his honour, stoned Anderton's house and St. Peter's Church, all strongly implying that only a military force could bring disorder to an end. [240] Matthew Fowler confirmed all this from his witness report, but also noted that a parallel race-meeting had been held by the loyal gentry of Cheshire at the Forest of Delamere. Some 500 attended with horses, dined well and behaved peacefully. [241] Quite possibly the nephew the rector employed as his spy was the John Fowler he so favoured in his will as the residue legatee of his property as a prebend of Lichfield cathedral. [242]

The success of the Duke at the race meeting and the honour he did the mayor of Chester were simple facts to Philip Henry when he made the entry in his diary on 15 September. He was just as impressed by the wonderful harvest of apples then being enjoyed in the district. Matthew Fowler, on the other hand, had considerable anxieties. He went so far as to comment on the prospects for James, Duke of York, in the light of Monmouth's visit locally.

> *"Give me leave, however, thus far to express my thoughts that by this progress of the Duke, though accompanied by much vanity and folly, it appears to me that the crown will sit very uneasily on the head of His Royal Highness, if he ever attain to it, unless he returns to the religion, for which his royal father was crowned with a glorious martyrdom."* [243]

The series of letters Fowler wrote to Secretary Jenkins was completed on 7 October when the whole Monmouth episode had run its course. The effect in London had been such that the king ordered Monmouth's arrest. This was duly carried out rather dramatically in Stafford after Monmouth had journeyed south via Madeley and Trentham. Fowler had meticulously named as many of the king's Cheshire enemies as he could throughout the correspondence and kept in touch with other loyal gentlemen such as Peter Shakerley to exchange news. He now confirmed that quiet had generally descended on the district.

> *"... only some grumbling words from the Whigs because the Duke of Monmouth, their great idol, met with so cold entertainment at his return. ... I hear of nothing yet done in Cheshire about the commission to inquire of the riot. The sessions are this week at Knutsford."* [244]

Fowler signed off with his last declaration of loyalty.

> *"Meanwhile I beg there be no more mention of repayment of charges, for that is a very inconsiderable thing to him that accounts it both his duty and honour to sacrifice his life and estate at his Majesty's feet."*

The ailments Fowler suffered from in 1682 are not known, but he lived another year, dying at Christmas time 1683. Conscious of his dignity and

Fowler's death

social pre-eminence he ordered that he be buried in linen *"and left five pounds in dole to the poor in consideration thereof [er]go either hee thought undergoing the Penalty satisfyes the law or hee dy'd in disobedience. D Zanchy succeeds"*, so wrote Philip Henry in his diary. [245] Woollen shrouds, as the law required, were for the common folk! Henry might also have been suggesting that the rapid appointment of Clement Sankey indicated his presence in the parish already. Perhaps Fowler's incapacity had been known for some time - he died worn out by care and sleeplessness according to his memorial in the church. The Earl of Bridgewater was certainly anxious not to leave Whitchurch without a rector and had Sankey lined up in anticipation of the inevitable. [246]

Matthew Fowler was eulogised by his wife as might be expected as a brilliant theologian, a man fearless in action and one devoted to his pastoral duties, eloquent and of shrewd judgment. His allegiance to the Stuart monarchs was undoubted and his sermons were worthy of printing.[247] His biographer, Rev. Gilbert Vane, assiduously avoided making a judgement on Fowler's impact on the parish of Whitchurch, somewhat discounting on the one hand the fulsome memorial carved out for display in the church and also Philip Henry's tart final comment as too much a sign of some bitterness left over from the excommunication episode.

Matthew Fowler's memorial in St. Alkmund's Church

This was a clergyman in the old Anglican tradition, however, who began his ministry in Whitchurch with the task of recovering his parishioners from their Presbyterian waywardness. He ended it fearing that it was not the dissenters who most put his church in danger, but his future sovereign. In so far as this was the case – and he made a point in his will of forbidding all *"encomiums or letters of recommendation from the pulpit"* at his funeral, following a good nonconformist example – he acquired wisdom from his experience.[248]

The mystery of just how much he conditioned the cultural and spiritual life of his parish during his twenty years service is deepened by the inventory of his personal possessions which included £700 of debts owed to him in bonds and loans of various unspecified kinds. Lettice, his widow and sole executrix, presumably had to deal with these. She was described in affectionate terms by Matthew as he wrote out the tasks she had to fulfil immediately. One of these was to pay out £20 to get poor boys in the parish put out as apprentices. Two harpsichords and £7 worth of books were luxuries indicative of a profitable living, but the coach and four horses he possessed put him into a higher social bracket than might be expected. Brewing vessels were testimony to the economic independence of a household big enough to require a constant beer supply.[249] But was he a banker to his parishioners as well? Did he use his cash income to lubricate the local economy and win friends and influence people? Of course, he might have been investing in fields further flung with no link to Whitchurch. We shall probably never know.

Chapter 10

A divided society in crisis: Whitchurch and 'The Glorious Revolution'

The arrival early in 1684 of a new rector in Whitchurch, Clement Sankey, after the death of Matthew Fowler, almost coincided with an even more momentous succession. The following year James II followed his brother Charles to the throne. For the first time in nearly one hundred and thirty years the monarch was an avowed Catholic in faith. He was also officially the Supreme Governor of the Church of England as by law established. Once again, no matter what the individual commitments of Whitchurch people with respect to religious beliefs and their public observance, national actions would impinge heavily on their activities.

Two contemporary documents contain evidence of the impact of a series of political crises in the 1685 – 90 period when James II attempted and failed to impose a new religious settlement. Philip Henry's diaries and letters recorded his response, while his eldest daughter, Sarah, married in 1687 to John Savage of Wrenbury Wood just over the Cheshire border, north of Whitchurch, provided another perspective in a journal she kept between August 1686 and December 1688. [250] They both reveal the anxieties of the dissenting congregations to which they belonged rather than the concerns of Anglicans such as those taking communion from Clement Sankey in St. Alkmund's.

In fact, James II failed to hold on to the loyalty of his principal subjects and a new religious settlement was arrived at by 1690, in his absence, entirely dependent on the requirements of new sovereigns, William of Orange and his wife Queen Mary. The course of events can be followed, in part at least, through the story of Whitchurch.

The new king's reign began quietly enough in February 1685. He called a Parliament, for instance, and promised that he would preserve the Church of England as it then stood. One man could *Monmouth's rebellion* not resist the temptation to call this into question. The Duke of Monmouth by June was in Dorset collecting men into an army of sorts and starting to march eastwards to claim his inheritance. James's reaction was swift, and habitual. All the usual suspects were rounded up and thrown in jail. In Philip Henry's case it was Chester Castle.

The editor of his diaries published no direct evidence from Philip's own journal, but Matthew Henry, his son, was quoted as reporting this event. [251] Numerous gentlemen and dissenting ministers from Lancashire and Cheshire spent three weeks in each other's company in no great degree of discomfort, apparently. Several were surprised that Henry's view was that

Philip Henry in Chester Castle

no good could ever come from the Duke of Monmouth. Indeed, Matthew Henry thought his father much more hopeful of another royal indulgence similar to that of 1672. Talking with a leading Anglican Philip Henry said as much. The reply was that he should place no trust in the king for he hated dissenters. Henry agreed, but pointed out that James had no more love of the Anglican clergy either! In a letter to his wife on 8 July 1685 Henry reported on conditions in jail with a certain calm acceptance.

> *"Our Afternoons, til late are fild with visitants, who love us and wish us well and are kind to us, but wee cannot doe with them what wee would. C[ou]sin Crue hath been an hour with me this morning shee brought me a quart of Aqu[a] Mirab[ilis] which I would have had her take back again, till more need, but she would not. I have not yet opened the little bottle I brought with mee, since I came, not wanting it … Mrs Wenlock was to see mee yesterday and brought me a bottle of wine. I bestow all of that kind in Common, my Companions strangers here."* [252]

Monmouth's adventure was ill fated from the start. On 15 July he was executed after losing a desperate battle at Sedgemoor in Somerset. James's revenge made operational by the infamous Judge Jeffries in a series of show trials of Monmouth's followers in western counties gained him a short-term advantage politically, and allowed Henry and his companions to be freed without difficulty. In the longer run, the king had displayed ruthlessness which was counter-productive.

The fate of Whitchurch people in the matter of religious practice was not decided locally. James II set out to reverse more than a century of religious

King James and freedom for Catholics

habit, but he had to work within a political system and avoid the mistakes of his father. People like Philip Henry, the Benions and Yates, could only respond to central government action and rely on the king's courtiers and bureaucrats defeating James's intentions. For example, in May 1688, quite unexpectedly, Philip Henry was invited by letter to join the magistracy. The exact reason for this and the mechanism by which he had the invitation may not be clear. But it was just the kind of move which fitted with King James's tactics. The first target for the king was to obtain freedom of worship for his fellow Catholics. They had been subjected to financial penalties for not attending their parish church for a century. Punishments had been enforced spasmodically and regionally variously, not consistently, but rigorously on occasions as quite recently. The law still stood, however, discriminating against people for the practice of their religious belief.

In addition, during Charles II's time, new legislation, the Test Acts, made appointment to offices of state, the armed forces and local government subject to taking communion in the Anglican form. This was anathema to Catholics. Again, individuals found ways around this in particular cases with royal help, but Charles had never pushed his luck too far. He knew the political cost could be his throne. Even so he exploited his prerogative power in favour of Catholics, as well as Protestant dissenters, when he found it necessary.

So, James tried his brother's trick of using royal prerogative to absolve all nonconformists from legal penalties for holding services and taking up government *Edict of Toleration* appointments. His Edict of Toleration early in 1687 met with the same opposition which Charles had faced. In law, it was argued, the king's prerogative might relieve an individual of some legal obligation: it did not extend to absolution *en masse*. Only Parliament could do this.

James had called a Parliament soon after his succession, but it was intractable on religious matters. He dissolved it and looked for ways of getting members elected more in sympathy with his objectives. He adopted Monmouth's tactic of 1682 and went on a provincial tour in the summer of 1687. There were two objectives, to meet the gentry who controlled Parliamentary constituencies, and to pray at the well of St. Winefride (Holywell) in Flintshire. The first was a short-term ploy to solve the election problem. The second was more long term. If Catholic supremacy could be achieved it could only be guaranteed if his barren wife produced a son. St. Winefride's waters had a history of miraculous cures, so why not seek a solution to Queen Mary's infertility there?

The king's route took him to Worcester and Ludlow, on to Shrewsbury heading for Chester. The Earl of Tyrconnel, Lord Deputy in Ireland, planned to meet him in Shrewsbury with a large body of supporters, and on 24 August when James arrived in Ludlow, Tyrconnel landed at Chester. On the 25th the Irish contingent processed south through Whitchurch and came into Shrewsbury where James appeared about five o'clock in the evening. The town was bustling with High Sheriff, Deputy

Lieutenants, JPs, and numerous gentry of the town and county. All gathered to watch the mayor, Corporation and *"Companies of the several Trades, ranked in order"* greet their sovereign with due pomp. The mayor took the king to his lodgings, but the reporter, observing all, wrote that

> *"the great Concourse of the People of all sorts, their Transports of Joy, and the different ways they had of expressing it, is what cannot be contained within the narrow compass of this short account."* [253]

Exactly this kind of account was given at every stopping place.

Not that everybody remembered it like this. Bishop Burnet was more impressed by the coldness of receptions James received. The Shrewsbury Corporation may have made the conduits run with wine and spent £200 entertaining the king, after checking up on what Gloucester and Worcester had done a few days earlier, but the gentry of Shropshire didn't display great enthusiasm. [254] None that Burnet gave credit to anyway.

The next day the greatly enlarged party moved on to Whitchurch where

> *"His Majesty arrived here this day, being still attended by the High Sheriff and Gentry of the County of Salop, within which we lie; and there was nothing omitted, whereby this little place could testifie their excess of Joy for the Honour of so great a Presence."*

Loyal Addresses at Whitchurch

The king clearly stayed overnight for he did not arrive in Chester until four o'clock in the afternoon of the 27th August. [255] Where could the king have eaten and slept? Was there bunting out over High Street? There were crowds for Sarah Savage saw them.

> *"1687. Friday, August 26, the king came into Whitchurch. James the Second, in his progress to Chester; great flocking to see him. Lord, order all consultations and actions for glory to thy name!*
>
> *Tuesday. I went to Whitchurch to see His Majesty in his return from Chester; saw him only in his coach; desired heartily to pray that he were as good as he is great."* [256]

A royal progress of this kind called for the gentry and institutions of nearby districts to present Loyal Addresses to affirm the strength of their allegiance to the person of the king. These were printed in the government's newspaper, the *London Gazette*. Philip Henry was among the many dissenters who made a special point of declaring their loyalty in a document handed to James while in Whitchurch. It was a joint effort by Whitchurch, Nantwich and Wem groups to thank James fulsomely for his *"late Royal Declaration of Indulgence to Proclaim Liberty to our Consciences and Practice, from the Restraints that lay upon us in God's Worship."* [257] It would be somewhat ironic if James had slept in Whitchurch rectory

To the King's Most Excellent Majesty,

The humble and thankful Addreſs of your Majeſties Loyal Subjects, the peaceable Diſſenters of the Towns and Neighborhood of *Nantwich* in *Cheſhire,* and of *Wem* and *Whitchurch* in *Shropſhire.*

WHereas it hath pleaſed your *Majeſty*, by your late Royal Declaration of Indulgence, to Proclaim Liberty to our Conſciences and Practice, from the Reſtraints that lay upon us in Gods Worſhip, we cannot but expreſs the joyful ſenſe we have of the ſame ; And in Teſtimony thereof, do in all humbleneſs caſt our ſelves at your Majeſties Feet, and give unto your Maieſty our humble hearty thanks for it, beſeeching your Maieſty, according to your Royal Goodneſs, ſtill to continue to us that Liberty; And we hope through God's Grace, we ſhall ſo demean our ſelves in the uſe of it, both towards God, and towards your Majeſty and your Government, and towards all Men, that your Majeſty ſhall have no cauſe to repent of, but to rejoice in your Royal Favor therein graciouſly extended towards us,

> Your Majeſties Dutiful and Loyal
> Subjects and Servants.

The Humble Address to which Philip Henry added his name as published in the London Gazette 5 September 1687 and then had this document presented to him after breakfast! There was a possibility that the king would offer compensation to all dissenters who had suffered distraint of their goods and other fines, but it was said that Philip Henry refused to consider taking this having long since forgiven those who had so roughly handled him. [258]

How much of this supporting sentiment would translate into Parliamentary votes is anybody's guess. A great fuss was made in Chester *St. Winefride's Well* and on 29 August when James and his Queen travelled over the sands of the Dee to Flint another show of loyalty was made by the Bishop of St. Asaph, plus clergy and gentry from all the surrounding districts. *The London Gazette,* perhaps calculatingly, did not say that James and Mary prayed for a boy child at St. Winefride's Well. Rather the report said they saw the waters and ate their dinner. But there, as in Chester and probably in Whitchurch also, James touched for the King's Evil. All this, and no one conceived the concept of spin doctoring!

James and his advisors were well aware, however, of the need to have sympathetic officials in local government posts. Town corporations which controlled Parliamentary elections were fixed by recalling their charters for amendment. Benches of magistrates which determined candidates for county seats in Parliament were culled of known Whigs and commissions issued appointing friendly figures to replace them. This was the context in 1688 for the offer in May to Philip Henry of a place among the magistracy. It was because he could see the reasoning behind such a move that he refused it.

Opinion throughout the country in late spring and summer 1688 was moving against James. His wooing of dissenters was a transparent trick. In *The king's orders to* May the king made his fateful move of forcing Anglican clergy to read out in their pulpits the *his clergy* Declaration freeing Catholics and dissenters from the penalties of not attending Anglican churches. Quite possibly Clement Sankey did just this for both the bishops of Chester and Coventry and Lichfield were pliant men and did not advertise objections. At any rate, his churchwardens paid the expenses of the bishop's special agent, his appariter, who delivered the necessary document. [259] Seven other bishops refused to order their diocesan clergy to obey. James reacted by having them arrested. What became known as the Glorious Revolution, or the dethroning of James II, was in train. [260]

Whitchurch people kept track of events to some extent by listening to the bells of St. Alkmund's. At Easter, a new set of churchwardens started their year's duty. At the end, they had to account for their income and expenditure, alongside their fellow parish officers.

> "The Accompts of Mr Richard Wicksted Mr John Gittins Ralph Lovell and Ralph Gregory Churchwardens and also of William Swanwick Peter Lee William Barrow and Robert Micklewright Overseers of the Poore of the Parish of Whitchurch Anno Dom 1688 of their Receipts and disbursements since the 17th day of April in the said yeare untill this present day being the second day of April 1689 as followeth (viz)"
> 261

It was the four churchwardens who had to act on news of royal activity as it arrived by whatever means. They could not have guessed that the celebration they had to arrange for the birth of a son to King James and Queen Mary in June was a critical link in a chain reaction ending in the 'Glorious Revolution'.

Churchwardens and the costs of revolution

Pd for a Proclamacon to forbid playing in the Churchyard	00	00	04
Pd for ringing the 23rd of Aprill being King James' Coronacon day	00	05	00
Pd for three Matts for the Bell Loft	00	05	06
Pd for a new Accompt Booke	00	09	06
Pd for Ringing the 29th May being the birth day of King Charles the second	00	05	00
Pd the Apparitor for the Declaracon about Liberty of Conscience	00	02	10
Pd for Ringing the 16th June being the birth day of the Prince of Wales	00	05	00
Pd for a forme of thanksgiveing for the birth of the said Prince	00	03	00
Pd for Ringing the thanksgiveing day for the said young Prince	00	05	00
Pd for the order for alteracon of the Com[m]on Prayer for the said young Prince	00	01	00

Special church services for royal events were, of course, nothing new. On 23 April 1688 the bells at St. Alkmund's were rung to celebrate the anniversary of James' coronation in 1685. On 29 May they were rung again on the birthday of the previous king, James' brother Charles II, dead three years now. News of a royal birth, however, was stunning.

James was 55 years old during the third year of his reign but his second wife, an Italian princess, Mary of Modena, was only 30. A good age for bearing children. So far, however, there had been five, all dying in infancy, from a marriage she began at the age of 15. Her health was reckoned to be too poor for hope of any more. The pilgrimage to St. Winefride's Well was a desperate last throw. If this failed, James would be succeeded by Mary, his daughter by his first wife Anne Hyde, and she in turn by her sister Anne. Both were known as devoted Protestants. There was considerable surprise, therefore, even at court, when, on 10 June 1688 an official announcement was made that the queen had been delivered of a boy child, a Prince of Wales. News spread rapidly and six days later the bell ringers in Whitchurch had another round of ale (no doubt) at the expense of the parish to lead public rejoicing on this wonderful occasion.

Childbirth was a dangerous business and at some time shortly after the first news arrived the ringers were in the church tower again to pull a peal in thanksgiving that the boy had lived so far. At the same time the churchwardens had to pay for alterations in the Prayer Books used on Sundays to include a new prayer for the infant prince. Nothing out of the ordinary, it might be thought, although Princes of Wales don't get born all that often. In fact, there had only been one other in the seventeenth century, and there were to be no more for fifty years at least. This particular birth, however, was subject to suspicion, rumour and political controversy. There were even those who openly discussed the chances of it being a fraud. Could a child have been smuggled into the Queen's bed in a warming pan as she simulated labour?

Only one of the dramatic events at the core of the political crisis in London that autumn cost Whitchurch's churchwardens extra money. They would have rung the bells for 5 November anyway, but rector Sankey felt it necessary to call God in aid of peace for the nation by commissioning a special prayer with regard to a threat of invasion by the Dutch William of Orange, the king's son-in-law.

Pd for a forme of Prayer upon the apprehension			
of the Invasion	*00*	*02*	*06*
Pd for Ringing the 5th of November & Candles	*00*	*07*	*06*

It's a nice question whether this took the form of a printed sheet distributed on a Sunday for parishioners to chant in unison, or for some other method of publicising the rector's plea. Did the rector charge for composing special prayers?

This was, of course, only one of the ways that Whitchurch people got to hear of actions resulting from threats to their king from the seven bishops.

Their arrest and trial for refusing to obey caused consternation among the nation's élite. A secret and high-risk plan was rapidly devised by James's critics to stop the king in his tracks. In short, on 30 June seven high-ranking politicians and members of the House of Lords invited William of Orange, ruler of the Netherlands, and husband to James's daughter Mary, to bring over an army to force James to change his religious and constitutional policies. On 5 November 1688 William's troops began to land at Brixham in Tor Bay, Devon. There could have been many who thought that this was 1642 all over again.

The order in which the churchwardens cast their accounts leaves it open as to when Clement Sankey got news of an impending invasion, but it does look as though this was before 5 November when rumours were rife, but nothing had been confirmed. By about 10 November William's invasion must have been common knowledge.

One can only assume that Whitchurch folk were on tenterhooks all winter wondering what conclusions would follow William's slow march towards London.

Pd for Ringing the 25th December	*00*	*05*	*00*
Pd for bindeing Bishop Jewells workes and Carriage	*00*	*05*	*06*
Pd for Ringing the first of January	*00*	*05*	*00*
Pd for Ringing the 6th ffeb[ruar]y being the day			
of King James's Inauguration	*00*	*05*	*00*

Christmas went by as usual and New Year's Day. One of the church's more valuable books had got a bit battered, presumably, and a binder charged five shillings and six pence for repairs. The rector must still have been assuming that it was in order to celebrate the accession date of King James on 6 February because the bell ringers had their normal reward for their efforts. In fact, James had fled first on December 11 and thrown away his Great Seal, and after capture, escaped again on 23 December (probably allowed to go) and thereafter he resided on the continent. Clement Sankey was pushing it a bit when he sanctioned another ringing for the king at St. Alkmund's.

Events moved rapidly as the next entry in the accounts shows.

Pd for the Bookes of thankesgiveinge and prayers			
for the Prince of Orange	*00*	*02*	*06*
Pd towards ransomeing some Merchants out of Turkey	*00*	*01*	*00*
Pd for Ringing the day K William & Queen Mary were			
Proclaymed K & Queen of England	*00*	*[?]*	*00*

William and Mary were declared joint sovereigns on 13 February 1689 and crowned on 11 April. New churchwardens took over on 2 April, so obviously Clement Sankey had to find copies of a new Prayer book sometime in late February – early March and let his bell ringers do their work again to rejoice in the arrival of a new sovereign. Incidental to their responsibilities for St. Alkmund's the wardens had to meet charity appeals organised nationally. It was not unusual for pirates to capture English ships in the Mediterranean and ransoms to be paid out of appeals to all parishes.

Only one more entry in the account book reports how Whitchurch bore the cost of the 'Glorious Revolution'.

Pd for an order to pray for K. William & Qu. Mary   00   02   06

It looks as though the parish had to pay the expenses of whoever delivered the instruction from central government that it was now King William and Queen Mary for whom prayers should be said each Sunday, and not King James, the king declared as abdicated, not deposed.

'The Glorious Revolution'

A recital of dates and bell ringing at St. Alkmund's slides over the complexities of the political deal made among courtiers and politicians popularly summarised as 'the Glorious Revolution'. One king was removed and joint sovereigns were installed in his place. The whole matter was registered in Parliamentary legislation and the main deals completed well within a year. And they were deals too, between groups and individuals, who all felt it necessary to accept the best bargain available to avoid 1642 all over again. Compromise on principles was crucial.

A Bill of Rights registered the detail. Of all the arrangements, the one with most immediate effect in Whitchurch was the Toleration Act 1689. This put Philip Henry and those like him in a new relationship with the rector of Whitchurch and the Anglican Church.

Tories and Whigs negotiated an arrangement in 1689 the upshot of which was to enshrine in legislation a major part of that policy of freedom to worship which Charles II and James II had toyed with – but restricted to Protestant dissenters only. Henceforth, Presbyterians and other Protestant groups such as Baptists were relieved of the penalties inflicted on them for non-attendance at Anglican parish churches on certain new conditions. For them it was toleration at a price: for Catholics there was no change.

An act for exempting their Majesties protestant subjects, dissenting from the Church of England, from the penalties of certain laws

IV. And be it further enacted by the authority aforesaid, That all and every person and persons that shall, as aforesaid, take the said oaths, and make and subscribe the declaration aforesaid, shall not be liable to any pains, penalties, or forfeitures, mentioned in an act made in the five and thirtieth year of the reign of the late Queen Elizabeth, intituled, *An act to retain the Queen's majesty's subjects in their due obedience*; nor in an act made i the two and twentieth year of the reign of the late King Charles the Second, intituled, *An act to prevent and suppress seditious conventicles*; nor shall any of the said persons be prosecuted in any ecclesiastical court, for or by reason of their non-conforming to the Church of England

V. Provided always, and be it enacted by the authority aforesaid, That if any assembly of persons dissenting from the Church of England shall be had in any place for religious worship with the doors locked, barred, or bolted, during any time of such meeting together, all and every persons or persons, that shall come to and be at such meeting, shall not receive any benefit from this law, but be liable to all the pains and penalties of all the aforesaid laws recited in this act, for such their meeting, notwithstanding his taking the oaths and his making and subscribing the declaration aforesaid.

VI. Provided always, That nothing herein contained shall be construed to exempt any of the persons aforesaid from paying of tithes or other parochial duties, or any other duties to the church or minister, nor from any prosecution in any ecclesiastical court or elsewhere, for the same

XVII. Provided always, and be it further enacted by the authority aforesaid, that neither this act, nor any clause, article, or thing herein contained, shall extend or be construed to extend to give any ease, benefit or advantage to any papist or popish recusant whatsoever, or any person that shall deny in his preaching or writing the doctrine of the blessed Trinity, as it is declared in the aforesaid articles of religion.

They had to register their meeting places with magistrates, leave them unlocked, and pay fees. They were still denied access to public office under the Test Acts, had to pay tithes and other dues to Anglican clergy and their ministers had no status unless episcopally ordained. They had achieved, nonetheless, the minimum degree of freedom Philip Henry had always wanted.

Almost immediately Henry registered a barn at Broad Oak as a meeting house and enjoyed for the last years of his life the opportunity to worship his God in public without interference or financial threats.

Chapter 11
Clement Sankey's Whitchurch

Rectors of Whitchurch were responsible for the spiritual welfare, moral standards, religious beliefs and therefore the behaviour of their parishioners. Moreover, they stood as models of what they preached. At least, that was the theory. In this, they were agents of a church as the law defined it. This theoretical position was not altered by the Toleration Act, even though alternative forms of religious observance were now allowed in public. In practice, dissenting ministers provided an alternative personification of a Christian life to that presented by Anglican clergy.

Clement Sankey was not without his problems. A section of his parishioners eventually found that he fell below their expectations. Explanations for this are difficult to unravel and more questions may be left open than are answered. It could have been a storm in a tea-cup; perhaps it was of much greater significance.

There could almost have been two Clement Sankeys (alias Zanchy), one an ambitious, garrulous and gregarious Cambridge college minor Fellow, the other a provincial clergyman, academic manqué, with interests in Yorkshire and Shropshire. The link which suggests they were one and the same person was a woman, Mary Archer.

On this assumption, Clement Sankey was London born about 1633, and Cambridge educated, getting his BA at Magdalene College in 1652. In the same year he was elected a Fellow of the College and re-elected in 1660. He was much tempted by life in London, however, for it was there that Samuel Pepys found him an agreeable drinking companion and *meetings with Samuel Pepys* fond of confiding his ambitions for a wealthy marriage. They were exactly the same age and obviously knew each other from their days at Magdalene. Pepys, who went up in 1651 and graduated in 1654, might have been an assiduous student but not one who aimed at an ecclesiastical career, nor was he overly puritanical in his habits. In fact, he and Sankey shared similar tastes in female company. Seven years later, Pepys recorded a day in London which brought back memories.

"Having this morning met in the Hall with Mr Sanchy, we appointed to meet at the play this afternoon … to dinner, at the Swan, in the Palace yard, and our meat brought from the Legg. And after dinner Sir

W.Pen and I to the Theatre, and there saw "The Country Captain", a dull play, and that being done, I left him with his Torys and went to the Opera, and saw the last act of "The Bondman", and there find Mr Sanchy and Mrs Mary Archer, sister to the fair Betty, whom I did admire at Cambridge. And thence took them to the Fleece in Covent Garden, there to bid good night to Sir W.Pen who stayed for me. But Mr Sanchy could not by any argument get his lady to trust herself with him into the taverne, which he was much troubled at; and so we returned immediately into the City by Coach, and at the Miter in Cheapside there light and drank, and then set her at her uncles in the Old Jury. And so he and I back again thither and drank till past 12 at night, till I had drank something too much – he all the while telling me his intention to get this girl who is worth 1000l, and many times we had her sister Betty's health, whose memory I love. At last parted, and I well home; only, had got a cold and was hoarse and so to bed." [262]

Sankey had revived acquaintance with Pepys the previous year, at Magdalene College, when Pepys spent time in Cambridge on family business. Pepys confided in his diary, *"I went to Magdalene College to Mr Hill, with whom I found Mr Zanchy, Burton and Hollins,"* but it was with Zanchy and two others that he met later that day *"at Morton's shop ..."* and then at the Three Tuns *"where we drank pretty hard and many healths to the king &c till it began to get darkish; then we broke up and I and Mr Zanchy went to Magdalene College ...".* A supper party then followed *"where in their discourse I could find that there was nothing at all left of the old preciseness in their discourse, specially on Saturday nights. And Mr Zanchy told me that there was no such thing nowadays among them at any time."* [263] No 'preciseness' any more - so much for Puritanism!

The following day Sankey avoided a church sermon by more drinking with Pepys at the Rose tavern, hailing the king's health until darkness fell. This was not the end. Pepys collected his father and a friend and he and Sankey returned to the Rose for a quart or two more wine, after which they had supper at a cousin's and sent out for more wine. [264]

Just what Sankey's ambitions were at this time is uncertain. He presumably continued to work as a Fellow and had something of a reputation as a scholar or teacher. He certainly found time to make visits to London, even if only occasionally. Pepys met him again in Cambridge in July 1661 and in August. [265] On that occasion, Pepys found Sankey and another Fellow critical of the restored college heads, returned after exclusion during the Commonwealth. This was hardly surprising for Sankey owed his Fellowship to the Puritan regime. [266]

A student's experience of Cambridge 1667-71

John Rastrick was seventeen years old when he went up to Trinity College, Cambridge, in June 1667. The son of a Lincolnshire self-identified yeoman he admitted that he was a weak scholar, too young to immediately grasp the significance of his lessons in *"Logick and Ethics"*. He was also much disturbed by the lack of good preaching anywhere in the town, and the formalities of services in his college chapel. He took time out when his mother was ill, but returned in the summer of 1669. He was *"furiously assaulted with the Temptations and injections of Satan and more deeply Melancholly than ever"* because he was uncertain about the nature of his future career as a clergyman. Rastrick was saved by taking long morning and evening walks in the fields around town. It concerned him that he preferred religious works to the books his tutors expected him to read and that he had no companions except the man he shared a room with.

Of the others he came across *"their Society was generally worse than none. … That very little which I saw of it (which could not be had but in Taverns) was a great deal too much : I was ever the object of their Scorn and derision: If I did but read a Greek chapter at Prayer times, or repeat my Sermon notes on a Lord's Day at night, in our Tutor's chamber, when he required it; my very tone was enough for them to laugh at and jeer me for afterwards. For a Scholler to intend the Ministry or order his Studys more directly that way was matter of Obloquy and Scorn enough for them. Comedies and Playbooks were in greater Reputation, and a greater Credit to Schollers, than Divinity Books: And I must have suited them, and drunk and been drunk with them, or have no company of their's. This seems hard for me to say; yet they that observe with what Ministers the Countrys are stored, will not I suppose be hard to believe it. Now if Society make an University, then was Cambridge no University to me: as things were."*

Andrew Cambers (edit) *The Life of John Rastrick 1650-1727* (Cambridge University Press for The Royal Historical Society, Camden 5th series Vol. 36, 2010) pages 45-58

In December 1661 Sankey was again in London and arranged to meet Pepys. Sankey *"should have brought his mistress, Mrs Mary Archer of Cambridge, but she would not come. But we had a good dinner for him; and so in the afternoon my wife went to church, and he and I stayed at home and drank and talked and he stayed with me till night and supped with me."* [267]

Mary Archer in London

Sankey had more luck the next day, for he collected *"his mistress, and with them went by coach to the Opera to see The Madd Lover"*. Back then to Pepys house for supper and merrymaking. There was no mention of Mary Archer staying with an uncle this time – how fortunate for the lady that she could make excursions to London and stay conveniently with a relative just at the same time that Clement Sankey could escape his Fellowship duties at Magdalene! [268]

Sankey may have been more regular in his trips to London than Pepys knew, but the two met less frequently as time passed. In April 1662, after a glut of theatre going Pepys and his wife agreed, *"We are resolved to see no more plays till Whitsuntide we having been three days together. Met Mr Sanchy, Smithies, Gale, and Edlin at the play, but having no great mind to spend money, I left them there. And so home and to supper, and then dispatch business, and so to bed."* [269]

Sankey remained at Magdalene at least until April 1664 for he met Pepys by accident in London – as Pepys wrote *"met Mr Sanchy of Cambridge, whom I have not met a great while. He seems a simple fellow – and tells me their master, Dr Rainbow, is newly made Bishop of Carlisle."* [270] Quite probably, Sankey's Fellowship was not extended in 1666, for in January 1667 Pepys learned that he had been given a living worth £200 a year *"which I wondered at, he [Sir R Ford] commending him mightily; but am glad of it."* This was at St. Clement's, Eastcheap. [271]

Pepys' warmth toward Sankey cooled somewhat at this point, perhaps as he himself became a hardened civil servant. He ran into Sankey in the street in April and at least gave him a lift in his coach. He recalled him *"as my old acquaintance at Cambridge"*, but now *"reckoned a great minister here in the city, and by Sir Rd Ford particularly, which I wonder at, for methinks in his talk he is but a mean man. I set him down in Holburne and I to the Old Exchange."* [272]

Pepys puts off Sankey

Ten days or so later Sankey and Pepys obviously fell out, though just why is unknown. Pepys simply recorded that *"Here comes Mr Sanchy with an impertinent business to me of a ticket, which I put off."* [273]

Big events in London might well have kept Sankey and Pepys apart in any case, for 1665 was the year of the great plague and 1666 was marked by the astonishing destruction by fire. In the first case, Sankey did well to stay out of the City altogether, but it may be that the fire gave him opportunities just when he needed them. Was this how the vacancy at St. Clement's occurred? The parish was close to the centre of the firestorm and the church completely destroyed. Did he have any part, however small, in the business of rebuilding the gutted portions of London? Pepys seemed to think he made a quick impact in his first parish post and one way might have been organising the means by which his neighbourhood recovered from the fire.

On the other hand, it might be argued that Sankey was not satisfied with his City parish, although £200 must have been a welcome income after Cambridge. He furthered his academic ambitions in 1668 when awarded a doctorate in divinity, but to boost his finances he acquired further livings. One in Essex, at Colne Engaine, and a second in Yorkshire have been credited to him. The first is unproven and it is a moot point as to which he actually lived in. Indeed, it is a touch uncertain as to whether he held them all simultaneously, and if so, for how long. It would seem that his Yorkshire living, at Settrington, led almost immediately to (or was accompanied by) a post as Prebend of South Newbald and canon at York Minster. This was a man who cultivated patrons with great care and skill. His patron for the prebendal job was the king himself.

The most intriguing move he made was to marry Mary Archer, of Bourn in Cambridgeshire, in 1669. Her family network may or may not have been a significant influence: *Sankey's marriage* she might or might not have brought him the £1,000 he boasted to Samuel Pepys that she was worth. It would seem though that the marriage was the achievement of a long held ambition. According to Pepys, he had been dallying with her in the early 1650s and it has been suggested that Sankey had a house in Bourn in the 1660s at least long enough to pay Hearth Tax on it. As a Fellow, of course, he was not allowed to marry. The mystery of his exact relationship to Mary before 1669 is heightened by Pepys description of the lady as "Mrs Mary Archer" and his use of the word "mistress" as an alternative way of reporting her. Certainly, Clement Sankey did marry a lady by the name of Mary for his wife was buried in Whitchurch by that name in 1688.

It is possible that Sankey moved out of London to the Yorkshire Wolds shortly after marrying and took up residence at Settrington, just east of Malton. York would not have given him the same theatre going opportunities London provided: perhaps he found some alternative entertainment in cathedral politics. It is not certain, however, that there was a residential requirement to his post as canon. Indeed, there must be a doubt about his residence at all in this relatively remote patch of rural England. In March 1675/6 a Mary Sankey was baptised in the parish of St. Botolph Aldersgate, London, to parents Clement and Mary Sankey. [274] This record at least allows the possibility that Clement and Mary never left London for either his Essex or his Yorkshire benefices. Whatever the case, and for whatever reason, Whitchurch in 1684 was a greater attraction for this fifty year old clergyman than anything east Yorkshire, Essex or London could supply. Maybe his former life style was catching up with him and he needed a lesser parish burden. By means unknown he found the second Earl of Bridgewater a generous patron and made the last move in his church career.

In Whitchurch, Sankey got through the crucial period of the so-called Glorious Revolution crisis and the arrival of joint monarchs in William

Sankey in Whitchurch

and Mary without any overt evidence of difficulty. There is a possibility though that in the new climate of a post-Revolution culture Sankey was vulnerable. The sexual excesses of Charles and James, the drift to a renewed Catholicism and moral laxity – as Puritanically inclined critics would have seen things – were over. The 1690s was a time of war against Louis XIV's Huguenot-persecuting Catholic France, of financial stringency, and the widespread flowering of Protestant nonconformity. Proof of the latter was the opening up of chapels across Staffordshire, Shropshire and Cheshire in startling abundance by Presbyterians, Quakers and Baptists at the very least. [275] It's a nice question as to what Whitchurch people knew of Sankey's past, and another as to how much his character had changed since moving from the excitements of London to the backwaters of the provinces.

Whitchurch was an extensive parish geographically, but the urban community huddled in a few streets south of a churchyard in which six centuries of dead were interred. The town was tightly packed, people deprived for the most part of private space. Everybody knew everybody else's business. Sankey's parsonage lay somewhat detached, beyond the graveyard and in a garden, almost a park-like open stretch of land. It was an old timber-framed, two-storey building, with additions and a gatehouse, all constructed within a moat. [276] What went on there was not so visible to those riding the highway to Chester as were the activities in, say, Wickstead's apothecary's shop off the High Street or the parlours of the town's numerous inns. These served as listening posts on the outside world and dens of local gossip for tradesmen and farmers. The rector was the nearest person the parish had to a social leader, a setter of standards and an epitome of taste. It was right that he was a bit remote: remoteness invited curiosity, however. His business was inevitably the object of all attention.

Crimes of theft, assault and trespass were among many misbehaviours covered by courts ranging from that of the manor, held in a town building in High Street, to the assize courts at Shrewsbury and indeed the court of Chancery in London. Moral depravities, or the sins of the flesh, on the other hand, were policed by the church. Those accused were taken before a bishop's court. The men who found the sinners were churchwardens, subject to the orders of the rector and inquiries by archdeacons on regular visitations. At the point where things were really getting out of hand churchwardens were responsible for alerting the bishop's officials who instituted proceedings in a court held, in the case of Whitchurch, at Lichfield. Nominally it was the bishop of Lichfield and Coventry who was the ruling authority. His Consistory Court proctors were the bureaucrats who took action. By the end of the 1690s Whitchurch was contributing

The Consistory Court room at Lichfield Cathedral now used as a display space and store for old pews.

more than its previous share of business to the Consistory Court's list of cases of moral degeneracy. In the space of eight years there were five cases (technically called 'causes') of immorality, six cases of defamation and one case of a clandestine marriage sent up to Lichfield from Whitchurch.

Whitchurch and Consistory Court causes

There was also a related case of an assault on a clergyman. Although there was the odd case of defamation thereafter, for the rest of the eighteenth century no Whitchurch person was hauled down to Lichfield on grounds of committing sins of the flesh. The concentration of cases in the last years of Clement Sankey's rectorship invites speculation. Just what was going on?

The question is made more intriguing by the fact that the fifth and final case of immorality centred on Clement Sankey's housekeeper, Jane Haines. This came up in the autumn of 1704 and was the culmination of some seven years of prurient curiosity, not to say vicious rumour-mongering, all around the town and district. There is an inevitable question raised by the case as to whether the principal target was Jane in her role within the rector's household, or the rector himself. It was not his sexually predatory behaviour which was in question, however, but Jane's. It was his refusal to dismiss her on the grounds that she was believed to be a whore that angered the 'sober' people in the parish. Whatever the circumstance, Sankey was in trouble and the written documentation left behind by the court case opens up to view a town society and a rector's household in rare detail.

The Consistory Court room at Chester Cathedral has its original furnishings. These illustrate the claustrophobic character of Bishop's courts.

Put simply, Jane Haines was suspected of having an affair with a mysterious itinerant singing master called Mr Cutler. He either fathered a child on her which she aborted, or more likely, as the gossip went, gave her a dose of venereal disease. This was bad enough, but when the rector was obviously not going to get rid of her the story was elaborated. Jane had been too familiar with the rector's curates. One in particular was reputedly caught in bed with her. Another spent time in fields and lanes with her, kissing and cuddling. There isn't a resolution to this simple story. It is not now of great significance as to what Jane's character actually was so much as what we can learn from the written record about Clement Sankey, his way of living and tensions in the town in which he resided. Needless to say, Jane denied all accusations of immodest behaviour, but admitted illness and seeking medical assistance.

the Jane Haines cause

At least thirty-seven witnesses, or deponents, provided the core of the story as it had developed from the arrival of Mr Cutler in or about 1697 to the hearings at Lichfield in 1704. The process of taking evidence appears to be that the witnesses made the trip to Lichfield in the period from July to the end of September 1704 to answer a list of prepared questions submitted in writing to Richard Rider, a public notary and court official. He had the answers recorded on separate sheets of paper, just as he had the lists of questions by which to interrogate the witnesses. Someone briefed the deponents carefully, or Rider (or Rider's clerk) took to recording what was said in a standard form. Many witnesses were quoted as saying the same thing in the same words. A modern forensic defence barrister would have a field day with the repetitions suggestive of collusion and conspiracy on the part of organisers of a campaign of vilification.

It seems reasonable to accept that Dr Sankey invited Mr Cutler to come and stay at the parsonage for several weeks, perhaps up to six months, in 1697 or 1698. He was there to teach Sankey's congregation to sing psalms. This in itself has intriguing religious implications. Anglican church services were not renowned for their music – not in provincial towns and rural parishes anyway. The singing of psalms, however, was an accomplishment which added solemnity, colour and emotional bonding to the congregation's experience of worshiping the Almighty. The tradition of going into battle with psalms ringing in the ears was reinforced during the civil wars of the 1640s. No doubt, some in Whitchurch could still recall tales of this told by their fathers. Unfortunately, it was the habit chiefly among Parliamentary troops, so the overtones were of radicalism and Puritanism.

On the other hand, to introduce such music into Anglican services in the 1690s might look like a hand of friendship or reconciliation, even an appeal to dissenters to return to the established forms of religious observance. Look, you can have your favourite psalms with us. Is this what Sankey had in mind? If it was, or something similar, he was among the early practitioners in a movement which gathered pace in the eighteenth century. At the time, it is also possible that Sankey aroused opposition from traditionalists who preferred the parish clerk to intone the psalms line by line for the congregation to repeat with whatever musical talent they had. It's a fair conclusion to draw from Cutler's activities that Sankey was innovating for whatever reason. And innovation can cause resentment. [277]

Secondly, the witnesses were all agreed – and there is no reason to doubt this – that Jane Haines was a well-established housekeeper with fourteen years service at least behind her by 1704. She was single, never married, and had previously been employed by a clergyman probably not too far away. One witness deposed that this had been at Ightfield, another that the man lived in Whitchurch. [278] Sankey needed a housekeeper after his wife, Mary, died in August 1688, for he did not marry again and he had a style to maintain. Certainly, several witnesses suggested that Sankey boarded curates as a matter of habit, kept indoor servants which is only to be expected and no doubt had frequent visitors for days at a time such as archdeacons and clergy friends, other acquaintances and even his bishop. [279] Not that he had many servants at any one time. Five, including John Sadler and two other men, paid five shillings between them to a charity collection in 1687. [280] He had a large house though, with outbuildings and a stable where Mr Cutler kept his horse. It was in these surroundings that Jane was courted by Mr Cutler to the point that, as several witnesses insisted, a license was sent for to authorise their marriage. John Sadler, head man servant in the Doctor's household, claimed to have ridden off to get it. [281]

All agreed that the license was not required. Mr Cutler, one Sunday morning, when all the Doctor's household were at divine service except certain servants, 'slipt away privately'. One witness even said "Cutler slipt away privately a back way thro the mote." [282] Circumstantial detail was piled upon detail, especially by Samuel Grindley who recalled his days as a servant living at the parsonage when Cutler lodged there and was familiar with Jane Haines. Grindley deposed

"that it was reported they would be married and about a week before
the said Cutler quite left the Dr's house the Dr's family being almost all
at Church one Sunday morning, and the said Cutler being then at

List of those giving evidence in the cause of Jane Haines

Name	Address	Age	Occupation/status
Banbury, Samuel			baker
Bostock, Nathaniel	Whitchurch	53	physician
Clewes, Jacob	Nantwich	32	surgeon
Comberbach, Robert	Whitchurch	51	maltster
Comberbach, Maria (Mary)	Whitchurch	47	wife of Robert Comberbach maltster
Crawford, Margaret	Whitchurch	50	shoemaker
Deaves, Edward	Whitchurch	31	gent
Drax, Tristram			apothecary
Edge, Maria	Whitchurch	37	spinster
Edgley, William	Drayton	35	barber and perukemaker
Gibbons, George	Whitchurch	28	curate
Gill, John	Whitchurch		miller
Gill, John	Whitchurch	45	yeoman
Grafton, Samuel	Whitchurch	67	pewterer
Grindley, Samuel	Whitchurch	45	maltster ; former servant to Sankey
Grindley, Joseph	Dodington	33	whitesmith
Harding Maria wife	Whitchurch	27	wife of Thomas Harding gent
Hare Thomas	Whitchurch	30	servant to Dr Sankey
Harpur John	Whitchurch	28	barber perukemaker
Heatley Elizabeth wife	Whitchurch	40	wife to Francis Heatley skinner
Heatley Francis	Whitchurch	53	skinner
Maisterson Richard	Whitchurch	39	mercer
Morris, William	Whitchurch		weaver : Parish Clerk
Morris, Sara	Whitchurch	49	wife to William Morris, weaver and Parish Clerk
Newton, Richard	Whitchurch	28	mercer
Owen, Maudelin	Whitchurch	41	wife to Thomas Owen labourer; former cook to Sankey
Pain, Elizabeth	Whitchurch	35	carrier [innkeeper?]
Paine, John	Drayton	49	medical man and surgeon
Price, Susanna wife	Whitchurch	60	midwife : wife of Thomas Price shoemaker
Sadler, John	Whitchurch	57	servant to Dr Sankey
Sankey, Dr Clement	Whitchurch	70	Rector Whitchurch
Turner, Adam	Whitchurch	49	brazier
Wettenhall, Anna	Whitchurch	34	wife of William Wettenhall yeoman
Whittingham, George	Whitchurch	19	domestic servant to William Bromhall
Wickstead, Sarah	Whitchurch	50	widow of apothecary [John Wickstead]
Wickstead Thomas	Whitchurch	17	apothecary
Wickstead Edward	Whitchurch	38	apothecary

Namptwich where he also taught to sing as the dept was inform'd, the deponent standing in the Dr's house at the foot of a stair case with Samuel Ely a Labourer since dead, Mandolini Owen the Dr's cook-maid came down staires weeping and the deponent asking her what was the matter she said we are all undone. Our Jane has got Susan Priest the midwife to look at her water and she is three weekes gon with child. And the Sunday following or the next Sunday but one in service time when the said Dr and most of his family were gon to church the said Cutler came to the said Dr's house and the said Jane and the said Cutler were in private together, but he staid not long for in a little more than an hour's time he slipt some private back way out of the house and got his hors out of the stable and went his waies ... " [283]

From this point on, fact and fiction are almost inseparable. Cutler did not appear among the witnesses and Jane herself was not interviewed for the record. The consistency of witness stories made the main thread of events then hinge on Jane being taken ill and leaving town. One variation in the accounts was that Jane claimed to be going to her sister's near Market Drayton. In fact, she went to Nantwich to be under the care of Jacob Clowes, a surgeon. Before going, she resorted to a Whitchurch apothecary according to Sarah Wickstead, the apothecary's widow. Sarah had problems with her evidence, though, for she reported that

"what medicines she took or what her distemper was the deponent cannot say for all the Physicians bills as soon as they were made up were taken away by the said Jane or her order and the deponent's Shopp book is torne to pieces soe that there are noe remains of any of the sd Jane's bills left." [284]

The consistory court officials were better informed than she knew for they then interviewed Edward Wickstead, who was almost certainly Sarah's brother-in-law. He was a well-known apothecary in the town who recounted that he

"received two bills from a reputed Physician one of [them] marked No. 1 [crossings out] dated May 23 : 98 : the other marked No. 2 dated 25. 98 and pursueant of the directions of the said bills the deponent or his servant made up the medicines for the said Jane which said bills [much crossing out] with the like ingredients are often made up and administered in venereal cases and he does not remember that he ever made up them or the like bills in any other cases tho' for ought he knows they may be proper or us'd in some other cases." [285]

This line of investigation was taken further and a seventeen-year old Thomas Wickstead was called to give evidence. He deposed that

*"having been almost 2 years an apprentice to Mr Edward Wickstead an
apothecary in Whitchurch and about 3 years immediately [blot] an
apprentice with Richard Smith an apothecary in Whitchurch aforesaid,
who is now gon into Ireland as the deponent has been informed and
believes, knows very well the character and handwriting of the said
Richard by seeing him write frequently whilst the deponent lived with
him, and the deponent having seen two recipes now shown to him by
the Examiner the one marked No. 1 dated May 23 98, the other
marked No. 2 dated 25 98 sais that he finds the said bills or recipes
enter'd into the said Mr Wickstead's Shoppe Book by the hand of the
said Smith who was the said Mr Wickstead's apprentice according to the
date of the said several bills charg'd to Jane Haines the party in this
cause and the deponent has known the like bills made up [words
crossed out] several time and the potio alba Baliena given to several
persons who have had the French disease, and the deponent never knew
that potion given in any other case ..."* [286]

Wickstead brought with him the doctor's two prescriptions and they were
entered into the court papers.

Long before now a reader of these documents can be excused for being
amazed by the persistence of the master-mind behind this investigation.
For in practice, this was more of a public inquiry than a criminal
prosecution. People were asked to record their stories and invited to
declare their truth, but the only official named as directing the
investigation was George Hand, consistory court proctor. It is difficult to
see him riding across to Whitchurch to conduct interviews prior to
drawing up questionnaires. It must surely have been the churchwardens
who asked around, inveigled the witnesses to make the trip to Lichfield
and followed the trail of gossip and rumour to get the witnesses lined up
in a sequence to gradually unfold the details upon which their accusations
were based.

Until Jane left the parsonage for a stay of several weeks in Nantwich there
was no great public problem. She was a woman disappointed in love at
worst. Maudelin Owen, of course, had another view. She confirmed that
Cutler had left Jane with a legacy of some kind – and as a servant in the
house at the time, though now long since left, she ought to know.
Maudelin reported that after she

*"had been in the Dr's service about a year and a half one Mr Cutler a
singing master was entertained in the said Dr's house and lodg'd there
near half a year and at his first coming he lay with Mr Pemberton one
of the Dr's curates in a building a little remote from the house and after
sometime the said Mr Cutler was remov'd into a room within the house
near unto the room where the said Jane lay, for the said Cutler courted*

Jane and the deponent believes he would have married her because the
deponent did diverse times see the said Cutler and Jane hugg and kiss
and embrace each other with great kindness and familiarity. However,
the said Cutler on a Sunday in time of divine service slipt away
privately from the house without the deponents knowledge, and after he
was gon the deponent found the said Jane weeping lamentably in her
chamber which made the deponent suspect the said Cutler had begotten
her with child for which the deponent believed she wept also, and went
down staires weeping, but what she ever said concerning such her
suspicion the deponent cannot now remember." [287]

That Maudelin herself was involved in bedroom swopping was not
admitted by this former cook. Her fellow servant Samuel Grindley,
though, deposed that it was Maudelin who told him that when Cutler first
arrived at the parsonage Jane Haines and she shared a bedroom. The
familiarity of Cutler and Jane was such, however, that Maudelin felt
obliged to abandon her bed. Nothing was said about where she went. One
possibility is that she left the household shortly after to marry a labourer,
Thomas Owen. [288]

Several sources of the rumour-mongering are now evident. Two former
servants of Clement Sankey had tales to tell, and the apprentices at the
apothecary's (Thomas and his colleague, Richard Smith) and the
apothecary's wife, all know something. Even Mr Pemberton, a curate
when Cutler was in residence, could have dropped remarks. But why
should they have had it in for Jane? Not that she was short of friends.
Several people came forward to say things in her favour. John Sadler, the
head male servant in the Doctor's household for at least eight years prior
to this inquiry, led the way. He declaimed that he
"never saw any indecent or immodest action betwixt the said Cutler and
the said Jane he believes he saw him salute her and he believes there was
some courtship [between] them in way of marriage because the said
Cutler employ'd the deponent to fetch a License for their marriage." [289]

Current knowledge does not allow Jane's career prior to 1697 to be
revealed. There may already have been animosity lurking in the
background arising from some previous actions. It could have been one of
those 'downstairs' quarrels or clashes of personalities among Clement
Sankey's servants which sparked off rumours. There is a hint in the
evidence of Richard Newton, a local shopkeeper, that she was a bit of a
termagant who ran the household to her own liking. He had that story
from several curates, he said. Newton was contradicted, however, by
George Gibbons, the only curate called to make a statement. He pointed
the finger back at Newton as the principal stirrer of trouble.

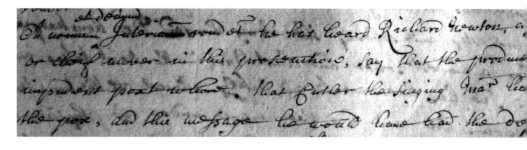

George Gibbons' deposition
"To the ninth and tenth questions answered that he has heard Richard
Newton, a great agent or chief mover in this prosecution, say that the
producant was an impudent poxt whore. That Cutler the singing man
had given her the pox, and the message he would have had the
deponent to have …."

Richard Maisterson, on the other hand, also a mercer in the town, similarly noted that among her faults was *"her having a very great sway and Power in the Dr's family gives great offence to the parishioners."* [290]

This last remark puts the whole story in another light. Before we get to the involvement of the curates, was there some fear in Whitchurch that the rector himself was too much under his housekeeper's thumb? Was it not so much Jane's mystery illness that gave rise to difficulties but Dr Sankey's weakness? In the sequence of events, however, it was the discovery by the rumour merchants in Whitchurch, during 1698 presumably, that Jane was with Jacob Clowes in Nantwich which next occupied attention. It was alleged she was living at a house with a back-street access to Clowes' home, allowing communication to be hidden. The suspicion was that she had the French pox, or the clap. That is, syphilis.

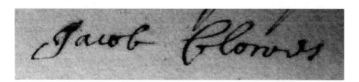

The treatment for this debilitating disease then common, but disputed and perhaps somewhat old-fashioned, was swallowing mercury. Richard Newton claimed he got the real story from Clowes himself when meeting him in the street at Whitchurch.

"… in a few daies it came to be known and twas discovered in
Whitchurch that she was sent to Namptwich 7 miles from Whitchurch
to be under the care of Jacob Clews, who twas said was to Salivate her
for a clap which the said Cutler had given her. And after the said Jane

had been at Namptwich as aforesaid and was returned to Whitchurch the deponent meeting with the said Jacob Clews in Whitchurch and suspecting that he had cur'd the said Jane of the pox and having a mind to be satisfied of the truth of it, asked the said Jacob in a josling way what [words crossed out] *the devil have you done with the wench (speaking of the said Jane) could no body cure her but you.* [last 6 words written over words crossed out]. *What's the reason she was taken out of Dr Edge's hands could not he cure her or to that effect. And the said Jacob at first deny'd that he had anything to do with her, but the deponent then replying what the devil did not M – Edge attend her, the said Jacob thereupon said God if it had not been for that* [word illegible] *or that squeamish bitch it had never been discovered or to that purpose, which confirmed the deponent in his beliefe that the said Jane was cur'd of a clap…".* [291]

Clowes himself was called as a witness and Jane's stay in Nantwich was confirmed by him. So was the administration of mercury. Clowes denied, however, that the disease he cured was the pox. On the contrary, Jane betrayed no signs of this. He diagnosed *"scorbichial and Rheumatig paines."*

This French medical text book, published in 1707, came too late to help Jacob Clowes and his Whitchurch colleagues. It illustrated the debate among some physicians as to the efficacy of mercury treatment for syphilis

Mercury treatment was a vile response to an evil condition, but Jane found little sympathy among her neighbours. Ingesting mercury led to excessive salivation of the patient lasting some time and horrid to observe. Mary Edge, who had gone with Jane to Nantwich as her carer, couldn't stand looking at the consequences of Jane's medication. She explained that before she left Jane
  "she had a great defluxion of Rheume which she evacuated by spitting, but the deponent having a weekness fallen into her own eyes left her in about a four[tnight] or 3 weeks time".. [292]

It was enough that Jane had committed the sin of fornication with a psalm singer; having the pox compounded her social crime. She was a pariah. Yet, Dr Sankey took no action.

Margaret Crawford, who ran a shoemaking business in the town, was the only person to try relieving Sankey of the ignominy of not sacking his servant. She told of a conversation she once had with the late Elizabeth Bathoe, another servant to Dr Sankey. Elizabeth spoke of Sankey in kindly fashion; *"My Master is a very good man hee knows nothing of these things, he is kept in the dark."* [293]

Jane Haines returned to her duties at the parsonage amid a welter of rumours and tittle-tattle. Witnesses were never exactly clear about dates, but if the assumption is that it was in 1697 and 1698 that all this happened, then another matter has to be raised. This was never mentioned by anyone concerned with the Haines cause in 1704, but it is now clear that Whitchurch was disturbed in 1699 by another scandalous tale. Of course, there may be no link between the cause taken to the Bishop's Consistory Court in November 1699 concerning Edward Wickstead and the malicious gossip focussed on Jane Haines culminating in her cause in 1704. Even if there is a connection, it cannot be certain as to what that might be. The one obvious fact though is that it must be the same Edward Wickstead, apothecary, who figured in both.

In November 1699 witnesses deposed to consistory court officials that some one had fathered an illegitimate child on Elizabeth Loton, a servant in Edward Wickstead's household. [294] The child was delivered in the girl's home parish of Prees to which Elizabeth had returned to live with her parents, they being her principal support at such a difficult time. Elizabeth refused to name the father but the rumour was that Edward Wickstead was responsible. The case was not essentially about identifying the father, important though that was, but about who was to relieve the parish of Prees of the maintenance charge for a bastard. In point of fact, one story put forward was that the parish was to be guaranteed freedom from charge by virtue of a bond put up by one Adam Turner of Whitchurch who acknowledged that the father was Richard Smith, also of Whitchurch. Indeed, Smith, identified to the court as Wickstead's apprentice, apparently admitted as much.

All the details of this court case are not important to the Haines business for the main matters have now been outlined. There was only one Edward Wickstead in Whitchurch at the time. From the Haines evidence it can be confirmed that Richard Smith was Wickstead's apprentice. Adam Turner, who was one of the accusatory witnesses in 1704, was a brazier or artisan shopkeeper, and neighbour to Wickstead. Very proper questions would be why it was that he offered to put up money to protect Richard Smith; was Richard Smith the actual father or the stalking horse for his master Edward Wickstead, and how come Richard Smith left the district soon after for Ireland? The evidence in the 1699 case was that Elizabeth Loton's parents were well known victims of poverty, but the girl during her lying-in was plentifully supplied with all that she needed. The rumour was that it was the real father who paid for this, and that he was Edward Wickstead.

The chronological sequence of events in the Haines case moves on to a number of parishioners applying to a justice of the peace, Mr Sandford, to lodge affidavits about the character and behaviour of the rector's housekeeper. Implicit in this is a prior appeal, or appeals, to Clement Sankey to dismiss Jane as a wanton woman. The point of involving the justice was to give authority to the charges made against her with a view to convincing Sankey that he had no option but to get rid of his housekeeper. Several deponents testified to George Hand, the proctor representing the bishop, as to this action.[295] The timing of this may have been determined by new elements in the allegations against Jane which now brought Sankey's curates into the limelight.

Just when, and indeed whether, George Gibbons saw Jane in bed with his fellow curate Mr Bowyer is not clear. This was a story it was alleged he repeated in public accompanied by strong language reflecting upon Jane's character. Probably this was in 1701 or 1702.

Gibbons appeared first in Whitchurch in 1700 having only recently left Cambridge and been made a deacon. He was a Shropshire lad, educated at Shrewsbury School and possibly known to Sankey through local people who knew Morton Corbet where his parents lived. Clearly, Sankey employed two curates at that time, and both slept at the parsonage, if not in the main house, then in some outbuilding. Neither had been there when Cutler lived in the same household.

One difficulty with the story about Bowyer, as Gibbons told it to acquaintances, was that he, Gibbons, was also subject to gossip about too great familiarity with Jane. In fact, this affair, if that is what it was, had been observed as late as August 1704 according to John Gill, a forty-five year old yeoman whose life had been entirely spent within two miles of Whitchurch town. He had been especially perplexed by Jane, when walking with the curate George Gibbons in a lane near Rowlands field, ducking down to squat alongside George for no evident purpose. When

Samuel Grafton of Whitchurch, pewterer

"… that within the space of 18 months last past the said Jane and George Gibbons late curate to the said Dr met twice at the dept's house in Whitchurch at both which times they the said George and Jane quarrell'd and the said George called the said Jane a whore over and over and at one of the said times said he had seen the said Jane in bed with Mr Bowyer a late curate to the said Dr and at that time one Mr Samuel Dasseny a clergyman was by and at the other time Ann Wetenhall was by and sometimes the said George and the said Jane were very amorous and fond of one another pretending they have a design of marriage but this their communication gives great offence to sober people of the parish … "

A short extract from the deposition of witness 15 who was 67 years old and had known Jane Haines for ten years. Grafton had a shop on the Bull Ring, next to the White Lyon Inn, and was a man who was trusted in business affairs. (see WHAG Newsletter January 2003) the pair left, Gill deposed, he went to inspect the site to find the wet evidence of her late activity! Any reader of the papers held now at Lichfield recording all these stories must conclude that the affaire Haines was a hot issue in the parish at that time and near to the point of explosion.

Before this episode there had been the legal move to get Jane turned out of her job. The intention was to force Dr Sankey to act. They succeeded to the extent of her going for a week, and then returning. Dr Sankey himself deposed that he could find nothing wrong with Jane's behaviour. It was presumably this which drove the churchwardens to place the whole matter before the archdeacon and press for an action in the consistory court.

So what relation did the case of 1699 have with that of 1704? Was it pure coincidence that Edward Wickstead was subject to gossip about his relations with female servants when stories were flying about that someone was supplying mercury to cure Jane Haines of the pox? Is there some indication here of a club of High Street shopkeepers, principally Adam Turner, mercers Richard Newton and Richard Maisterson, and Edward Wickstead, acting in concert to defend the reputation of one of their number? It is difficult now to be certain, but emotions were running high in the parish. None of those accusing Jane Haines of lewdness can be identified as nonconformists. It is not impossible to see charges laid against Jane as an expression of some puritanical streak characteristic of successors to Thomas Porter, Edward Lawrence and Philip Henry. It seems much more likely though that the divisions and tensions which took so many men and women off to Lichfield to speak their minds were confined to the Anglican congregation.

One sign of this may be that at least two of the deponents reported that they felt deceived by Edward Deaves, a gentlemen, who also gave evidence, when he rounded up people to go to Justice Sandford with a petition. They put their names to the document at the time, but claimed in their written statements to George Hand that they believed they were only petitioning for a new curate qualified to administer the sacrament.[296] They didn't realise it was a manoeuvre to get rid of Jane. George Gibbons was not admitted to full orders until 21 July 1701, which raises the possibility that Sankey was rather too casual in his spiritual duties.[297]

An intriguing sidelight on Sankey's lifestyle may have been shown by Susanna Price who deposed that Jane Haines and George Gibbons had been known to ride around the countryside in Sankey's coach. Matthew Fowler died possessed of a coach and four horses and the possibility is that Sankey bought them off Lettice Fowler as essential items of equipment for his new life in north Shropshire. Quite innocent explanations are available for Gibbons being accompanied by the rector's housekeeper when using this form of transport about the parish. The image of Sankey as a man who could afford to run a coach and horses, and let his curate have the use of them, is one that can only come from reading papers such as those found in the Haines cause. At the time, his behaviour put him out of favour with a significant section of his flock. Perhaps Whitchurch rectors have often had to comfort themselves with the thought that they couldn't please everybody all the time. Only a few got into such deep trouble as Clement Sankey though.

Sankey, in fact, had not been a well man for a long time – at least, Dr. Nathaniel Bostock, a respected physician from Whixall, told George Hand in 1704 that he had been attending Sankey for twelve years at least. Bostock's role appears almost to be that of expert witness in the case, for much turned on whether the prescription of mercury to induce salivation was only ever given for venereal disease. If it was, then Jane Haines had suffered the pox. On the other hand, if as Bostock said, it was given to those suspected of having other conditions then Jane could well have been subject to some innocent complaint such as gravel in the bowel. In that case, Jacob Clowes told the truth.

Susanna Price, a midwife and part-time cook for Dr Sankey on particular occasions (as she deposed), was especially questioned about Jane's health over a long period. Jane had always had poor health, weak, sickly and victim of pains. *"Always under the hands of a physician"*, according to Susanna. She claimed to have inspected Jane's waters to see if she voided gravel. She also believed that Jane, some time after Cutler left Whitchurch, had consulted with a Mr Edge, in Dr Bostock's absence. He pronounced Jane to be suffering rheumatic pain and stones.

The alternative opinion was advanced by the apothecaries, Edward and Thomas Wickstead. In their experience, doctors prescribed mercury, or *potio alba Baliena*, only when treating venereal disease. The apprentice was decided in his view, but his master admitted that *"for ought he knows they may be proper or us'd in some other cases."*

Whoever masterminded the accumulation of witnesses in the Haines case was thorough. Another medical practitioner was found to testify about the state of Mr Cutler's health, but he added more to confusion than clarity. John Paine was a forty-nine year old doctor in Market Drayton (simply known as Drayton at the time). He remembered the stories of seven years ago about Haines and Cutler, about Haines going to Nantwich into the care of Jacob Clowes and of how Clowes dealt with the supposed pox.

Doctor Nathaniel Bostock

Nathaniel Bostock of Bostock Hall, Whixall, was about 49 years old in 1704. As a physician he had a reputation which stretched into Lancashire at least. In July 1702 Nicolas Blundel of Little Crosby, near Liverpool, required assistance to deal with his father taken suddenly ill. He sent for Dr Farrington at Preston on 28 July, and the next day went to Wigan to fetch Dr Worthington when the Preston man could not be found. Nicholas was clearly desperate for he then sent his butler to Whitchurch. As he wrote in his diary *"I sent Thomas Howard to Whitchurch for Dr Bostock, but he came not"*. On August 2 his father died.

Despite not responding in 1702 Dr Bostock was still a man in whom Nicholas Blundell had faith. On 18 August 1709 Blundell recorded in his journal *"My Wife & I began our Journey toward Whit-Chourch, we came too late for the Boats at Leverpoole so we went over at Runkhorne, after which we lost our way & went to Windy Weston where we got a Guide that brought us to Frodsom where we Lodged: After we went from home Mally was ill hurt on her face by the Rowling Stone. 19 Aug We went from John Websters the Signe of the Bears Paw at Frodsom where we lodged last night to Whitchurch, to Mr Benbows the Signe of the Red Lyon where we dined and discoursed Dr Bostock about my wives Paine in her back, from Whit Church we went to Chester where we Lodged at Mr Taylors the Signe of the Golden Lyon."*

Blundell must have talked to Bostock about his daughters because on 25 August, back at home, Nicholas noted that after helping with the bottling of seven dozen of ale and entertaining guests, he saw *"The children took Phisick by directions of Dr Bostock."* He also calculated his monthly expenditure which included a fee to Dr Bostock for the consultation with his wife of £1-16-0, medicine for his wife at 15/6d and £1-14-11 for the costs of the trip to Whitchurch, presumably ferry, lodgings and transport charges.

F. Tyrer & J.J.Bagley (editors) *The Great Diurnal of Nicholas Blundell of Little Crosby, Lancashire* vol. 1, 1702-1711 in Record Society of Lancashire and Cheshire vol. 110 (1968)

Indeed, Paine met Clowes, as he did fairly frequently, and asked him why he used the salivation treatment. He said to Clowes *"if it had been a French pox there had been noe need of a salivation"*. Paine, further, reported that he had himself been consulted by Cutler who feared he did have the pox. Paine agreed and prescribed accordingly, that is, *"gave the said Cutler physic proper for it"*. As a cautious professional, Paine did not state what the medicine was. Cutler came back to him, however, and *"acknowledg'd to the deponent he had cur'd him and paid for his cure."* [298] This testimony was no help to Jane Haines and was irrelevant to the question of whether mercury treatment was specific to venereal disease or more widely used.

Dr Sankey died in post in Whitchurch in 1707. For the last ten years he had been close to the centre of a whirlwind of speculation, innuendo, 'nudge-nudge do you know what the rector's housekeeper has done now' kind of gossip? Could she shop in the market down High Street on a Friday without the stares and winks of her neighbours giving her a fright? According to one account, at any rate, Jane felt able to frequent a drinking parlour with George Gibbons where the deponent

> *"has seen them in different humours sometimes kissing and embracing each other and sometimes in great heats and quarrels, and in their quarrels the deponent has heard the said George call the said Jane a whore and pockified whore to the best of the deponent's remembrance but the deponent not having seen them together for the last half year or three quarters of a year last past cannot be particular in any other ill names the said George gave the said Jane tho' she heard a great deal more ill language - by him ..."* [299]

If the witnesses are to be taken at face value then Jane was a brazen hussy of the first order. Close study of the written evidence, however, raises numerous doubts.

The question at the present time is, does this pile of paper reflect what the town and Sankey's parsonage were really like, or was much of this made up to achieve an objective? And was the target Jane or Dr Sankey? Further, who was responsible for amassing the evidence, perhaps tutoring the witnesses, shepherding them first of all before

Questions raised by the case of Jane Haines

Justice Sandford and then down to Lichfield in September 1704. Was this the culmination of some longer running, deeper rooted conflict within residents in Whitchurch town – perhaps across the parish as a whole – or a storm in an Anglican pint pot? Were these shopkeepers, yeoman, servants, surgeons, apothecaries, shoemakers, barbers and perukemakers, and artisans paraded before George Hand in Lichfield simply spiteful nosey parkers? Were they anything other than jealous of one woman's role in the rector's household? Did they exaggerate beyond belief some innocent pleasures Jane Haines took, keen as she might have been to marry and create a household of her own? The role of Edward Wickstead in the light of his earlier difficulties before a church court cannot be disregarded. The truth we shall never know. The insight into Whitchurch life and Dr Clement Sankey's affairs is, nevertheless, unique albeit tantalising in its partiality.

It was by no means unknown for clergy to fall out with their parishioners. Sometimes the causes are easily traced and the people in conflict identified. John Rastrick, in the parish of Kirton in Lincolnshire, in 1678, had a spectacular row with one of the leading gentlemen in his congregation. Rastrick confided the details to his journal making all plain – albeit confidential at the time. Rastrick simply refused to administer the bread and wine at communion to a William Hunt because he would not admit and repent of sins. As Rastrick was also in the habit of refusing baptism to the children of sinful women who would not publicly acknowledge their shortcomings it is hardly surprising that his parishioners grew fed up. He was taken to his bishop's court and left his benefice in a fit of pique. [300]

In Whitchurch it is not so certain who was the principle prosecutor of Jane Haines. Francis Heatley might have been as he was one of the churchwardens in 1704. He was a fifty-three year old skinner and with his wife, Elizabeth, gave evidence in court. Both, however, strenuously refuted the charges against Jane Haines. In Francis's words "*he never saw any immodest and uncivil act don or offered by her in this life and a modest civil and chast woman the deponent takes and believes the said Jane to be.*"[301] He was the only churchwarden in office during the 1700-1704 period to give evidence. Indeed, the only other holder of this office to appear in court was Richard Maisterson (Masterson), churchwarden in 1697. In his view, the common opinion of Jane was that she was a lewd woman who had too great a power in the rector's household. This was accusatory, but hardly marked him out as her principal persecutor.

Who led the charge against Jane Haines?

Edward Deaves, on the other hand, another witness, and hostile to Jane, was the reported organiser of the petition to Justice Sandford to get Jane removed. As an acknowledged gentleman, he was socially superior to all involved in the Haines case (except Sankey, of course) and is the likeliest prospect for leadership in the matter. Deaves was active in the local land market from 1697 with property in High Street and so was a

Edward Deaves

man of substance. He also had an interest in *"an Engine House"* in Newtown which he surrendered in 1713.[302] This was a project to supply the town with fresh water and suggests Deaves was something of an entrepreneur. He was certainly a man of action, for above all, he was charged with assault on George Gibbons in another case brought before the Bishop's Court in 1704. Gibbons, in fact, alleged that Deaves attacked him twice in the churchyard before the Haines case came on. By an Edward VI statute these attacks, in March and then again in September, were religious offences and the penalties Deaves had to pay were public denunciation in church, excommunication and the costs of the case. Witnesses were said to observe the attacks, but none were called into court. [303] What cannot be discovered is how far all these events related to another matter before the Bishop of Lichfield's court in 1705 when Edward Deaves was found guilty of marrying without the proper licence. Apparently, he had taken Eleanor, his bride to be, off to Sandbach in 1795 to marry under a licence from Chester when he should have had one from Lichfield.[304] This was another misbehaviour warranting excommunication! If it was depriving the rector of Whitchurch of marriage fees, was this a case of revenge for Deaves' part in the Haines affair?

One footnote to this *cause célèbre* deepens the mystery. In his will of 27 September 1706 Clement Sankey left bequests to his *"faithfull servant"*, Jane Haines, and to John Sadler as well as to George Gibbons. Jane got £200 and Sadler two thirds of what was left after other bequests were met. Gibbons had the other third. These sums cannot be discovered, but the poor of the parish had £100 and there were other people who shared £85 between them. One was another servant, Rachell Haines, Jane's sister, who had £20. Sankey clearly valued Jane Haines very highly, and could have left John Sadler comfortably off also. Interestingly, the will said nothing about a library and its disposal. [305]

Sankey's will

The bishop's officials did betray some anxiety about Sankey, irrespective of the court action focussed on his housekeeper. He had to face an extraordinary number of archdeacon's visitations judging by the glebe terrier inquiries he had to deal with. There is nothing in the listing of such inquisitions in the history of Whitchurch to compare with the three inquiries in six years to which Sankey replied until a similar close examination took place in the 1770s. [306] He had been asked to supply information first in 1686, but in 1701, 1705 and again in 1706 there were further papers for his attention. In 1686 and in 1706 the details Sankey supplied were minimal, but he made a very full return in 1701. In fact, this was the most comprehensive listing of what lands, rents, tithes and fees the rector could expect to possess made by any incumbent between 1612 and 1725. [307]

These terriers provide a major clue as to why Sankey would have wanted to come to Whitchurch for they list the assets and income he took over on his appointment. His parsonage, stables, outbuildings and gardens, the few cottages he leased and the twenty or so acres he also rented out were one thing, his claim for tithes from his parishioners quite another. These were paid in kind, not cash, but were levies on animals and crops such that the more his neighbours prospered as farmers the more valuable his annual take from their produce. He had money at Easter as well, and fees, of course, for burials, marriages and other religious acts. One calculation is that this was among the ten richest benefices in the diocese, although it's impossible to say what that meant to Sankey in coin in any one year. [308] Just as interesting is the answer to the question, what did Sankey do for Whitchurch? He did not deepen controversy and divisions between Anglicans and nonconformists, but he came ultimately to clash with some among his near urban neighbours in what was clearly an unpleasant way. Interestingly, it was not the churchwardens who paid the £33-12-9 court costs of the Haines' cause out of parish rates. [309] It would be nice to know if Sankey supplied the money.

Chapter 12

Church and Chapel in troubled times

The extent to which the religious settlement arrived at in the epoch-making legislation of 1689 was anticipated in north Shropshire, and approved by local opinion, is difficult to assess. It brought immediate benefit to Philip Henry and his colleagues, but was probably hardly pleasing to Clement Sankey and the local 'establishment'. So long as the main nonconformist congregation met outside the town, and beyond the bounds of the parish of Whitchurch, however, there was little that Sankey could do to mitigate the impact of the 1689 Toleration Act. In any case, as time went on, as already indicated, Sankey had other matters to worry about.

The continued tensions between groups devoted to different forms of public worship and private conviction were made very obvious in 1715. A major riot in Whitchurch and the burning down of the dissenting meeting house in Dodington has to be seen as witness to a religious divide of significant proportions. The rapidity with which St. Alkmund's was rebuilt after the collapse of its tower in 1711 may also reflect the anxieties of the Anglican establishment in the parish to maintain supremacy in the community. Despite the severe political limitations imposed upon those who would not conform to the Anglican Church, alternative forms of public religious observance nevertheless survived in Whitchurch throughout the eighteenth century. North Shropshire society was permanently divided.

Almost immediately the Toleration Act was published Philip Henry used its protection. He had only gradually accepted the necessity for him to preach regularly at Broad Oak, and also to administer the Last Supper. His attendance at the Anglican Whitewell Chapel was unfailing but it was an outpost, not *Broad Oak licensed* a parish church as such. Services there could not be relied upon, so he was under pressure from his congregation to conduct worship at his house. Matthew Henry reported that his father registered a barn or outbuilding at Broad Oak as a meeting place under the terms of the Act, *"fitted up very decently and conveniently for the purpose"*.[310]

This regularised the situation and gave all those in Whitchurch who continued the tradition of Porter and Lawrence a fixed place for their religious practices. Until Philip Henry died in June 1696 there was no

Philip Henry's death and Samuel Benion's ministry

particular problem, but, thereafter, those attending relied upon a visiting minister, Samuel Benion from Whixall. He has been mentioned previously as a pupil of Philip Henry and his teaching assistant in the small school Henry ran at Broad Oak. As a dissenter, Samuel could not go to Oxford or Cambridge Universities despite his fluent Latin scholarship honed at a Free School in Wirksworth. Instead, he went up to Glasgow University and in 1696 got a Master of Arts degree. His return home to Whixall more or less coincided with Philip Henry's death and the vacancy for a minister. Matthew Henry later described the situation:

> *"The beheaded congregation presently cast their eye upon him as the most likely person to succeed Mr Henry, being one of themselves, and one that upon all accounts promised well."*

He was twenty-three years old and had never preached, let alone been certificated by a classis. Like Henry, he too now also looked to run a school to earn a living. Given that eventually he had thirty pupils he obviously won a good reputation. [311]

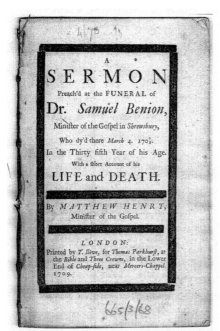

Shropshire Archives 665/3/68

According to Matthew Henry (in the sermon he preached at Samuel's funeral) Samuel's mother was in the habit of acting as a medical adviser and practitioner in the Whixall area. She inspired Samuel to take a serious interest in her work and he added this to his way of earning an income. He went further and in 1703 returned to Glasgow to study medicine and its associated disciplines. The mechanics of this are not quite certain, but he very quickly obtained his doctorate in medicine and a wide circle of people appreciative of both his skills as a physician and his probity as a preacher.

After his return to Shropshire he married Grace Yates, the daughter of a faithful member of his congregation, who soon produced two sons. [312]

Perhaps it was economic necessity rather than naked ambition which determined that he left Broad Oak for a ministry in Shrewsbury in 1706. Whatever the case, he enjoyed his new place for but a short time, dying there in March 1708.

Samuel Benion was followed at Broad Oak by a young successor, Mr Robert Pell, another Whixall man. Unfortunately, he soon left and also died in Shrewsbury, in 1707 aged 25.[313]

In September 1706 Matthew Henry wrote in his journal *"Went to Broad Oak. Some of the congregation met me. They are building a meeting place at Whitchurch where there are many Adversarys."* [314] The omens for such a move were not good despite the funeral service for Philip Henry, and his burial, at St. Alkmund's ten years before. The rector, Clement Sankey, had even allowed a memorial to him on the wall.

1707 a watershed year?

The year 1707 was something of a significant date in the history of Whitchurch. At St. Alkmund's a new rector arrived after the death of Clement Sankey, and in Dodington the Presbyterians opened their new chapel. Neither event did anything to change the character of the community immediately. Both, rather, were symptomatic of the new situation as established by the Toleration Act. If anything, the construction of the first nonconformist chapel in the town advertised the confidence its promoters had in their future. Hitherto they had sought shelter in a scatter of meeting places in rural areas. It was a relatively bold move to put up a purpose-built meeting hall in town. The reaction of the Anglican congregation depended a lot on the views of Peter Leigh, the new rector. His theological inclinations, political preferences and strength of personality were potentially critical to the stability of the parish.

It was precisely the assertion of their freedom by nonconformists generally throughout England which contributed to the continued political tension not by any means fully removed by the revolutionary settlement of 1689-90. Whitchurch did not escape all the consequences of that tension, but it did not feel the worst of it either. Unfortunately, it is not possible to trace the unfolding of events which led to four days rioting in the town in July 1715, but that very occurrence itself is testimony enough to the divided state of the community for years beforehand. Church opposition to chapel was the new reality. The legal right to exist was the chapel's essential defence.

Peter Leigh, who took over as rector in 1707, is thought to have achieved this appointment as a result of his marriage to a niece of the third Earl of Bridgewater. He had already been rector of Lymm in Cheshire and vicar of Great Budworth in the same county. He was of

Peter Leigh good gentry stock and there is no reason to suppose that he was anything other than a firm supporter of the political settlement which brought Queen Anne to the throne in March 1702. In common with his fellow clergy, though, he would have been aware that all Anne's children had died and that legislation determined that on her death the crown would pass to a German princess from Hanover. Anne's legitimacy lay in being the daughter of James II, and arguably the inheritor of that divinity which surrounded monarchs. There was a boy wandering around France in the meantime, claiming not only to be her brother, but by gender the rightful sovereign as James III. He had been brought up as a Catholic, but he still asserted his rights as against Anne and a future Parliamentary-defined monarch whose blood link to kingship derived from a sister of Charles I. Peter Leigh and his Church of England colleagues could be sure that the position of their institution would not be fully resolved until the possession of the crown, and hence the governorship of the Church itself, was secure. Given the

'The Church in Danger' rash of chapels appearing across the land serving the interests of those refusing to acknowledge the monopoly of the Anglican Church it is no wonder that the contemporary political cry was 'The Church in Danger'.

There were numerous other complications determining the course of events, not the least being a war with France from which, for example, John Churchill would emerge as Duke of Marlborough. Finding the money for huge investment in military and naval activities in conjunction with continental allies was a significant cause of political conflict between Whigs and Tories. Neither 'party' was at all united yet some divisions between them were fundamental. Whigs stood by the constitutional settlement reached with William and Mary even though Queen Anne was personally more inclined to favour Tories in government. The Tories, on the other hand, despite submitting to the necessity of the 1701 Act of Settlement, included politicians undoubtedly hoping to engineer the accession of James III and the rejection of the Hanoverian heir named in the statute. The term for them was 'Jacobite'. Richard Cresswell, MP for Bridgnorth, and John Kynaston, successively MP for Shrewsbury and then Shropshire county, were two such men.[315] Nonconformists could not trust Tories to maintain the religious freedom they had won under the 1690 settlement and they were no doubt apprehensive during Anne's reign at the substantial majorities Tories won at general elections in 1710 and 1713. The conclusion of the war in 1713 with a Treaty of Utrecht was also politically controversial and not a healer of domestic political wounds.

One man who passed through Whitchurch at the end of June 1710 exemplified the religious dimension of the current political situation – Dr Henry Sacheverell. He was certainly in Shrewsbury, Ellesmere and Oswestry while *Dr Henry Sacheverell* en route to and from a new living he had obtained at Selattyn, just inside Shropshire near Oswestry. In effect, he was on a triumphal provincial tour and just before a general election which brought Tories back to power. It is possible to see him as a catalyst for local conflict, if not actual violence, in every town he passed through.

Sacheverell was formerly vicar at Cannock in Staffordshire, but made his national reputation with sermons he preached in Derby and at St. Saviour's in Southwark.[316] He was high church and vehemently Tory. On 5 November 1709 his sermon at St. Paul's Cathedral in London, which was published under the title *The Perils of False Brethren,* brought a storm of criticism about his head and a government-led charge of sedition. He was tried in Westminster Hall in February 1710 in circumstances more resembling a Cup Final football match than a solemn inquiry into the truth of Sacheverell's opinions.

The gist of the matter was that on the very day when the country celebrated its deliverance from a Catholic plot to subvert the rule of law and restore the Pope to supremacy, Sacheverell chose to spend almost literally hours of his pulpit diatribe denouncing Protestant nonconformists for being the principal threat to the Anglican church. This was anathema to the Whig ministry then in power, but the trial for sedition merely served to pour petrol on the fire of political conflict already burning. Sacheverell's point was that, despite the Test Acts and other legislation of Charles II's time still legally debarring nonconformists from holding public office in town, county and national government, they did so by adopting the habit of occasional conformity. In other words, to legitimise their appointment they would deign to accept communion in their parish church once a year. These were the *'false brethren'* of Sacheverell's sermon. These were the vipers in the nest – his language was virulently inflammatory, politically vicious and deliberately anti-government in anticipation that a general election was in the offing. Sacheverell was found guilty, but subject to such piffling penalties that the nation had no doubt where the sympathies of the Establishment lay. Numerous riots in and around London targeted at nonconformists - at least six chapels were destroyed - appeared to show that popular opinion was on his side too.

Almost immediately after the disturbances and destruction in London consequent on Sacheverell's trial and ludicrous punishment, the Tory hero set off into the provinces to visit his recently *provincial tour* acquired parish in Shropshire. In effect, he was repeating the tactics of the Duke of Monmouth in 1682 and James II in 1687. In every place he stopped, he sought to demonstrate the political support he had garnered. At Ellesmere the civic authorities entertained him, this being but one of ten such events he enjoyed in a six-week journey. One account, using a pamphlet of the day, tells of his reception in Shrewsbury in July, returning to London after his short stay at Selattyn. This could well give us a picture, by implication at least, of how he might have been met in Whitchurch.

> *"He notified his intention of entering Shrewsbury, says that authority, on Tuesday the 3d of July, about noon. Hereupon ' the cryer was sent about to make proclamation through the town and adjacent villages. The bells began to ring to call the rabble together, and the gentry assembled in the market-place, and went out of town in this order to meet him'."* [317]

The pamphlet was perhaps somewhat satirical in character, making fun of the town's notables in their procession to *'Monford Bridge'*. The claim then was that here were gathered about 7,000 horsemen! Sacheverell lodged at the Raven, so it was said, and bonfires and bells played all evening. [318]

Unfortunately, there is no direct evidence as to how Peter Leigh behaved in this set of circumstances. It's known that Sacheverell stopped over night at a *stopped in Whitchurch* High Street inn, and presumably dined there. How much of a commotion in the town did that cause? In his seven weeks on the road Sacheverell only spent seven nights sleeping at inns. He was almost invariably wined and feted by prominent gentry when friendly peers were not available. The number of his entourage demanded a large house. Perhaps the parsonage was too small. Perhaps Leigh refused to accommodate the notorious Doctor on principle. Possibly, Sacheverell thought Leigh too insignificant to warrant political patronage. The visit of such a high church Tory showman could hardly have passed without notice in the town. The noise in the stables and the cash take at the inns would be enough to arouse interest, if not disturbance. [319]

At the election in October the Whig government was swept away on a surge of anti-nonconformist rhetoric and Queen Anne got her beloved

Tory ministers back in attendance. Now it was her health and life expectancy which determined how far and how quickly the Tories could act against occasional conformity.

Collapse of St. Alkmund's tower July 1711

In Whitchurch, though, one event now occurred which focussed minds on an entirely different problem. Here the church was literally in danger: in fact, it was destroyed. On 31 July 1711 St. Alkmund's tower collapsed. The old church was useless. And on a Sunday too!

This was not an unusual happening. Buildings resting on foundations four or five hundred years old were subject to self-destruction. St. Mary and St. Andrew at Condover, near Shrewsbury, fell down in 1660. In 1690 the central tower of the parish church of Selby, in Yorkshire, formerly the abbey church, crashed down taking the South Transept with it. Whitchurch churchwardens had always been fighting rain seeping into the stonework and joints where the roof met the tower. Re-pointing was almost an annual expenditure.

There was a well-established mode of obtaining money to finance rebuilding. Authority was obtained to make a diocesan and even a national collection under the terms of what *the Brief* was known as a 'Brief'. In other words, a begging letter went off to every parish in the land. Whitchurch wardens habitually recorded the sums they collected in response to these briefs. They raised £1-4-2 in October 1692, for example, in response to a request to subscribe to a fund to help Betley people, in Staffordshire, rebuild their church steeple. In November they similarly sent in money for the same purpose at Sheinton in Shropshire.

Now it was the turn of Whitchurch to go a-begging. The first step was to submit an application to Quarter Sessions which the magistrates considered on October 2. A month later Queen Anne formally approved a brief to make the appeal national. Of course, all the great and the good locally supported this – and their names were listed on the impressively decorated Letters Patent. Scroop, the Earl of Bridgewater, headed the list of trustees who were to receive and pay out the money. The men of the town most actively engaged, led by Peter Leigh, the rector, were John Eddowes and Alexander Duncombe, who almost certainly were agents for the Earl, and George Sandford and Thomas Ball. John Whitehall and John Hill may also have been in this group. [320]

Contributions to the fund were expected from parishioners, the wider neighbourhood and those of wealth and influence. Individual amounts from those responding were meticulously recorded, and with the names have been publicly displayed on painted boards in the church ever since. On examination it seems justified to say that not only were the local people separately listed, but that an appeal was deliberately made to habitual travellers on the road to Chester. Did someone write begging letters, or were notices posted at High Street inns explaining how cash could be donated? The treasurer keeping the accounts was Alexander Duncombe. Perhaps tourists were directed to his door to put their coins or promissory notes personally into his hands. At all events, some £2,322-6-1 was recorded on the church boards as the final total.

The names are fascinating. Was the Mrs Jane Haynes who gave five shillings the former rector's housekeeper? *contributors to the fund* Adam Turner (£1-10-0) must have been he who was prepared to stump up for Edward Wickstead in 1699 in his little spot of bother, and then speak out against Jane Haines in 1704. Robert Comberbatch who put in one pound could have been the maltster in 1704; Francis Heatley (£1), William Morris (five shillings), John Gill (£2), Samuel Grafton (ten shillings), Mr Maisterson (£2-10-0) and Mrs S Wickstead (£2-3-0), widow, are all names familiar from the Haines affair of 1704. All told, 201 parishioners had their names advertised in perpetuity as contributing their mites to St. Alkmund's rebuilding fund. Included in this group were the rector, Peter Leigh, who gave £50, as did Richard Hill, Esq., one of the Hawkstone Park family. Other neighbouring gentry who made substantial gifts were Rowland Cotton Esq., Thomas Boycott Esq., and Luke King. Alexander Duncombe put up £10, presumably in addition to the silver communion table dish his wife gave. The minimum sum to ensure a name on the boards seems to have been five shillings. Smaller gifts were simply totalled up as £17-10-0. The Lady of the Manor, Jane, Dowager Countess of Bridgewater, headed the list at £200, with her son, Scroop, in for £100.

A lot could be made, in similar fashion, of the people who probably only knew the town because they passed through it, *socially eminent contributors* regularly or even occasionally. Men with Irish connections such as the Earl of Montrath, Dr Swift, Dean of St. Patrick's, and the Earl of Donegall are obvious examples of frequent travellers. Henry, Viscount Newport, Lady Grosvenor and Charles, Duke of Shrewsbury, had historic links in one way or another with the town. Hugh, the Earl of Cholmondeley, would have had good knowledge of the place. They have

St. Alkmund's Church in 2011 is externally much as designed in 1712.
The gallery as photographed by D. Stevens (WHAG Collection) is no
longer to be found in this form.

Left board

Voluntary Gifts by the Pari[sh]

Name	£	s	d
The Revd Peter Leigh Rec	50	0	0
Richard Hill Esqr	50	0	0
Rowland Cotton Esqr	10	15	0
John Whitehall Esqr	20	0	0
Thomas Boycott Esqr	21	10	0
Luke King Gent	10	0	0
Mr Duncombe	10	0	0
Thomas Ball Gent	5	0	0
Mr Thomas Ienkes	2	10	0
Mr George Edge	2	10	0
Mr Churton	1	0	0
Mr Hughes School Mr	1	1	6
Mrs Martha Payne	0	10	0
Samuel Cooper	1	10	0
Mrs Susan Williams	0	5	0
John Mathers Iunr	0	5	0
Thomas Lowe	0	5	0
John Owen	0	5	0
William Capper	0	5	0
John Rodes	0	10	0
Mrs Roycroft	1	0	0
Mr George Walker	0	5	0
Mr George Payne Senr	0	7	6
Mrs Iane Haynes	0	5	0
Hugh Barrow	1	10	0
Richard Barrow	0	5	0

Top board

Name	£	s	d	Name	£	s	d
Mr Higgins	0	5	0	Adam Turner	1	0	0
Simon Lawson	0	0	0	John Bradshaw	1	0	0
Mrs Taylor Wid	0	5	0	Wid: Dickin	0	2	0
Hugh Roe	0	5	0	Willm Bradshaw	0	5	0
William Taylor	1	0	0	Mr Thos Buckley	3	0	0
John Nevett Iunr	1	0	0	Mr John Golborn	1	0	0
John Nevett Senr	0	0	0	Mrs Sandford Wid	1	1	6
Wid: Hare	0	0	0	Mrs Sr Wickfeed Wid	2	5	0
Wid: Woods	0	5	0	John Phillips	0	5	0
John Parry	0	5	0	Ambrose Johnson	0	5	0
William Bartho	0	7	6	Thomas Hankey	0	5	0
Tho. Williamson	0	15	0	Stephen Memory	0	5	0
Thomas Garrett	0	7	6				
...Evans	0	5	0	More by Small			
...ht	1	0	0	Sumes of Others			
...ates	3	0	0	of the Parish			
...rare Tist	2	0	0	amounting to	17	0	0
...ghall	1	1	6				
...reston	0	5	0				
...Gregor	0	5	0				
...ndford	5	0	0				
...er	0	5	0	Paid by Assesments			
...utters	5	0	0	upon the Parish	882	8	1
...eaver	0	0	0				
...Holt	2	0	0				
...okes	0	15	0				
...indley	0	5	0	The Whole Summ	2322	6	7

The boards recording the names of parishioners and the amount they each donated to the church rebuilding fund have suffered the passage of time. These people were undoubtedly the core congregation who gathered to hear Peter Leigh preach. Those heading the list were among the socially preeminent, but they were not ordered according to the amount they paid, nor alphabetically. Their ranking is an intriguing puzzle.

to be imagined as people who lodged overnight at one or other of the High Street inns, perhaps on several occasions. Did they ever attend for divine service, one might ask? On the other hand, somebody must have done a bit of pressing to get contributions from New College, Oxford, as well as Brasenose and Magdalen Colleges. Likewise, Dr Finch, Dean of York, and Lord Chief Justice Parker, the ex-MP for Derby, tormentor of Henry Sacheverell, and later the first Earl of Macclesfield were successfully tapped. Not Dr Sacheverell it seems!

It has been said before that the Tudors made no great effort to construct additional churches. Buildings that fell down were replaced, and seventeenth century architects had opportunities to design new places of worship. This was particularly true in London even before the Great Fire of 1666 brought them considerable business. By the reign of Queen Anne, however, as already indicated, the Anglican authorities woke up to the dangers of not having churches in the right places – that is where new aggregations of people had emerged out of reach of ancient parish churches. True, the House of Commons voted money in 1711 to finance new churches only in London suburbs to meet the challenge of nonconformist chapels. It was a sign, though, of current anxieties. The speed of action in Whitchurch, the amount of money raised and the form of the replacement for the old St. Alkmund's speak of a rector and his gentry allies determined to show the Anglican faith in the very best light. Or was Sacheverell's 'Church in Danger' cry more resonant with them?

The next step was to get an estimate of costs. Just who did this remains a mystery, but it was done by 26 November 1711 for the Letters Patent for the brief claimed the likely cost to be £5,497 and upwards. Possibly this came from the man who was able in January 1712 to present designs to subcontractors, one John Barker.

estimates of costs : John Barker and William Smith

At that stage the total costs were thought to be around £3,700. The builder with whom Barker worked was William Smith. Both of them must have been efficient, effective operators to have advanced as far as they did by January 1712, for the proposal they made was for a quite different sort of church from that which fell down. It was discussed as of *"the Doricke Order"* and therefore well within the latest fashion. What did the parishioners think of that?

Neither Barker nor Smith were local men. Both were Midlanders, though, and William Smith at least was well-known in aristocratic circles for work on country houses. [321] Cholmondley Hall and Trentham Hall were only two of the contracts for large-scale rebuilding on which he was currently engaged. He only had one church to his credit, though, that of St. Mary in Warwick completed in 1704. His brother, Francis, became better known and is usually referred to as 'of Warwick'. In fact, their family base was The Wergs, near Tettenhall in Staffordshire, from which William chiefly operated. John Barker was a former carpenter and architect who became the steward to the Duke of Rutland in 1723. He was based in Derbyshire in the Bakewell area. [322] Just before getting work in Whitchurch he had started building St. Ann's Church in Manchester as the contractor in charge and probable designer. Which of them was the first to be contacted cannot be determined, nor who was the patron making the recommendation. It was a commission worth some investment in time and energy. William Smith subsequently had four church commissions, including All Saints' at Derby – now the cathedral. Barker had a commission in 1711 from the Duke of Devonshire to rebuild the baths at Buxton. What they had as financial profit is undiscoverable. Barker certainly moved later into estate management and money lending so it's not likely he made a loss!

The new St. Alkmund's was consecrated on 8 October 1713. Entertaining the bishop that day cost £9-14-11. It might have been a bit of a tight

entertaining the bishop

schedule for workmen were paid six shillings *"for night work against the consecration"*! There is no contemporary comment available to show what impact it had on Peter Leigh's parishioners. Externally it was then more or less what it is now. Internally, it was not given any coloured glass so the contrast in lightness with the former building would have been considerable. And that despite galleries on three sides. There was no chancel arch or remains of a rood screen to obstruct the view of the choir and rector performing services. An organ was seriously discussed and costed once the church was opened. It is tempting to see a different theology underpinning this classically inspired preaching box from that structure originating in the Catholic doctrines prevalent in the fourteenth century. This is not the place to speculate on how far this represented the outlook of Peter Leigh and his principal parishioners. One thing is clear, and that is the determination to get Whitchurch people back worshipping in an Anglican building as rapidly as possible. [323]

Virtually contemporary with the reopening of St. Alkmund's was the end of the war with France and a general election at which the Tories scored an even more emphatic victory than in 1710. The peace treaty was highly controversial and the election viciously divisive. In Whitchurch the Presbyterian congregation in the Dodington chapel had survived for seven years, although a recent sign that the level of religious enmity in the town remained high had been the failure to re-erect in the new church the memorial to Philip Henry placed in the old St. Alkmund's. Even more contentious, his grave had been relocated as well. [324] Still, there was a regular, if small, accumulation of baptisms at the chapel and through the record of these some glimpse is possible of the nature of the community which gathered there on Sundays.

One later writer judged that the Dodington Presbyterians were an extremely wealthy and important group. About 1720, he thought, they numbered something like 300, of whom 30 were voters on the Parliamentary electoral list, six being gentlemen. [325] He counted 30 tradesmen, 44 farmers and 20 yeomen. Just how he came to this conclusion he didn't say. [326] Their wealth was judged by the bequest in 1707 of Thomas Benyon to the trustees of the chapel of land in Alkington producing about £50 a year income. This was to be spent towards the instruction of 30 boys in reading, writing and arithmetic by a master appointed by the trustees. In effect, this could have meant setting up a school.

the Dodington Presbyterians

There isn't a list now available of those worshipping in the Dodington Chapel, but there is a register of public baptisms conducted there which supplies an initial group of parental names. The Table below (page 151) covers the years from 1707 to 1716. It numbers 57 entries in order, and then re-arranges them into an alphabetical sequence. Most importantly, township addresses were recorded.

Register of baptisms

Some individuals appeared more than once as bringing a child for blessing. Only eight people had Whitchurch as their address, though among those without an address there could have been a few from the town itself. Similarly, in addition to the 15 people with addresses outside the town others could be included in the group of country dwellers. Some names and townships stand out. John Butler of Ash came in every two years with a new baby; Joseph Ralph must have been his neighbour. Incidentally, there was no Benion of Ash producing children in these years, or they went elsewhere for baptisms. Tilstock had three families attending, those of Thomas Hilditch, John Parry and the Swanwicks. John Lee of Whixall and John Bradshaw of Black Park both appeared more than once, as did John Griffiths of Marbury. Thomas Huxley from Alkington was another regular with four children brought to the font. Of the town residents William Watson, Isaac Poole and Samuel Eddowes were the most prolific.

The minister who kept this record was Samuel's younger brother, David

Benyon, who died at Bath in 1725. He recognised that some of his congregation were somewhat hesitant about advertising their nonconformity too openly – or had some other social reason for not going for a public ceremony at particular times. He listed, therefore, those parents who organised private baptisms separately (page 152).

Once again, the majority of parents having children baptised by a nonconformist minister had a rural address. Indeed, only five were of the parish of Whitchurch, and two of them had brought other children for a public service. It is, of course, perfectly possible that the bulk of the Dodington congregation were beyond the child conceiving age, or took their children to an Anglican church for this particular purpose. Nothing prevented them from doing this. For whatever reason, this quick look at the baptismal record of the nonconformist group does not suggest a large community of young married couples within Whitchurch parish eager to enlarge their gatherings with children. Does the evidence support the view that the bulk of the congregation resided in the town? Did they really pose a threat to the Anglican supremacy?

Searches for biographical material relating to members of the Dodington congregation have so far found little for certain and that insufficient to judge the social status or wealth of the chapel's adherents. The first probability is that the John Swanwick, who had a child baptised in 1709, was the John

John Swanwick

whose will was proved in April 1713. He was a 'chirurgeon'– in other words, another medical man practising in Whitchurch. According to the inventory of his personal possessions he wasn't worth a great deal - £19-13-0 to be precise. His house had one main ground floor room, with a buttery and a *'Little roome'* attached. Over the house place there was one bedroom with two feather beds. Another bedroom with a bed in it was *'over the gates'*. In a garrett there was a bed for a servant. There was also a *'shop'*, so he was likely to have been a barber-surgeon. His instruments were valued but not specified and the chairs in his sparsely furnished shop were *'old'*. Given the baptism of his son John, in 1709, he could not have been too old a man, so he had perhaps taken over a business from some relative. [327] This was not likely to have been his father, William, who survived until 1719, and lived in a house adjoining the town mill. He was a maltster with land at Moss Meadows in Dodington. [328] William and his wife Mary had another son, William junior, and three married daughters. If these four had children they did not take them to the Dodington chapel for baptism – at least not before 1718. How they were related to the Swanwicks of Tilstock – if they were – has not been traced.

"An Account of the Children yt were publickly Baptiz'd att the New Chappel in Whitchurch, & at Broad Oak & Danford, & at Hampton Lecture Day By D.B."

Date	Name and address		No.
1711	Boid, Andrew	of Whitchurch	29
1716	Bradshaw, John	(dead)	52
1714	Bradshaw, John	of ye Hollad	44
1710	Bradshaw, John of Black Park (at house of Elin Eddowes in Whitchurch)		20
1715	Butler, John	of Ash	50
1711	Butler, John	of Ashe	27
1713	Butler, John	of Ashe	35
1709	Butler, John	of Ashe	11
1709	Dumbole, Jonathan	at Hampton	15
1710	Eddowes, Samuel	of Whitchurch	18
1714	Eddows, Ralph	of Whitchurch	45
1712	Eddows, Samuel	of Whitchurch	32
1708	Edwards, James		1
1708	Elson, Robert,		2
1714	Ferriman, Benjamin	of Bronington	43
1710	Gandy, Thomas	of Whitchurch	19
1710	Griffiths, John	of Marbery	17
1713	Griffiths, John	of Marbery	37
1713	Harris, John		42
1716	Hilditch, Thomas	of Tilstock	56
1711	Hilditch, Thomas	of Tilstock	24
1715	Hilditch, Thomas	of Tilstock	49
1713	Holditch, Thomas	of Tilstock	39
1709	Hulson, Samuel		6
1711	Hulson, Samuel	of Whitchurch	25
1711	Huxley, Thomas		22
1715	Huxley, Thomas	of Alkington	48
1712	Huxley, Thomas	of Alkington	33
1713	Huxley, Thomas	of Alkington	41
1708	Johnson, Hugh		4
1710	Latebrook, Richard	of Marbery	16
1716	Lee, John	of Whixall	57
1715	Lee, John	of Whixall	47
1713	Milward, Nehemiah	of Whitchurch	40
1709	Morgan, Samuel		7
1712	Morgan, Samuel	of Hadley Heath	34
1709	Paelin, Joseph		8
1709	Parry, John		10
1716	Parry, John	of Tilstock	55
1714	Parry, John	of Tilstock	46

1712	Parry, John	of Tilstock	30
1710	Poole, Isaac	of Whitchurch	21
1709	Poole, Isaac Mr	(dead)	5
1709	Powel, Caleb		12
1711	Powel, Caleb		28
1716	Ralph, Joseph	of Ash	53
1713	Ralphs, Joseph	of Ash	38
1709	Swanwick, John		13
1711	Swanwick, Joseph	of Tilstock	26
1708	Walford, John		3
1711	Walford, John		23
1713	Walford, John		36
1716	Walford, Joseph		51
1709	Watson, William		9
1716	Watson, William		54
1712	Watson, William	of Whitchurch	31
1709	Yates, Thomas	of Dearnford	14

Private baptisms: parental names ordered by entry and rearranged alphabetically

Date	Name		No.
1708	Barker, Timothy	Wem	2
1709	Basnet, Mr Roger	the Ditches, near Wem	7
1708	Boid, Andrew	Whitchurch	4
1710	Cook, George	Woodhouses	14
1709	Cook, Joseph	Newtown (Whitchurch?)	10
1708	Eddowes, Mr John	of Nantwich at his own house in absence of Mr Lawrence	1
1709	Evans, Rev Mr Jeu (sic)	Oswestry	8
1708	Griffiths, John	Marbury	5
1708	Grindley, Robert	Woodhouses	3
1709	Higginson, Allen	Wem	13
1711	Jack, Timothy	Welsh Hampton	19
1709	Key, Richard	Whixall	12
1709	Lathrop, Mr Ralph	Wem	9
1711	Lathrop, Revd Mr Ralph	Wem	16
1711	Lewis, Samuel	Bronnington	17
1709	Ravenlea, Thomas	Broad Oak	11
1711	Ravenlea, Thomas	Broad Oak	18
1708	Reynolds, Francis	Ellesmere	6
1710,	Richards, William	Lineal	15
1711	Yates, Thomas	Danford	20

The Register was published by the Shropshire Parish Register Society in 1903, and edited by W P W Phillimore

The most interesting individual was Samuel Eddowes. His two children, John and Sarah, were baptised in the Dodington chapel, in 1710 and 1712 respectively. Their mother, Anne, was of a Mountford family likely to be of Tilstock.

Samuel Eddowes

Samuel was a glover, who died in 1713. He was almost certainly a grandson of that Ralph Eddowes excommunicated in 1670, and son of Roger, an ironmonger in the town. Samuel's mother was Elizabeth (formerly Nevett), daughter of a Presbyterian minister ejected from Oswestry in the great purge after the restoration of the monarchy in 1660. Samuel had four brothers and one sister, but only one of his brothers, Ralph, stayed in Whitchurch, running a grocery business. This family seem to have been stalwarts of the Dodington congregation in its Broad Oak as well as its Dodington days. [329] Their relationship with John Eddowes, manorial steward, has been commented on previously.

More can be said about Samuel Eddowes because there were problems with his estate after death. His wife, Anne, as executor, had to produce accounts for the Bishop's Court at Lichfield. [330] Ostensibly, Samuel's personal wealth was of the order of £456. Something like £98 of this was reckoned to be debts impossible to collect, and Anne's actions were subject to a law-suit – hence the documentation filed away by the Consistory Court. There is no way of knowing how Samuel's assets compared with other tradesmen at the time, but he was undoubtedly among the wealthier men. Nonconformity in religious observance was no hindrance to accumulating capital. He possibly started with some advantages for he had not been in business on his own for all that long. He was apprenticed in Chester in 1698 and, assuming this was for seven years, he couldn't have started much before 1705 when he was presumably twenty-one years old. [331] This gave him only about seven years or so to build up his list of customers. In fact, his business career might have been shorter, for his dated list of debts started with sums owing to him from January 1707.

This might explain why he had a far from ostentatious home. A parlour, kitchen, and shop occupied the ground floor. Three bedrooms, a garret and closet, were arranged above. His kitchen had no luxuries – pewter dishes and wooden trenchers – but there was a curtain at the window. There was more style to the parlour which had six pictures and an oval table, a looking glass and white curtain. The provision for children was intriguing – two nursing chairs, two children's chairs and a cradle, all in the kitchen. The closest things to luxuries were a few books in the closet (at third floor level), six white cups and a case of knives and forks. All told, his household goods were valued at a little over £22. Somewhere he had a brewhouse, a bakery, a workhouse and, below the main building, a cellar.

Samuel's stock in trade, and a few other goods, including a silver watch from his father, Roger, came to just over £100. He had a large variety, and number, of finished gloves for children and adults, as well as gloves partly made up. He had invested in numerous skins of goats, dogs and sheep. There was an Indian buck skin as well as *"shammy"* leathers and doe skins. These seemed mostly to be dressed, but he may have been working on some in the final stages of preparation. Much the largest asset was property which his widow sold for £150 to Mr Thomas Ravenshaw.

More might be made from these records about the trade of glove makers and the process followed by a widow who had to sell off everything in her husband's possession to fulfil her obligation as executrix. One final comment, however, which can be made concerns the distribution of Samuel Eddowes' clients. He kept a book recording those owing him money and the date the debt was incurred. In a substantial number, but by no means the majority, of cases he noted a township address and/or an occupation for his debtor. Local ones such as Mr Sandford of Black Park and Mr Yates of Danford are expected. People from Malpas and Chester are not surprising. To find a tanner at Nantwich, Mr Daxon, is a clue to where Eddowes bought his skins. Customers in Knutsford, Market Drayton, Stone, Macclesfield and Warrington, on the other hand, are very suggestive of Samuel's skill and reputation – perhaps even his business acumen, if looked at in one way. With four exceptions the sums owed were small, mostly a few shillings only. They are just the kind of grants of credit most tradesmen had to allow their customers to keep sales ticking over. It was not very clever of Samuel to allow these to pile up, nevertheless, although, to be fair, he would not have expected to die young. One of the key business skills was debt management, of knowing who to give credit to, and when to go out actively collecting in the cash. It was good to have Sir Robert Cotton as a customer, but not sound practice to have him owe over £8. Mr Billinge of Chester owed over £23, and Mr Bird of Warrington just over £5.

Thomas Yates (1672-1765) came only once with a child for baptism to Dodington chapel – his son, John, in 1709. Along

Thomas Yates

with his father, Thomas (1634-1709), already described as a prominent member of the dissenting community led by Edward Lawrence, this Thomas is taken to be a key figure in the story of how a Presbyterian minority in Whitchurch parish survived the persecution initiated in 1662. Again, as already noted, there is something of a problem with Thomas (1634-1709) for his father was also a Thomas (baptised 1603) who lived in Whitchurch until 1682. Information relating to a Thomas Yates from about 1660 to 1682, unless qualified by some independent identifier, could apply to either of these two men. Similarly, from about 1695 to 1709 there were two Thomases difficult to distinguish. For the period 1672 to 1682 all three were alive.

The location of the proposed new chapel planned to replace the converted barn at Broad Oak was determined by Thomas Yates (1634-1709). He provided premises at the rear of a house on the west side of the street named Dodington. That's not the building as seen now, but the site on property occupied by Thomas Yates is the same. The wealth and social status of Thomas Yates was not measured by his houses on the Dodington street, and the space there for building a chapel, but by Dearnford Hall in Alkington township. The grandeur of this stylish house is in marked contrast to the contemporary townscape of Whitchurch and to the contents of the inventory of personal possessions drawn up on Thomas's death in 1709. Nominally he was worth £266, but £200 of this was in loans he made from which he may well have been due interest. His clothes, small amount of kitchen-ware and simple furniture were valued at £12, and his farming, cheese making and other equipment, possibly for brewing, came to £10-6-0. He had animals worth £29, including a bull, which presumably indicates an interest in building up a dairy herd. Given that it was April, before the manufacturing season began, the existence of 400 cwt. of cheese in store suggests a considerable capacity for cheese making for sale rather than domestic consumption. The barley and muncorn (a mixture of cereals) probably came from his land and at £9 was not an exceptional amount. Even with the contents of his summerhouse, the grand total, apart from his money out on bonds, at just over £66 was hardly commensurate with the appearance of Dearnford Hall. One possible explanation for this, of course, is that he had already handed over most of his furniture and moveable goods to his son, Thomas (1672-1765).

Land and a house in Heath Lane and another similar property in Whixall were also left to Thomas (1672-1765). There was no mention of the Dearnford house in the will, nor of properties in Dodington street. Possibly these had already been conveyed to Thomas as a whole, or in part to Samuel, the younger son, who had nothing specified in the will. Samuel's children were provided for, however, and also Samuel's wife.

All these people who brought their children to be baptised at the Dodington chapel were still objects of some suspicion for refusing to conform to the practices of their parish clergyman. It was more than just not attending communion services. There was a political dimension tied to the religious affiliation of the monarch. Queen Anne died on 1 August 1714 and a middle-aged, protestant German prince was peacefully set upon the throne in September to the chagrin of a sizeable minority of gentry folk and politicians at court and in Parliament. A new king meant a new set of government ministers – not surprisingly, mostly of the Whig party. Riots in October in Birmingham, Bristol and Norwich are thought

George I, a new royal dynasty and new political circumstances

to show some popular antagonism to the arrival of a Hanoverian dynasty. A drawn-out general election campaign in the spring of 1715 was marked by prominent Tories fleeing

to France to join James Stuart, the 'Old Pretender'. Their party lost control of the House of Commons. By the end of May rumours abounded that James Stuart intended an invasion to seize the throne by force.

Actions in Staffordshire and Warwickshire which followed immediately on the heels of rumours provoke thought. Just why did mobs of the lower

attacks on nonconformist meeting houses

social orders attack and burn down nonconformist meeting houses? Who led them? How were they brought together, and why in some towns and not others? Was there a copycat element to the spread of destruction? Could these

riotous assemblies have been a release for economic tensions arising from trade slumps and high food prices, with any excuse for a punch-up eagerly accepted? The questions are endless. The fears they raised were well expressed. In July, the House of Commons heard the following part of a letter read out by Mr Bracebridge, the Member for Tamworth.

> *"Undoubtedly you will have heard of several Passages, that followed upon the Performance of the Wolverhampton Mob; as namely the Demolishing of the Presbyterian Meeting-houses at Stafford and Walsall, and ('tis said) at Stone and Longdon: Yesterday a Parcel of the Wolverhampton Folks set forth in order to attack Bromwich Meeting-house: These people took Bilston, Dorlaston and Wednesbury in the way; so that they were a great Number: But the Dissenters, having Notice of what was intended, came together in great Numbers, Horse and Foot, furnished with Guns, Swords etc, and attackt the Rioters, and drove 'um off; several of whom were wounded..."*[332]

One later historian quoted a rioter in Wolverhampton as climbing on the meeting house roof and shouting, *"God damn King George and the Duke of Marlborough and God bless King James. Fall on my boys."*[333]

The reaction of King George's government was fierce, as a letter sent to the High Sheriff of the County of Warwick on behalf of the king shows:-

> *" The king having heard that riots have begun to take place at Birmingham, and fearing that they may spread as they have done in the county of Stafford, desires him to put the laws against riots duly into*

execution. He is to call out the posse comitatus, and repair to Birmingham, or any other place in the county of Warwick where riots are threatening, and if he finds such riots still going on, to quell them at once, and punish the offenders with the utmost rigour of the law. Whitehall 20 July 1715.” [334]

One new weapon in the hands of authority was a recently passed Riot Act, due to come into force on 1 August 1715, This greatly strengthened the legal powers at the disposal of magistrates.

Crowds acting violently in provincial towns were far from new phenomena. On the other hand, a series of such actions across the Midlands, very specifically targeting one minority group, destructive of life and property, ostensibly expressions of religious enmity and occurring within such a short space of time, must be revealing of the communities within which they took place. One such place was Whitchurch.

There is insufficient evidence about the obvious riot and attack on the Dodington chapel to allow individual people to be identified. The baptismal register kept by David Benyon recorded the bare fact of destruction, after noting that the latest ceremony had taken place at Broad Oak, when John son of John Lee of Whixall was baptised - *"The chapel at Whitchurch being demolished by ye mob on July 15th, 16th, 18th & 19th, before”.* [335]

Dodington chapel destroyed

Even if this explosion of anger in Whitchurch is attributed to spontaneous combustion, it still involved a lot of particular people – activity over four days, with a pause in between the first two and the second two days. Again, fire requires materials to burn, metaphorically speaking first of all, quite apart from the pews and roof timbers of the chapel itself! The event implies a pent up, latent antagonism needing only a spark to cause a conflagration. Was the spark news from Wolverhampton on 30 June of the events there the day before, so dramatically reported a fortnight later to the House of Commons? Or were Whitchurch people not moved until news came of the riot in Shrewsbury on 6 July when the chapel Samuel Benion had gone to serve was demolished?

Conversations over the dinner table among the chattering classes were heavy with conflicts over the respective roles of 'Tories' and 'Whigs', Anglican clergy and nonconformists, in fomenting trouble. Dudley Ryder, in London in June 1715, well known to Matthew Henry's widow as the son of a nonconformist, recorded one such in his diary. He visited his uncle, a vicar in Kentish town, and *"soon got upon public affairs and a little warm dispute followed."* The vicar and his family took offence at remarks to the detriment of Tories, and

> *"When I talked of the insults and riots that had been committed by the high church mobs throughout England they said they were well assured that many of the mobs were hired by some Whig lords. The breaking of windows in London upon public nights was laid entirely on the glaziers whose interest was that it should be so and tories suffered equally by it with the whigs."*

According to this view it was the Whigs who had torn down the nonconformist meeting house at the time of the Sacheverell disturbances in London! [336]

There is no reason to suppose that Whitchurch people were not equally split in their opinions about dangers to the realm, and where fault lay. Did the socially superior of the town adopt the attitude of one of Dudley Ryder's acquaintances who thought *"the common people are so poisoned with Jacobitism and so much set against the present government"* that if the Pretender's invasion took place George I would have to bring in foreign troops to defend his position? [337] Certainly, this opinion attributed a high degree of ideological commitment to the *'common people'* difficult, in practice, to believe. Evidence elsewhere, from trials of alleged rioters and ringleaders, pointed rather to a deliberate organising of mobs by gentry and clergy taking advantage of the propensity of the crowd, given drink and violent speeches, to despoil the property of the current minority outsiders. Newcastle-under-Lyme was a case in point. Here the churchwardens were said to have rung the church bell as the signal to begin an attack on the meetinghouse, and one of those named at the Assizes as directing events was Ralph Sneyd, of Keele Hall, a major Tory land owner in the district. [338]

The only clue to high Tories and potential 'Jacobites' in Whitchurch is the Poll Book for the 1713 general election. Out of the 30 freeholders who went to vote for two MPs, nine supported John Kynaston, the candidate most likely to have been of this persuasion. True, none plumped for him, three voting also for Lord Newport (the county's leading Whig) and six for Sir John Astley. Newport came top with 2,036 votes and Kynaston second with 1,707. But it was a narrow margin over Astley who had 1688.

Most unusually, the government moved to repair the damage, once the foolish Jacobite adventure of 'the 1715' was dismissed. Towns in eight counties had been seriously affected. A Commission investigated and the Treasury paid out cash to victims. Places in Staffordshire, Shropshire and Lancashire headed the list. Staffordshire had £1,722, Shropshire was second with £1,063. Wem and Oswestry as well as Shrewsbury and

Presbyterian Chapel, Dodington

David Benyon's congregation rebuilt their chapel behind Thomas Yates' house using a government grant paid in 1717. It survives in a much altered form in 2011, but with the original simple rectangular box structure still evident, defined on its eastern side by the stone quoins at two corners. The western wall, without quoins, was at the rear. Part of the external face of the south wall is found in an upper room of an extension. It shows a timber A frame and semi-circular headers for two windows. Areas of fire blackened brickwork suggest that parts of the 1697 chapel building were retained.

Whitchurch qualified, in the case of Shrewsbury to the tune of £429. The entry for Whitchurch in the Treasury accounts is quite clear –

> *"the meeting house demolished being the property of Thomas Yates: damages £303-6-9. Anne Jennings widow damaged to the value of £5-0-0; Timothy Seymour damaged £1-1-6".* [339]

More than likely Anne Jennings and Timothy Seymour suffered collateral damage as neighbours to the target building. Newcastle-under-Lyme people had just over £500 between them. In Wrexham two meetinghouses were compensated for with £312.

Dodington chapel rebuilt

If nothing else, one thing should be clear. This was no ordinary event in the history of Whitchurch, nor one that can be set aside as a quirk or matter of no import. It's not a footnote, but a crucial element of the main story. The absence of more evidence does not devalue it either. It does invite questions about the tensions in Whitchurch society, about the culpability of particular people – the churchwardens and the rector for a start – and the speed at which David Benyon and his congregation were able to find a sufficient reconciliation with their neighbours to avoid a repetition of violence. They were not driven out, but rebuilt their place of worship with government cash.

The shell is still there. It was built as a simple brick box, about 27 feet by 40 feet, with a restrained, classically inspired, front wall now much altered. Even if its seats were of the simplest it was not anticipated that the congregation would be large. Perhaps the most impressive furniture would have been the pulpit on the end wall, opposite the entrance. It was a fixture in Whitchurch's cultural environment thereafter for a century, well patronised by the Benion and Yates families. Moreover, it was but the first in a series of buildings housing congregations of people who could not be comfortable in their Anglican parish church. But, as they say, that's another story.

*A*fter thoughts

Nearly three hundred years have passed since the Dodington Chapel was burnt down. Tolerance of considerable religious diversity, let alone simple nonconforming to the Church of England is, today, considered our major virtuous characteristic as a society. The first thought after reading this book must surely be, therefore, how does the story continue. Has intolerance taken most of the three hundred years to disappear, or did it evaporate quickly. The law may say one thing, but how people behave can be quite another. If the first stage was completed by about 1720, and dissent from a state approved way of publicly expressing religious belief had been accepted in law, where do Methodist chapels, Catholic churches and Jewish synagogues fit in? Whitchurch today does not contain all the available varieties of religious organisations and the histories of the various congregations that have existed in the district remain to be written. Nevertheless, some day their stories should be told and explanations should be offered for why sub-divisions took place. Is it the case that intolerance was never again a significant feature of public life in the town?

Daniel Defoe, writing about 1722, almost certainly never stayed in Whitchurch but somehow he had heard that there were Catholic gentry in the neighbourhood.[1] If there were any such families of much significance they remain to be investigated. One way, not adopted in this present work, would be to systematically analyse the opening statements of all the last wills and testaments of Whitchurch people from, say, 1530 to 1615. This would parallel a study recently published by Ludlow Historical Research Group of three Shropshire parishes, Easthope, Shipton and Stanton Long, just south of Much Wenlock.[2] It can be argued that a useful indicator of religious allegiance can be derived from the preambles of wills where near deathbed statements were normally made about an afterlife. Convinced Catholics phrased their beliefs quite differently from firm Protestants. In this way some measure might be obtained of the extent of support among Whitchurch people for the new faith and the length of time over which some families clung on to the old.

---

[1] Daniel Defoe, *A tour thro' the whole island of Great Britain, divided into circuits or journies,* Letter 7, Part 1: Cheshire and North-West Midlands (1724)
[2] Wendy Brogden, *Glimmers of Dissent: Reactions to the Reformation in the south Shropshire parishes of Easthope, Shipton and Stanton Long,* Ludlow Historical Research Group 2010.

Robert Gyll, for example, in 1537, conventionally in the Catholic tradition, bequeathed his soul to almighty God, Saint Mary and the holy company of heaven. He also left money for a priest to say Saint Gregory's trental for him – thirty masses for his soul. [3] Thomas Padye left sixteen pence for a fund for St. George in 1533. [4] By 1540, William Hitchen remained true to the same tradition by leaving sixteen pence to buy a lamp for St. Alkmund's church and a taper for the chapel at Tilstock. He felt it necessary to show that he knew all about King Henry being head of the church in England, however. [5] He wasn't the only one who seems to have felt pressed to record an understanding of the politics of the day. In contrast, William Constantine the younger, in 1572, gave his soul to God as his creator and redeemer hoping to be acknowledged as one of the elect in the kingdom of God. This could be read as a certain sign of Protestant convictions, but traditions were still powerful. William left six shillings and eight pence to his parish church, though not for any stated purpose. [6]

This present work has not been concerned with searching for evidence of Catholic dissent or hostility towards families who refused to conform. Such evidence does not jump out in the way that the record of the 1715 riot does. As a group though, Catholics remained severely disadvantaged until 1829. It was the occasion of their political emancipation that year which brought out the residual antipathy towards them of an influential section of Whitchurch society. The Dod, Brookes and Corser families headed moves in February 1829 to petition Parliament to reject Catholic emancipation. At least, they had no recourse to violence. [7]

On the other hand, one characteristic feature of the Church of England in the eighteenth century was that it continued to generate nonconformity. The movement led by John Wesley, initially not intended to separate from the Established Church, did in the end do just that. Methodists, in fact, became the largest independent Protestant sect in England. In 1799 a visiting Archdeacon reported that there were numerous dissenters in Whitchurch, meeting in three chapels, one being the old Dodington Presbyterian building now occupied by Unitarians. Of the two Methodist chapels, one was for those separated from the Anglican church completely, the other for those still attending at St. Alkmund's on occasions. Their sites are uncertain. One was possibly in Tilstock, the other in Broughall. [8]

---

[3] Lichfield Record Office probate for Robert Gyll 11 April 1537.
[4] Lichfield Record Office probate for Thomas Padye 18 August 1533.
[5] Lichfield Record Office probate for William Hitchen 21 April 1540.
[6] Lichfield Record Office probate for William Constantine 21 September 1572.
[7] *Salopian Journal* 25 February 1829.
[8] R.F.Skinner, *Nonconformity in Shropshire 1662-1816,* Appendix 4. Shrop A, *Shropshire Quarter Sessions Orders* vol.3, 1783-1839, July 1799 and April 1805.

*Congregationalists
(top), Anglicans
(centre), and
Methodists (bottom)
all erected new
buildings in the
nineteenth century.
There are interesting
stories of the people
involved and the
reasons for their
actions awaiting a
local historian.*

John Wesley passed through Whitchurch six times on his famous tours of Britain, first of all, but not stopping, on 4 April 1751. He was heading for Alpraham in a snow storm. He preached on three occasions, the first time in March 1771 when his congregation was too large for the house. The story of who met him, gave him shelter and helped set up one of his classes will be a significant part of some future investigation into the history of religious observance in Whitchurch. [9]

The characteristics of the prevailing culture of a community are not just moulded by religious belief, nor expressed only in church attendance. The story of schooling in Whitchurch, inside and beyond the grammar school, in private schools and also Sunday schools, must be integrated into the history of church and chapel. One might guess that change was slow and a long time coming in Whitchurch with respect to the availability of books through lending libraries, access to London and provincial newspapers, hosting touring theatrical companies and forming self-education groups. These were all probably essentially mid-to-late nineteenth century developments. Merely to recite the topics is to show what an open field there still is for the local historian of Whitchurch. There are people aplenty to identify, interactions to record and impacts to measure, sufficient to keep a small army at work for quite some time yet. If this current work provokes others to carry on historical investigations in new areas it will be worthwhile.

[9] *The Journals of John Wesley A.M.*, 4 vols. Everyman's Library .

Further reading

Very few earlier published works exploring topics related to aspects of this current book have Whitchurch as their focus. The following, taken together, make a significant contribution to a history of the town either by outlining the Tudor and Stuart centuries or filling out many details not previously made available.

Paul Anderton, *Exploring Whitchurch History: growth of*
 a Shropshire town (2009)
Jean North, Madge Moran & Joan Barton, *The Old Rectory,*
 Whitchurch, Shropshire (2007)
Madge Moran & Joan Barton, *Dearnford Hall* (2003)
Joan Barton, *A Millennium History of Whitchurch* (2000)
Madge Moran, *Vernacular Buildings of Whitchurch and Area*
 and their occupants (1999)
T.C.Duggan, *The History of Whitchurch* (1935)

Of the many books on the emergence of nonconformist congregations and Protestant dissent from the Church of England as established by Henry VIII and Queen Elizabeth the most apposite is
Margaret Spufford (editor), *The World of Rural Dissenters 1520-1725*
 (1995)

End Notes abbreviations

Shrop A	Shropshire Archives
LJRO	Lichfield Joint Record Office
Staffs CRO	Staffordshire County Record office
M. Moran, *Buildings*	Madge Moran, *Vernacular Buildings of Whitchurch and Area and their occupants* (1999)
ODNB	*Oxford Dictionary of National Biography* (2004-6) continued on line
Watts, *Shropshire Terriers*	Sylvia Watts, *The Glebe Terriers of Shropshire*, 2 vols. (Shropshire Record Series VI 2002)
Henry Diaries	M.H.Lee, *Diaries and Letters of Philip Henry MA 1631-1696*, (1882)
SPD	State Papers Domestic
Latham *Pepys Diary*	R. Latham & W. Matthews, *The Diary of Samuel Pepys*, (1976)

End Notes : Prologue

1 Whitchurch parish was not separately analysed in the official Religious Census Report as it was not policy to publish statistics parish by parish. The preferred unit was a Poor Law Union and Whitchurch parish was a Union in its own right.

End Notes : Chapter 1

2 Thomas Bilney (1495c – 1531). In August 1531 he was burned for heresy in Norwich after condemnation before Wolsey and others in 1527. He was released, only to be re-arrested and further pressured about his religious beliefs. He was a priest and Cambridge educated theologian, friend to Hugh Latimer and Matthew Parker, who preached throughout the Ely diocese after 1525 promulgating Lutheran opinions.

3 Tim Cooper, *The Last Generation of English Catholic Clergy*, (Boydell 1999) pages 140-43.

4 Sincere thanks go to Nigel Coulton who drew my attention to this case, provided me with a summary of the entry in the Bishop's Register and pointed out secondary literature setting it in context. In particular, this was to Tim Cooper, *The Last Generation of English Catholic Clergy*, (Boydell 1999) from page 140 to 143. The incident, however, had been reported by J.Fines in an article in *Transactions of Shropshire Archaeological Society*, 4th Series vol. LVII (Part II) 1962-3 issued April 1964 pages 166-168. Fines had seen Bishop Blythe's Register and quoted directly the Latin reference to Whitchurch, but placed no emphasis on this – "et maxime cum quodam Georgio Constantino in villa Whitchurch et Atcham". This account by Fines is a source used here for further details.

5 *Transactions of Shropshire Archaeolgical and Natural History Society*, 2nd Series 1888-9 for a copy of 'Lichfield Wills and Administrations 1516-1652' published by the British Record Society (1892).

6 M.A.Faraday, *The Lay Subsidy for Shropshire 1524-7*, Shropshire Record Series vol. 3 (1999) Centre for Local History Keele University ; see also John Wright, 'The Military Survey 1522' in *The Glaven Historian* No. 12, (2010), the Journal of the Blakeney Area Historical Society, quoting S.H.A.Hervey, 'Suffolk in 1524: Return for subsidy of 1523' in *Suffolk Green Books* (1910).

7 See Madge Moran, *Vernacular Buildings of Whitchurch and Area and their Occupants*, (1999), page 208, hereafter M.Moran, *Buildings*.

8 Tim Cooper, *Last English Catholic Clergy*.

9 Oxford Dictionary of National Biography (2004-2006 continued on line) entry by Anthony Hope, hereafter ODNB.

10 Constantine was named as a distributor of illegal books in 1527 by Robert Necton in a confession dated May or June 1528. He bought at least 16 copies of the New Testament in English from a London dealer, Mr Fish. See C.H.Williams, *William Tyndale*, (1969) pages 23-24.

11 John Foxe, *Book of Martyrs*, (1563 edition) Book 3, page 443.

12 Williams, *Tyndale* page 47 : also David Daniell, *William Tyndale: a biography*, (Yale 2001) page 178. Neither of these two authors knew of Constantine's earlier tour of north Shropshire in 1528, both taking him to be London or East Anglia based.

13 *Dictionary of National Biography*, vol 12, (1887),Thompson Cooper states that George Constantine was the author of '*Instructions for my Lord Privy Seale as towchinge the whole communication betwixt John Barlow, Deane of Westbury, Thomas Barlow, Prebendary there, clerkys, and George Constantine of Lawhaden, in their journey from Westbury unto Slebech in Sowthwales*' (1539), see *Archaeologia* xxiii, pages 56-78. Slebech is in Pembrokeshire. Constantine became vicar at Llawhaden in the 1540s after successfully making peace with the Established Church. He was not necessarily connected to this parish by origin just because he got the living there.

[14] The Constantine family had origins in Tushingham, Cheshire, holding a lordship there until the mid-thirteenth century. They may have had French ancestry in the Cotentin and be traceable back to Domesday Book, see G. Ormerod, *The History of the County Palatine and City of Chester,* vol. II pages 654-657.

[15] M.A.Faraday, *The Lay Subsidy for Shropshire 1524-7*, Shropshire Record Series vol. 3 (1999) Centre for Local History Keele University.

[16] Lichfield Joint Record Office, B/C/11 William Constantine 15 May 1544. Hereafter this office is noted as LJRO.

[17] Andrew Hope ODNB article on Constantine.

[18] see M. Moran, *Buildings*.

[19] Nigel Coulton's translation of Bishop Blythe's Register.

[20] J. Fines, *Shropshire Archaeological Society* 1962-3.

End Notes : Chapter 2

[21] This case has been investigated by Nigel Coulton who has very generously made his translations and researches available, and to whom sincere thanks are given. See LJRO B/C/2/1/f70v; /f75v; f88r. See also Tim Cooper, *Last English Catholic Clergy,* page 182.

[22] This summary translation was generously provided by Nigel Coulton.

[23] LJRO probate B/C/11 Margaret Bentley 6 May 1553.

[24] LJRO probate B/C/11 William Bentley 30 May 1554.

[25] This account relies heavily on Ernest Clarke, *A History of Whitchurch Grammar School 1550-1950,* (Sheffield University M.A. 1953) seen in Whitchurch Library. Hereafter Clarke *Grammar School.* On page 18 he quoted from Chapter Acts (Lincoln) to show the reasons Talbot gave for resigning as *"on account of the cure of souls committed to me, lest perchance through my absence or negligence the flock committed to me should seem to perish or err, and on account of my bodily ill-health, and the repairs in my benefices which I am bound to make, and other urgent and legitimate causes."*

[26] Clarke, *Grammar School,* page 12.

[27] Ibid., page 17.

[28] Ibid., page 13 quoting Lichfield Register (Sampson), 13/14,f.58.

[29] Quoted from Clarke's thesis by Joan M. Barton, *Whitchurch Schools 1550-1950,* (Whitchurch History and Archaeology Group, 1989, new edition 2001) page 3.

[30] M.Moran, *Buildings* page 210.

[31] Clarke, *Grammar School,* page 334.

[32] Jean North, Madge Moran and Joan Barton, *The Old Rectory, Whitchurch, Shropshire,* (2007) page 52. The other three were James Nitzens instituted 1571; Thomas Mawdesley DD, instituted 1585, and James Brookes instituted 1589 (or he was James Gourde alias Brookes, MA, of 1579).

[33] LJRO B/C/11 John Estwyke 5 May 1574.

End Notes : Chapter 3

[34] 5/6 Edward VI c 1. The second Act of Uniformity to pass through Parliament was the first to require attendance at church, ordering that *all ... persons .... shall diligently and faithfully having no lawful or reasonable excuse to be absent, endeavour themselves to resort to their parish church or chapel accustomed, or upon reasonable let thereof to some usual place where common prayer ..... shall be used ... and there to abide orderly and soberly during the time of common prayer ... upon pain of punishment by the censures of the church.* The Elizabethan Act 1559 added the financial penalties of 12 pence per Sunday absent to be collected by the churchwardens and used to relieve the destitute.

[35] Sylvia Watts, *The Glebe Terriers of Shropshire,* vol. II, (Shropshire Record Series VI 2002) page 164. Hereafter Watts, *Shropshire Terriers.*

[36] J. North, M. Moran and J. Barton, *The Old Rectory Whitchurch Shropshire*, (2007) page 52.

[37] Nicholas Tyacke, *The History of the University of Oxford* vol. IV *Seventeenth Century Oxford,* (1997) pages 184, 574-5.

[38] Watts, *Shropshire Terriers* page 163. Buckley does not come up on the Clergy Church of England database, but he signed the terrier in 1612. See http://www.theclergydatabase.org.uk/jsp/search/index.jsp

[39] ODNB http://www.oxforddnb.com/view/article/23191

[40] ODNB http://www.oxforddnb.com/view/article/23191

[41] J. North, M. Moran and J. Barton, *The Old Rectory Whitchurch Shropshire*, (2007) page 52: The Rector's Book (St Alkmund's, Whitchurch), loose paper, terrier 1849 listing benefactions. Bagshaw's *Directory 1851* page 346 states that this property became known as Alport's land, and that the money was handed out on St. Thomas's day. Rawlinson's will, drawn up on 29 January 1630/31, left £20 cash for the poor which must have been in addition to the charge on land left to Alport, an action registered in the manor court on 26 January 1630/31 according to the 1849 terrier. Rawlinson died on 3 February, having organised his bequests in a sequence when at death's door. He was also presumably in Whitchurch at the time, for he was buried there on 10 February.

[42] Madge Moran & Joan Barton, *Overton Hall: 'A Handsome House'*, (2000) page 4.

[43] John Rawlinson's will in PCC in TNA PROB 11/160.fol.47.

[44] Probate John Rawlinson in TNA, 1631 PROB 11/160 fol. 47.

[45] Clergy Church of England Database for date of Dudley's first appearance in Whitchurch.

[46] Shropshire Archives (hereafter Shrop A), Parish 303 microfiche card 258.

[47] Shrop A 6001/2743 and Parish 303 microfiche cards 256, 257, 258. Part of this account is based upon work done by Ernest Clarke, *Grammar School.*

[48] Shrop A 6001/2743 and Parish 303 microfiche cards 256, 257, 258. Part of this account is based upon work done by Ernest Clarke, *Grammar School.*

[49] Shrop A Parish 303 microfiche card 258. One of these burials was for the wife of Mr John Benyon for which he paid 3/4d.

End Notes : Chapter 4

[50] J. North, M. Moran and J. Barton, *The Old Rectory Whitchurch Shropshire*, (2007) page 53.

[51] H.Owen and J.B.Blakeway, *A History of Shrewsbury*, (1825) vol.1 page 417 quoting Peter Studley MA, minister of God's Word in Shrewsbury, '*The Looking-Glasse of Schism',* London 1635.

[52] Lambeth Palace Library, Court of Arches B 3/108, 2 December 1639.

[53] W Phillips, 'Ottley Papers relating to the Civil War' in *Transactions Shropshire Archaeological and Natural History Society,* 2nd series vol. VI (1894) page 34 quoted by E. Clarke, *History of Whitchurch Grammar School 1550-1950,* (University of Sheffield MA thesis 1953) page 58.

[54] *Letter Books of Sir William Brereton,* editor R.N. Dore, in *Record Society of Lancashire and Cheshire* vol. CXXIII (1984) Nos. 396 : 401. Dore confidently described this man as Rector of Whitchurch, though no other evidence is available to confirm Thomas Fowler as a Doctor of Divinity.

[55] This biographical account of Thomas Fowler, except where stated otherwise, is based upon Rev. G. Vane, 'Two Rectors of Whitchurch' in *Transactions Shropshire Archaeological and Natural History Society* vol. XII (1900). J. Hall, *History of town and parish of Nantwich,* (1883) page180 quoted Malbon's *Memorials* for 1 March 1645 for a list of persons brought from Shrewsbury to be imprisoned in Nantwich. They include a

"Doctor ffowler." Some moved to Manchester shortly after, and others were sent to Eccleshall Castle. On page 184 Hall quotes a list of all delinquents whose lands in Nantwich Hundred were sequestered. Among these was "Parson [Thomas] Fowler of Whitchurch, [Salop] ; noe order etc". In a footnote Hall states that Fowler was fined £130. [See Harl. M.S.2128] Possibly the property that Thomas Fowler held was a wich house, for on page 172 Hall quotes a Catalogue of Delinquents in Nantwich Hundred for whose lands Marc Folineux was responsible, where a "Mr Fowler" for "walling rents in Nantwich " paid £4-0-0. [See Harl. M.S. 2166] There is no other evidence to support this speculation.

56 David Hutchinson Smith, 'Two Rectors of Whitchurch', in *Newsletter* Whitchurch Archaeology and History Group No. 62 (1996). The inscription refers to Fowler as *"a man well renowned in the world of letters, a living model of piety, uprightness, gentleness and purity; a most obedient son of the English Church; a distinguished theologian; eloquent and determined; in short, a man notable for every kind of virtue. He was buffeted by many disasters, tossed here and there, when at last he had seen his country despoiled by brigands, and his noble king put to the axe by scoundrelly foes and the English Church almost destroyed; tired of life, he translated to the gods on the 27th February in 1652 AD."*

57 E. Clarke, *History of Whitchurch Grammar School 1550-1950,* page 70.

58 Eric Hopkins, 'The Bridgewater Estates in North Shropshire during the Civil War' in *Transactions Shropshire Archaeological and Natural History Society* vol. LVI Part III, (1960).

59 R.N.Dore, *Letter Books of Sir William Brereton,* vol.1 in *Record Society of Lancashire and Cheshire* vol. CXXIII (1984).

60 R.N.Dore, *Letter Books of Sir William Brereton,* vol.1 in *Record Society of Lancashire and Cheshire* vol. CXXIII (1984), items 183, 184.

61 Shrop A, P303/B/1/1/3.

End Notes : Chapter 5

62 The most useful outline of Porter's career can be found in Janice V. Cox, *The People of God: Shrewsbury Dissenters 1660-1699,* Shropshire Record Series 2 vols. (2006, Centre for Local History Keele University). This relies on A.G. Matthews, *Calamy Revised,* (1948) as well as on manuscript sources such as probate documents. R.N. Dore, *Letter Books of Sir William Brereton,* vol. 2 in *Record Society of Lancashire and Cheshire* vol. CXXIII (1984) page 545 for May 1642 refers to Porter in Chester.

63 For his lectureship at St.Lawrence see Paul S.Seaver, *The Puritan Lectureships: the politics of religious dissent 1560-1662,* (Stanford University Press 1970) page 50.

64 T. C. Duggan, *History of the Parish Church of Whitchurch,* (1935) page 28.

65 Shrop A, 665/3/61

66 J. Walker, *An attempt towards recovering an Account of the numbers and sufferings of the clergy of the Church of England,* (1714) I, page 89 : J.E. Auden, 'Ecclesiastical History of Shropshire during the Civil War, Commonwealth and Restoration' in *Transactions Shropshire Archaeological and Natural History Society,* 3rd series, vol. VII, (1907) page 263, both quoted in E Clarke, *History of Whitchurch Grammar School 1550-1950,* page 70-73, with Auden using a pamphlet in the Bodleian Library of 29 April 1647 as his source. See also Barbara Coulton, 'The Fourth Shropshire Presbyterian Classis 1647-62' in *Transactions Shropshire Archaeological and Historical Society* vol. LXXIII (1998) page 34. Coulton explains that there were six 'classes' in Shropshire, of which the one in which Porter served was the Fourth.

67 For Hotchkis see Shrop A, P303/F/2/4/1, and for Wittar see Shrops A, 212/Box 108, John Eddowes, Rental of freeholders, copyholders and fee farmers Manor of Whitchurch,

Dodington, Marbury and Lyniall 14 July 1667 (hereafter Eddowes Survey 1667) entry no. 160.

[68] J. Walker, *An attempt towards recovering an Account of the numbers and sufferings of the clergy of the Church of England*, (1714) I, page 89 : J.E. Auden, 'Ecclesiastical History of Shropshire during the Civil War, Commonwealth and Restoration' in *Transactions Shropshire Archaeological and Natural History Society*, 3rd series. vol. VII, (1907) page 263, both quoted in E Clarke, *History of Whitchurch Grammar School 1550-1950*, page 70-73 with Auden using a pamphlet in the Bodleian Library of 29 April 1647 as his source. Probate for the will of a Daniel Benyon of Ash, gentleman, was granted on 16 September 1670 (LJRO). He died possessed of wealth to the value of £234, about £150 of which was in cattle, corn and husbandry equipment. His will was worded in the simplest of terms and gave no clue as to his religious affiliation. He left a son, Daniel, and four unmarried daughters. A Daniel Benyon had property on Pool Dam listed by Eddowes in his Survey 1667, No. 46. William and Ralph Jackson were witnesses to the will alongside one who appeared to sign himself R. Dutton. A Joseph Wittar was an appraiser for the inventory of Randle Eddowes dated 25 March 1663 (LJRO probate date 1663 April 4). Ralph Eddowes, brother to Randle, married Sarah the daughter of John Hotchkis, both of whom were excommunicated for non-attendance at church in 1670.

[69] Shrop A, P303/B/1/1/3.

[70] E Clarke, *History of Whitchurch Grammar School 1550-1950*, page 78.

[71] For discussion of the significance of the 'Testimony' see Ann Hughes, *Gangraena and the struggle for the English Revolution*, (Oxford 2004) pages 368-79. For a copy online see http://www.covenanter.org/TestimonyBearing/Saloptestimony.htm. This latter reference was kindly supplied by Ian Bolton of Birmingham Library and Archives Services in advance of finding the Library's copy among Civil War pamphlets at History C/86.

[72] R. Parkinson (editor), *The Life of Adam Martindale, written by himself*, Chetham Society, 1st Series. vol. IV (1845). Martindale had developed a reputation for Calvinistic preaching around south Manchester from 1646 to the point where he was invited by a congregation at Rostherne to take up the benefice there. His memoirs of that time record the struggle he had to obtain full possession of the house and property against local opposition.

[73] The account of correspondence between Oliver Cromwell and the Earl of Bridgewater about Thomas Porter given by Antonia Fraser in her book *Cromwell Our Chief of Men* (1973) relies upon the papers held in the collections of the Duke of Bridgewater at Mertoun in Scotland. Unfortunately, she drew the wrong conclusion from them.

[74] *Dictionary of National Biography*, (1887) John Egerton, quoting State Papers Domestic 1651 page 162.

[75] Ellesmere Papers, Huntington Library. No.8044, quoted by Antonia Fraser, *Cromwell Our Chief of Men*, (1974) pages 491-93.

[76] Ellesmere Papers, Huntington Library, No. 8045, Fraser Ibid.

[77] Ellesmere Papers, Huntington Library, No. 8047, Fraser Ibid. Fraser stops the story at this point claiming that Cromwell's withdrawal of support left Bridgewater's man in place. Clearly this was not the case.

[78] *Transactions Shropshire Archaeological and Natural History Society*, vol. XLVII Part 1 (1933).

End Notes : Chapter 6

[79] J. Aubrey, *The Natural History of Wiltshire*, editor J. Britton (1847) quoted in Margaret Spufford, *The World of Rural Dissenters 1520-1725*, (1995) page 44.

[80] Spufford, *Rural Dissenters,* page 46 quoting F. J. M. Lloyd Thomas (editor), *The Autobiography of Richard Baxter,* (London 1931) : F. J. Powicke (editor), 'The Rev. Richard Baxter's Last Treatise' in *Bulletin of John Rylands Library,* 10 (1926) page184. Baxter was born in Shropshire and was minister at Kidderminster, a weaving town, for a long period before moving to London and becoming involved in the Savoy Conference 1661. He refused a bishopric from Charles II, and remained outside the Established Church. See also Tessa Watt, *Piety in the Pedlar's Pack; continuity and change 1578-1630,* quoted in Spufford, *Rural Dissenters,* page 235.

[81] Spufford, *Rural Dissenters,* page 48.

[82] Spufford, *Rural Dissenters,* page 48 quoting Horsfall Turner (editor), *Autobiography* page 84. See also R.C.Richardson, *Puritanism in North-West England,* (1972).

[83] Spufford, *Rural Dissenters,* page 49 quoting P. Edwards, 'The Horse Trade of Chester in sixteenth and seventeenth centuries' in *Journal of Chester Archaeological Society* 1962 (1979). Margaret Spufford makes a strong argument for the dissemination of religious reading matter and dissension via trade routes not only infecting towns, but also rural settlements, through a network of itinerant salesmen.

[84] Cambridge University Library copy of a calendar of the Ellesmere Papers in the Huntington Library microfilms 771- 772, item nos. 8538, 8539, 8540, 8541, 8542. More detail would be available if these documents were studied in the original.

[85] E. Clarke, *History of Whitchurch Grammar School 1550-1950,* page 70.

[86] Shrop A, *Quarter Session Orders 1638-1708 Abstract,* vols.1 & 2 pages 7-8. George Wittingham (sic) occupied property in Newtown according to Eddowes Survey 1667 No. 68.

[87] E. Clarke, *History of Whitchurch Grammar School 1550-1950,* page 79. Clarke quotes a High Ercoll School Master who was parish registrar as well, and the churchwarden's regulations which forbade the Registrar, or parish clerk, running a pub.

[88] John Hotchkis was a draper at Dodington who made his will in November 1657. He prefaced it with a rather more personal statement than most people : *"my assured hope is, that through the merits of Jesus Christ my blessed redeemer my soule and body shall at the last day be reunited, and eternally glorified in heaven."* He had four sons, John, Thomas, Samuel and Joshua, and four daughters, Susannah, Barbara, Sarah and Elizabeth. Hotchkis died in January 1666 and probate was granted 1665/6 March 15. (LJRO)

[89] E. Clarke, *History of Whitchurch Grammar School 1550-1950,* for brief biographies in an Appendix.

[90] Barbara Coulton, 'The Fourth Shropshire Presbyterian Classis 1647-62', in *Transactions Shropshire Archaeological Natural History Society,* vol LXXIII 1998 page 36 quoting Calamy and J. E. Auden.

[91] *A True and faithful Narrative (for substance) of a Publique Dispute between Mr Thos. Porter and Mr Hen. Haggar concerning Infant Baptism* ... Shrop A, Eyton Collection 665/3/52. A. G. Matthews identified Mr Haggar as a Baptist minister from Stafford. See A. G. Matthews, *Calamy Revised,* (1934: 1988).

[92] Barbara Coulton, 'Fourth Shropshire Presbyterian Classis' page 36.

[93] Ibid., quoting Auden.

[94] Ibid. Indeed, Baxter apparently recommended that Porter be considered for a bishopric in 1660 when refusing such a position for himself during negotiations with the new royalist government – see Coulton, 'Fourth Shropshire Presbyterian Classis' page 40.

[95] Ibid., page 36 on reading Thomas Porter, *Spiritual Salt,* (1651).

[96] A. G. Matthews, *Calamy Revised,* (1934: 1988).

[97] Quoted by Barbara Coulton 'Fourth Shropshire Presbyterian Classis' pages 38-9.

[98] Others ordained at the same time were Mr John Wilson, Mr David Jenks, Mr George Burraston and Mr Thomas Soley. The printed sermon can be found in the John Rylands Library as published in London 1656.

[99] W. Urwick, *Historical Sketches of Nonconformity in Cheshire,* (1864) page 150. quoting E. Calamy, *The Nonconformists' Memorial,* (1712 : 1775 edition edited by S. Palmer), revised by A. G. Matthews, *Calamy Revised,* (1934: 1988).

[100] Janice V. Cox, *The People of God: Shrewsbury Dissenters 1660-99.*

[101] A. G. Matthews, *Calamy Revised* (1934: 1988).

[102] R. F. Skinner, *Nonconformity in Shropshire 1662-1816, (1964)* page 18 for Porter's last sermon.

[103] Janice V. Cox ,*The People of God: Shrewsbury Dissenters 1660-99,* in Shropshire Record Series (2006 Centre for Local History Keele University).

[104] A. G. Matthews, *Calamy Revised,* (1934: 1988). See also Barbara Coulton 'Fourth Shropshire Presbyterian Classis' page 40.

[105] M. H. Lee, *Diaries and Letters of Philip Henry MA 1631-1696,* (1882) page 202 Hereafter *Henry Diaries.*

[106] Janice V. Cox, *The People of God: Shrewsbury Dissenters 1660-99,* in Shropshire Record Series (2006 Centre for Local History Keele University).

End Notes : Chapter 7

[107] The most readable introduction to Philip Henry is that by David Hayns, *Heavenly Henry: the life and times of Philip Henry 1631-96,* (1996). This section relies heavily on Hayns' research papers generously provided for study, and for which sincere thanks are given.

[108] *Henry Diaries* page 74 and quoted by W. Urwick, *Historical Sketches of Nonconformity in the County Palatine of Chester,* (1864) page 111.

[109] P. Crawford, 'Katherine and Philip Henry and their children: a case study in family ideology' in *Transactions of Historic Society of Lancashire and Cheshire,* vol. 134 (1984) pages 39-73.

[110] Ronald Hutton, *Charles II,* (1991) pages 210-11.

[111] David Hayns, *Heavenly Henry: the life and times of Philip Henry 1631-96,* (1996) page 19.

[112] *Henry Diaries* page 135.

[113] E.Calamy, *The Nonconformist Memorial* vol. 3 page 162.

[114] *Henry Diaries* page 136.

[115] *Henry Diaries* page 134.

[116] *Henry Diaries* page 176.

[117] *Henry Diaries* page177.

[118] *Henry Diaries* page 166.

[119] From an online source Open Church Network about churches in Wrexham area. Sir Thomas Hanmer is highly regarded in garden history circles for his book on gardening which is the focus of all biographical accounts. His religious outlook remains unexplored.

[120] *Henry Diaries* page 228. Philip Henry clearly kept an eye on Sir Thomas Hanmer. In June 1670 he noted that Sir Thomas was ill with a swelling between his neck and his shoulder, *"lord lay not his sin to his charge."*

[121] *Henry Diaries* page 189. Information for Thomas Tanat drawn from an unpublished essay (1997) analysing Malpas inventories for the 1660s by the late Gerrard Barnes.

[122] Hon. Rev. Gilbert Vane, 'Two Rectors of Whitchurch' in *Transactions Shropshire Archaeological and Natural History Society,* vol. XII (1900) page 295 for the full entry in Latin.

[123] LJRO probate B/C/11 Joshua Lee 7 April 1663.

[124]   Henry Diaries page 134.

[125]   This section on Fowler owes much to Hon. Rev. Gilbert Vane, 'Two Rectors of Whitchurch' in *Transactions of Shropshire Archaeological and Natural History Society,* vol. XII (1900).

[126]   Possibly this was the same Doolittle to whom Philip Henry sent his son Matthew in 1680 for tuition at the age of eighteen, see David Hayns, *Heavenly Henry,* page 22.

[127]   Vane, 'Two Rectors' page 293 reported Fowler as instituted as rector at Whitchurch by Bishop Hackett on 13 February 1667 having been instituted by the same bishop on 28 January 1664 to the rectory at Hinstock. Philip Henry reported Dr Fowler as arriving in April 1663 to replace Dr Heylin, see *Henry Diaries* page 134.

[128]   Probate papers for Francis Darlaston of Edgeley show that his executrix signed an oath before Matthew Fowler DD on 4 May 1663, see LJRO B/C/11, 4 May 1663. The Clergy Church of England Database notes that he was first appointed to be Rector at Willey in November 1660, rector at Hinstock near Market Drayton in January 1664 and rector at Whitchurch in February 1667. However, the local evidence is that he was in Whitchurch first as preacher and then as curate. See http://www.theclergydatabase.org.uk/jsp/search/index.jsp

[129]   *Henry Diaries* page 226 for Henry's reporting of the Act which he thought limited the attendance of strangers to four, whereas the Act actually stated five.

[130]   *Henry Diaries* page 226.

[131]   Vane, 'Two Rectors', page 296; *Henry Diaries* page 232.

[132]   There is no reference to this incident in the Consistory Court Records for the Lichfield diocese for 1669-70, for a search of which thanks are due to Nigel Coulton.

[133]   This quotation is from M. H. Lee, *Diaries and Letters of Philip Henry MA 1631-1696,* (1882) page 227.

[134]   Ibid., page 227.

[135]   Ibid., page 227. The fine of £5.00 as transcribed by M.H.Lee is puzzling as the penalty per adult for the first offence was five shillings.

[136]   Rev. Geoffrey Nuttall, 'The nurture of nonconformity: Philip Henry's diaries', in *Transactions of the Honourable Society of Cymmrodorion,* New Series vol. 4 (1998) page 15 - hereafter Nuttall, 'Nurture'

[137]   *Henry Diaries* page 227

[138]   *Henry Diaries* page 217 for death and burial of *"Uncle Benyon of Ash".*

[139]   *Henry Diaries* page 232

[140]   This paragraph relies upon R.F.Skinner, *Nonconformity in Shropshire 1662-1816,* (1964) pages 17-18 and a quotation from Lambeth Mss found in Lyon-Turner, I, pages 54-55 [presumed to be Professor G. Lyon Turner, *Original Records of Nonconformity under Persecution and Indulgence*]. Richard Greaves in his biography of Philip Henry in the Oxford Dictionary of National Biography states that there were four preachers to a congregation of 80.

[141]   ODNB article by C.D.Gilbert.

[142]   *Henry Diaries* page 232.

[143]   *Henry Diaries* page 236-7.

[144]   *Henry Diaries* page 209.

[145]   *Henry Diaries* page 232.

[146]   Ronald Hutton, *Charles II,* (Oxford 1991) page 284-5.

[147]   *Henry Diaries* page 250.

[148]   *Henry Diaries* page 250.

[149]   *Henry Diaries* pages 251-2.

[150]   *Henry Diaries* page 262.

[151] R.F.Skinner, *Nonconformity in Shropshire,* page 18 included John Smith as one of the men registering buildings, but an earlier listing, published by F.Bate, did not mention Smith. See F.Bate, *The Declaration of Indulgence 1672: a study in the rise of organised dissent,* (1908) Appendix VII.

End Notes Chapter 8

[152] Inventory only available LJRO B/C/11 Thomas Eddoes 1634/5 March 5.

[153] LJRO 25 March 1663 for will and inventory. A later reference to a Sarah Eddowes, widow of a Randle, however, claimed him as a tanner, see Shrop A, Mellington Deeds 1044/16, dated 2 February 1675/6. This causes confusion for the Randle or Randulph who died in 1663 made no mention of a wife or children in his will, making Ralph, his brother, executor and naming another brother William for a bequest.

[154] The clue is the name of Joshua Witter appearing in a pamphlet published in April 1647 which gave details of the creation of a Shropshire Classical Presbytery for which Thomas Porter, minister at Whitchurch, was eligible along with John Hotchkys and Joshua Witter also of Whitchurch. William Cotton of Bellaport and Daniel Benyon of Ash were among others similarly named, see E. Clarke, *History of Whitchurch Grammar School 1550-1950,* pages 70-73 quoting J. Walker, *An attempt towards recovering an Account of the numbers and sufferings of the clergy of the Church of England,* (1714) I, page 89, and J.E. Auden, 'Ecclesiastical History of Shropshire during the Civil War, Commonwealth and Restoration' in *Transactions Shropshire Archaeological and Natural History Society,* 3rd series vol. VII, (1907) page 263.

[155] See will of John Hotchkis LJRO B/C/11 1665/6 March 15.

[156] Nuttall, 'Nurture' page 16.

[157] Survey of Whitchurch Manor 1667 by John Eddowes, Shrop A, 212/Box 108.

[158] *Henry Diaries* page 188-9, *"An unhappy difference between Uncle Hotchkis and cosin Raph Eddow".*

[159] See Whitchurch Parish Register and Marbury Parish Register. Nuttall, 'Nurture' page 19 claims that this marriage of Martha Eddow was to Joseph Hanmer and was in 1659. He notes Joseph Hanmer as conforming, having earlier been curate at Whitewell chapel and later rector at Marchweil. Ralph Eddowes's third son, John (1656-1729), has been identified as matriculating at St. Edmund's Hall, Oxford, in 1672 and being awarded BA in 1675-6. He married Anne Jenkins and had five daughters. By a deed 11 November 1726 he and his second wife Alicia gave his house and property at Terrick House to his daughters. His will and inventory on his death 1729 noted him as of Terrick in the county of Salop. Joan Barton kindly provided notes from records seen in Shropshire Archives with this information. In addition, Henry's diary referred to a Sarah as daughter to Ralph Eddowes who had a connection with Chester.

[160] See J. Hall, *History of the town and parish of Nantwich,* (1883) using a pedigree of the Eddowes family of Nantwich found in British Museum Add. Mss 24,444f.106.

[161] Ibid., page 507

[162] Not to be confused with a John Eddowes who was an almost contemporary resident of Bridgenorth.

[163] The site of this house is almost certainly the one shown on a sketch map dated 1739, see Paul Anderton, *Exploring Whitchurch History* (2009) page 79.

[164] The National Archives E/170/255/21, f21v. *Henry Diaries* page 249 has a reference to a John Eddow going along with Joseph Mainwaring to start an academic career at Oxford with Henry wishing them well.

[165] From notes made on a copy of an Eddowes family tree suggesting that churchwardens' accounts may be the source, but the origin of the tree is lost, and the accounts do not appear to confirm this project.

[166] Cambridge University Library microfilm copy of a calendar of the Ellesmere Papers in the Huntington Library, microfilms 771 and 772 item nos. 8134, 8135, 8162.

[167] Shrop A, 212/Box 32 Index to Surrenders and Admissions : Box 425 for original surrender documents.

[168] This speculation and information from various surrender documents is based upon notes supplied by Joan Barton following work done by R.B.James.

[169] Rev. Geoffrey Nuttall, 'The nurturing of nonconformity: Philip Henry's diaries 'in *Transactions of the Honourable Society of Cymmrodorion*, New Series vol.4 (1998) page 6.

[170] Mary Beard's property was close to Pepper Street and next to a half-burgage plot occupied by John Maddox in 1659, see Shrop A, 103/1/4/130. She was a widow at the time.

[171] For Mr Lawrence at Nantwich see Edward J. Law, 'A chance discovery: genealogical and other extracts from the diary of Sarah Savage of Wrenbury Wood for the years 1688-95', in *Cheshire History* No. 50 (2010-2011) page 11. John Beard witnessed the will of Elizabeth Hotchkis in February 1675, probate 21 April 1675 in LJRO B/C/11.

[172] *Henry Diaries* page 130.

[173] J.Eddowes Survey 1667 in Shrop A, 212/Box108 and LJRO probate 16 January 1681-2.

[174] LJRO probate B/C/11 John Lovell 15 March 1665/6.

[175] LJRO probate B/C/11 Thomas Chetwood 1697 July 8.

[176] Lichfield Consistory Court Records, LJRO B/C/5/1676.

[177] *Henry Diaries* page 187. In March 1667 Henry noted the death of Robert Bickley, who drowned and was deeply in debt. See also LJRO probate Elizabeth Yardley 1676 September 23

[178] Nuttall, 'Nurture' page 16.

[179] 1667 Survey of Whitchurch manor drawn up by John Eddowes, Shrop A 212/Box 108. Two Kettles, John and William, were included as tenants on the Bridgewater estate in Dodington township on a map 1651 by William Fowler, see P.Anderton, *Exploring Whitchurch History: growth of a Shropshire town* (2009) page 48, and Shrop A, 212/Box 466/13. William Kettle of Alkington (LJRO probate B/C/11, 2 June 1665) was a husbandman who died worth £106-11-8, one appraiser being John Kettle.

[180] LJRO probate B/C/11, 18 July 1672.

[181] F. Bate, *The Declaration of Indulgence 1672,* (1908) Appendix VII, page xiv.

[182] *Henry Diaries* page 217.

[183] LJRO probate B/C/11, 16 September 1670.

[184] LJRO probate B/C/11 Robert Bennion 1691 October 2.

[185] *Henry Diaries* page 203 reports how Philip's son John got his name from John Benyon, his great grandfather. See also Sarah Lawrence, *The Descendents of Philip Henry MA,* (1844), page 58.

[186] *Henry Diaries* pages79-80.

[187] *Henry Diaries* pages 136, 139, 143.

[188] *Henry Diaries* page 172.

[189] *Henry Diaries* page 201. Rowland Hunt lived at Boreatton, married a daughter of Lord Paget, and was a friend of Henry. Here Henry consulted with Members of Parliament sympathetic to the Presbyterian cause, for example in 1670 with Richard Hampden and John Swynfen. In August 1680 he was the guest of Lord and Lady Paget at Boreatton, meeting MPs Philip Foley and John Swynfen, see ODNB for R. Greaves on Philip Henry.

[190] J. Foster, *Alumni Oxonienses 1500-1714,* (1887-92). Daniel's uncle, Joshua, matriculated at Oxford in 1634 and had his MA in 1640.

[191] *Henry Diaries* page 146. "*September 2 Cousin Butler call'd for ye hundred pounds which I owe him, also Mr Yates for £30. I am in strayts, but wayt upon God. September 3 I heard of £100 which I may have of Robert Benyon's brother*".

[192] Sarah Lawrence, *The Descendents of Philip Henry MA*, (1844), page 58. Joshua Benyon, son of John Benyon of Ash, gent, matriculated at Oxford in 1634 and had his MA in 1640 see J. Foster *Alumni Oxonienses 1500-1714*, (1887-92).

[193] *Salop Quarter Session Order Books 1638-1708*, vol. 1 & vol. 2, no date in Shrop A.

[194] Information from Helen Kerridge from family history research.

[195] *Henry Diaries* page 263.

[196] *Henry Diaries* pages 152, 180.

[197] *Henry Diaries* page 152.

[198] *Henry Diaries* pages 188-9.

[199] There is a problem here of too many men with the same name.

[200]   Clergy Church of England database http://www.theclergydatabase.org.uk/index.html : Parish Registers of Stanton Fitzwarren, confirmed by Wiltshire and Swindon Archives Service searches.

[201] This Samuel Hotchkis is presumed to be the one who married Martha Benyon, for Daniel Benyon noted Samuel as his brother-in-law in his will 1690. By that time Samuel Hotchkis was a citizen of London.

[202] LJRO probate B/C/11 John Hotchkis 1681 July 27.

[203] This Alice may be the one whose probate date is 1694 April 26 in LJRO. She was of Dodington.

[204] *Henry Diaries* page 116-117.

[205] Parish Registers of Stanton Fitzwarren, confirmed by Wiltshire and Swindon Archives Service searches.

[206] Clergy Church of England database http://www.theclergydatabase.org.uk/index.html : J. & J. A.Venn *Alumni Cantabrigienses: A Biographical List of All Known Students, Graduates and Holders of Office at the University of Cambridge, from the Earliest Times to 1900*, Part I, vol. II.

[207] Early English books STC II 1640-1700: Wiltshire and Swindon Archives 1762/1.

[208] *Henry Diaries* page 174.

[209] *Henry Diaries* pages 158-9.

[210] *Henry Diaries* page 174.

[211] *Henry Diaries* page 216.

[212] Biographical work on the Yates family on which this account is based was originally done by Joan Barton for whose efforts grateful thanks are due.

[213] LJRO probate B/C/11, 4 May 1709.

[214] This transfer was reported by Joan Barton without a reference on the basis of notes made by R.B.James.

[215] A story from Rev. G.E.Evans, *Whitchurch Long Ago*, (1893).

[216] *Henry Diaries* page 255.

[217] From manuscript Brief Books 1686-1723 seen in St. Alkmund's Church archives.

[218] *Henry Diaries* page 200.

[219] These references to the Yates children are owed to Joan Barton who used parish registers.

[220] Information from Joan Barton.

[221] F. Bate, *The Declaration of Indulgence 1672: a study in the rise of organised dissent*, (1908), Appendix VI page xlv. R.F.Skinner, *Nonconformity in Shropshire 1662-1876*, (Shrewsbury 1964) page 18 included the house of John Smith in his list, but this did not appear in Bate's list. John Smith was appointed executor of Elizabeth Yardley's will along

side Robert Bennion which may be a clue to Smith as a prominent member of the dissenting community.

[222] A. Whiteman (editor), *The Compton Census of 1676: a critical edition,* (1986).

End Notes Chapter 9

[223] Anne Whiteman, *The Compton Census 1676: a critical edition,* (1986).

[224] Elizabeth M. Halcrow (editor), *Sir Peter Leicester, Charges to the Grand Jury at Quarter Sessions 1660-77*, Chetham Society 3rd Series, vol. 5, 1953.

[225] *Henry Diaries* page 276.

[226] *Henry Diaries* page 279.

[227] *Henry Diaries* page 296.

[228] *Henry Diaries* page 298.

[229] *Henry Diaries* pages 307-309.

[230] The date on Matthew's memorial in St. Alkmund's Church is taken to be decided by the old calendar when January 1677 is January 1678 by the modern calendar.

[231] Ronald Hutton, *Charles II,* (Oxford paperback 1991) page 390. For more details see Robert Dunning, *The Monmouth Rebellion,* (1984).

[232] Ronald Hutton, *Charles II,* (Oxford paperback 1991) pages 390, 411.

[233] State Papers Domestic Car. II. 419, No. 171. Hereafter SPD with the number as given here in the printed version for 1682 with a page reference. The papers found in manuscript versions at The National Archives have an alternative number for recall purposes.

[234] SPD 419, No. 171 page 314.

[235] SPD 419, No. 171 page 313.

[236] SPD No. 420, No. 22 page 343.

[237] SPD Entry Book 68 page 124; page 371.

[238] SPD 420. No. 61 page 390.

[239] *Henry Diaries* page 317.

[240] SPD 420.No. 63 page 391.

[241] SPD 420. No. 73 page 398 dated 16 September.

[242] Rev. G.Vane 'Two Rectors', page 294. For the will see LJRO probate B/C/11 Matthew Fowler 1683/4 March 3, in which he noted two other nephews, Thomas Fowler and Walter Fowler, the latter of Penford with children.

[243] SPD 420, No. 83 page 409.

[244] SPD 420, No. 154 page 458.

[245] *Henry Diaries* 1684 January 3 page 322

[246] J. North, M. Moran, J. Barton, *The Old Rectory Whitchurch Shropshire,* (2007) page 54.

[247] Shrop A, 665/3/64.

[248] Rev. G.Vane 'Two Rectors', page 298.

[249] LJRO probate B/C/11 Matthew Fowler 1683/4 March 3.

End notes : Chapter 10

[250] Cheshire Record Office ZBASTEN/8.

[251] *Henry Diaries* page 340.

[252] *Henry Diaries* page 340.

[253] This account and quotations are from the *London Gazette* issues 2272, 2273 of 25 and 29 August 1687.

[254] A.Owen & J.B.Blakeway, *A History of Shrewsbury,* vol.1 (1825) pages 494-97. These authors also found that Richard Gough in his *History of Myddle* noted that a local woman was touched by James for the King's Evil at Shrewsbury, but it did her no good.

[255] *London Gazette* issues 2272, 2273 of 25 and 29 August 1687.

[256] From the diary of Sarah Savage quoted in Matthew Henry, *The Life of Rev. Philip Henry AM,* (1698; 1712) corrected and enlarged by J.B.Williams (1828) reprinted 1974 page 173.

[257] *London Gazette* 29 August 1687 issue no. 2273 page 2.

[258] *Henry Diaries* page 327.

[259] Churchwardens' Account 1688/9 in Shrop A, P303/1/1/4.

[260] Henry and Barbara van der Zee, *1688 Revolution in the Family,* (Penguin 1988) pages 68-70.

[261] Shrop A, P303/1/1/4.

End Notes : Chapter 11

[262] R.Latham & W. Matthews, *The Diary of Samuel Pepys* (1976) vol. ii, pages 219-20, 25 November 1661, hereafter Latham *Pepys Diary.*

[263] Latham *Pepys Diary* vol.i, page 67.

[264] Latham *Pepys Diary* vol. i pages 68-9, 25 and 26 February 1660.

[265] Latham *Pepys Diary* vol. ii page 136.

[266] Latham *Pepys Diary* vol. ii page 146.

[267] Latham *Pepys Diary* vol. ii page 225,1 Dec 1661.

[268] Latham *Pepys Diary* vol. ii page 226,1 Dec 1661.

[269] Latham *Pepys Diary* vol. iii page 58, 2 April 1662.

[270] Latham *Pepys Diary* vol. v page 135,27 April 1664.

[271] Latham *Pepys Diary* vol. viii page 17,16 January 1667.

[272] Latham *Pepys Diary* vol viii page 151, 5 April 1667.

[273] Latham *Pepys Diary* vol. viii page 167, 15 April 1667.

[274] Ancestry.co.uk London England baptisms, marriages and burials 1538-1812.

[275] See Ian Atherton, 'An early list of the registrations of Dissenters' meeting houses in late seventeenth century Staffordshire' in *Staffordshire Studies,* Vol. 11 (1999) pages 51-69.

[276] For a history of the rectory building see Jean North, Madge Moran and Joan Barton *The Old Rectory, Whitchurch, Shropshire,* (2007).

[277] For information on psalm singers I am grateful to Sally Drage.

[278] LJRO, B/C/5/1704 John Gill witness No. 20: also Clement Sankey. Francis Heatley said she had been employed by Mr Jenkes. There had been a curate of that name in the parish who paid into the French refugee charity in 1688. The papers in this cause bundle B/C/5/1704 are identified by a further number with the top paper as /123b. They are tightly folded into one another and not kept in strict sequence so witnesses are hereafter named and only numbered when the clerk to the court gave them a number.

[279] The first of his known curates presumably did not live in, for in January 1688 when a charity collection was made for French Protestants, Mr Jenkes, the curate, was married and had his wife's mother living with him, see Brief Books in parish collection held in St. Alkmund's. The bishop came in 1698-9 for the churchwardens had to spend £4-17-0 on his entertainment, see P303/B/1/1/4.

[280] Brief Books, Whitchurch parish collection held in St. Alkmund's, for January 1687 when money collected for payment to French Protestant refugees.

[281] John Sadler witness No. 11.

[282] Richard Newton witness No. 2.

[283] Samuel Grindley witness No. 9.

[284] Sarah Wickstead witness No. 12.

[285] Edward Wickstead witness No. 13.

[286] Thomas Wickstead witness No. 17.

287   Maudelin Owen witness No. 10.

288   Thomas Owen married Maudelin Griffiths on 16 November 1699 see Whitchurch Parish Register.

289   John Sadler witness No. 11.

290   Richard Maisterson witness No. 7.

291   Richard Newton witness No. 2.

292   Mary Edge witness No. 1.

293   Margaret Crawford witness No. 8.

294   LJRO, B/C/5/1699/117b and associated papers.

295   Edward Deaves witness No.4, Samuel Grindley witness No. 9 and Maudelin Owen witness No. 10.

296   Robert Comberbach, and Francis Heatley neither being numbered by the clerk to the court.

297   Clergy Church of England database online.

298   John Paine witness No. 21.

299   Elizabeth Pain wife of Ralph Pain, a carrier, witness No. 16. The Paynes were a family well known for being landlords in High Street inns, and since Elizabeth said that it was in her house that Jane and George met it is quite likely that this was one of the town's principal inns.

300   Andrew Cambers (edit), *The Life of John Rastrick 1650-1727*, (Cambridge University Press for The Royal Historical Society 2010, Camden 5th series, vol.36) pages 3-4, 94.

301   Francis Heatley B/C/5/1704/133.

302   Shrop A, 212/Box 32.

303   LJRO, B/C/5/1704/97.

304   LJRO, B/C/5/1705.

305   The National Archives, Prerogative Court of Canterbury PROB11/498 Clement Sankey 26 November 1707. Sankey had two nephews, John Eldridge, gent, of London and Humphrey Newbury, a clergyman. His two kinsmen who had bequests were Dr John Lawrence and Dr Samuel Sankey of Greys Inn, London.

306   Sylvia Watts, *The Glebe Terriers of Shropshire*, Part 2 (2002) in Shropshire Record Series vol.6 page164.

307   See J.North, M. Moran, J.Barton, *The Old Rectory Whitchurch Shropshire*, (2007) page 93 for Chapter 2, footnote 6, for a reference to a terrier 20 April 1669 copied into the Rector's Book and not listed by Sylvia Watts in *The Glebe Terriers of Shropshire*, (Shropshire Record Series VI 2002).

308   For more information see J.North, M. Moran, J.Barton *The Old Rectory Whitchurch Shropshire*, (2007) pages 49-50.

309   LJRO, B/C/5/1704/123b

End Notes : Chapter 12

310   *The Register of Dodington Presbyterian Chapel, Whitchurch 1708-1812*, Shropshire Parish Register Society (1903), Introduction.

311   This biography of Samuel Benion is taken from the published sermon preached at his funeral by Matthew Henry, Shrop A, 665/3/68 Eyton Collection

312   This marriage has been misread by others as between David Benion and Grace Yates. The source here is Matthew Henry's sermon at the funeral of Samuel Benion when he is hardly likely to have had Samuel's wife's parentage incorrect. The source of the error is a misreading of the signatures to the will of Thomas Yates (1709) when both David and Grace were witnesses, They had different spellings of their surnames, however.

313   Nuttall, 'Nurture' page 25.

314   Ibid., page 25.

[315] David Szechi, *Jacobitism and Tory Politics 1710-1714*, (1984) page 201.

[316] Clive Holmes, *The Trial of Dr Sacheverell*, (1973) is the principal source for this section.

[317] Quote from H. Owen & J. B. Blakeway, *History of Shrewsbury*, (1825) pages 501-3.

[318] H. Owen & J.B. Blakeway, *History of Shrewsbury*, (1825) pages 501-3 quoting '*A New Map of the Travels of Our High Church Apostle*', London 1710 price 2d, page 16.

[319] Clive Holmes, *The Trial of Dr Sacheverell*, (1973) pages 244-5.

[320] This account owes much to the careful researches by the late David Hutchinson Smith into the rebuilding of St. Alkmund's, and generously shared with an Adult Education Class run by the present author for the University of Keele.

[321] Information on Smith and Barker was collected from John Betjeman's *Collins Guide to Parish Churches in England and Wales* (1980), B.F.L.Clarke, *Church Builders of the Nineteenth Century*, (1938), H.M. Colvin *Dictionary of British Architects 1600-1840*, (1978). The most authoritative work on Smith and St. Alkmund's is Andor Gomme, *Francis Smith, architect and master builder*, (2000).

[322] Sheffield Archives, Papers of the Barker family of Bakewell.

[323] For papers in Shrop A consulted for this account see 212/1-6 and 212/Box 446.

[324] Nuttall, 'Nurture' page 25.

[325] The source for these figures is not known, but the 1713 printed Poll Book for Shropshire shows only 30 residents of the parish voting, and only one could remotely be linked to the nonconformist congregation, see Shrop A, c55.7.

[326] Rev. George Eyre Evans, *Whitchurch of Long Ago*, (1893) page 18.

[327] LJRO probate John Swanwick 15 April 1713.

[328] LJRO probate William Swanwick 15 April 1719.

[329] This set of family connections has been deduced from probate evidence and James Hall, *History of the town and parish of Nantwich*, (1883).

[330] LJRO, B/C/5/1716/12 –14. Probate date for Samuel 7 October 1713.

[331] Chester City Records: Apprentice Books

[332] A. Boyer, *A compleat and impartial history of the impeachment of the last ministry*, (1716) reproducing a letter dated 13 July 1715 from Richard Hines of Bilston to William Ward M.P. for Staffordshire, from which this is an extract. This letter was read to the House of Commons by Mr Bracebridge, M.P. for Tamworth, on 16 July.

[333] A.G.Matthews, *The Congregational Churches of Staffordshire*, (1924).

[334] Calendar of Treasury Papers CXCI (1714-19).

[335] W.P.W. Phillimore, *Nonconformist Registers*, Shropshire Parish Register Society (1903) as transcribed by Rev. George E. Evans.

[336] W.Matthews, *The Diary of Dudley Ryder 1715-16*, (1939) pages 40-41.

[337] W.Matthews, *The Diary of Dudley Ryder 1715-16*,(1939) pages 61-62.

[338] J.A.Y. Briggs, '1715 July: The burning of the Meeting House, Dissent and Faction in late Stuart Newcastle' in *North Staffordshire Journal of Field Studies*, vol.XIV (1974).

[339] Calendar of Treasury Books vol. XXXI. Part II. Jan-Dec 1717.

❖❖❖❖❖❖❖❖❖❖❖

Index

Boycott, Thomas 144
Bracebridge, Mr 156
Brackley, Viscount 39
Bradford North, Hundred of 46, 48, 50
Bradshaw, John 149
Breda 59
Brereton, Sir William 41, 42, 43–4
Bridgewater, Earls of see Egerton family
Bridgnorth 140
briefs 143, 147
Bristol 156
Brixham 107
Broad Oak
  Benyons in 81
  conventicles at 88
  Henry in 61, 63, 73, 82, 91
  meeting house 110, 137–9, 155, 157
Bromley, Mr 63
Brookes family 162
Broughall 162
Broughton, Lady 92
Bruce, Mr 56
Buckley, Anthony 30
Bunbury 58
burial fees 37
Burnet, Bishop 102
Bury, Edward 91
Butler, John 149
Buxton, 148

Calamy, Edmund 57
Cannock 141
Capper, Mary 81
Castle Well 78
Catholics 72, 89–92, 108–10, 1
  61–2
  freedom of worship for 100–1
census (1811) 8
Charles I, King 31, 40, 41, 43–4, 53
Charles II, King 59, 61, 71–2, 89–93, 101, 105
Charlton, Alan 23, 25
Chester
  bishops of 58, 104
  in Civil War 42, 43–4
  Consistory Court 118
  debtors of Samuel Eddowes from 154

Eddowes (Samuel) in 153
Henry in Castle 99–100
horse fairs 52
James II in 102, 104
Monmouth in 93, 96
Porter in 45
riots 96
Chetwood, Ann 79
Chetwood, Anna 64
Chetwood, John (brother of Thomas) 78
Chetwood, John (son of Thomas) 78
Chetwood, Thomas 64, 78
Chetwynd, Walter 94–6
Cholmondeley, Hugh, Earl of 144
Cholmondeley Hall 42, 147
Christide Book 37
Church, William 34
church attendance 27
church buildings
  construction 147, 160–1
  significance 6, 27–8
Church of England
  abolition 53
  restoration 56, 58, 59
Churchill, John, Duke of Marlborough 140
churchwardens
  accounts 32–4, 55, 106–8
  duties 34
  and Glorious Revolution 104–8
  income-raising 34, 36–7
  and Jane Haines case 123, 134
  period 1619–40 35
Civil Wars 41–4, 119
Clarke, Ernest 22, 42
Clibery, William 34
Clive, Mary 57
Clive, Robert 57
Clowes, Jacob 122, 125–6, 131–3
Colne Engaine 115
Comberbatch, Robert 144
communion, taking 64
Compton Survey 88
Condover 143
Congregationalists 163
Consistory Courts 9, 19, 117–33, 134–5, 136, 153
Constable, Sir William 44
Constantine, George 9–18, 19, 22
Constantine, Joan 17

Constantine, John 18
Constantine, Philip 17
Constantine, Thomas 12
Constantine, William (elder) 14,
    15–17, 18, 22
Constantine, William (younger)
    16, 17, 25, 162
Conventicle Act (1664) 60, 62
Conventicle Act (1670) 68
Corser family 162
Cotton, John 12, 17
Cotton, Katherine (neé Constantine)
    12
Cotton, Ralph 25
Cotton, Richard 10–11, 12, 14, 18,
    22
Cotton, Rowland 144
Cotton, Sir Robert 154
Cotton, Thomas 10, 12, 17, 18, 22,
    24–5
Cotton, William 46
Court of Arches 40
courts 117
    see also Consistory Courts
Coventry, Sir Henry 93
Coventry and Lichfield, bishops of
    67, 104, 117
Crawford, Margaret 127
Cresswell, Richard 140
crime 117
Cromwell, Oliver 46, 49–50
Cromwell, Thomas 17
cultural environment 8
curates 30
Cutler, Mr 119–22, 123–4,
    131

dairymen 51
Danford 154
Davies, Thomas 62
Daxon, Mr 154
Dearnford Hall 84, 85, 88, 155
Deaves, Edward 130, 134–5
Deaves, Eleanor 135
Declaration of Indulgence 71–2, 78,
    80
Defoe, Daniel 161
Derby 141, 147
Devonshire, Duke of 148
dissent, spread 51–2
dissenters

families of 75–88
freedom of worship 72–3,
    108–10
meeting houses 88, 110
Dod family 162
Dodington
    Constantines in 12, 16, 17
    Henry in 63, 88
    houses 155
    named residents of 46, 76, 78,
        83, 85, 150, 153
    Vestrie men 37
Dodington Chapel
    baptisms 149, 151–2, 153, 154
    destroyed 137, 157
    opened 139
    premises provided for 155
    rebuilt 159–60
    Unitarians in 162
Donegall, Earl of 144
Doolittle, Mr 66
Dorchester 28
Drayton see Market Drayton
Dudleston 56
Dudley, Arthur 32
Duffy, Eamon 28
Duggan, T. C. 46
Duncombe, Alexander 143, 144
Dunham Massey 94

Easter Dues 37
Easthope 161
Easton-in-Gordano 84
Eaton Constantine 51
Eddoes, Thomas 75
Eddowes, Anne (neé Mountford)
    153–4
Eddowes, Elizabeth (neé Nevett)
    153
Eddowes, John (son of Ralph) 76,
    78, 143, 153
Eddowes, John (son of Samuel)
    153
Eddowes, Joshua 84
Eddowes, Marie 76
Eddowes, Mary 77
Eddowes, Ralph 64, 67–9, 70–1,
    75–7, 79, 153
    and Henry 76
    home of 88
Eddowes, Ralph (brother of

Newport, Lord (1713) 158
Newton, Richard 124–6, 130
Newtown 78, 135
nonconformists 116, 139, 141, 162
  meeting houses destroyed 156–
    60
  see also dissenters; *specific*
    denominations
Norbury 20
'northern rebellion' 61
Norwich 156

Oates, Titus 90–1
Orton 91
Oswestry 141, 153, 158
Overseers of the Poor 34, 37
Overton Hall 31
Owen, Dr. John 84
Owen, Maudelin 123–4
Owen, Thomas 124
Oxford, Parliament in 91
Oxford, University of 30, 31
  college contributions to St.
    Alkmund's 147

Padye, Thomas 162
Paine, George 88
Paine, John 131–3
parish government 34–8
Parker, Lord Chief Justice 147
Parliamentary Committee for
  Plundered Ministers 46
Parry, John 149
parsonage repairs 40–1
Payne, widow 91
Pell, Robert 139
Pemberton, Mr 123, 124
Pemerton (high constable) 91
penance 20
Pendeford 39
Pepys, Samuel 90, 111–12,
  114–15
Poll Book 158
Pool Dam 78, 80, 81
Poole, Isaac 149
poor, bequests to 32
Popish Plot 90
Porter, Jabez 56
Porter, Mary 56
Porter, Samuel 56

Porter, Susanna (neé Clive) 57
Porter, Thomas
  arrival in Whitchurch 46–9
  at work in Whitchurch 51–8, 76
  early life 45–6
Porter, Thomas (son of rector) 56,
  58, 62
Prayer Book (1662) 60, 65
Prees 80, 88, 127
Presbyterian classis 45, 48, 55–6,
  60, 75–6
Presbyterians 45–6, 54–6, 108,
  148–9
  see also Dodington Chapel
Price, Susanna 130, 131
priesthood, educated 24
Protestant outlook 24
Protestant Reformation 11
psalms, singing of 119–20
Puleston family 56, 60
Puritanism 39–41, 51

Quakers 54

Ralph, Joseph 149
Ranshall, William 34
Rastrick, John 113, 134
rates *see* lewnes
Ravenshaw, Thomas 154
Rawlinson, Catherine 32, 40
Rawlinson, John 31–2, 36, 37–8,
  40
rectors of Whitchurch 25, 30, 111
Religious Census (1851) 7
Richardson, Joshua 87
Rider, Richard 119
Ridley, Nicholas 23
Riot Act 157
riots 96, 137, 139, 141, 156–7
Robertson, William 84
Robinson, Elizabeth 78
Robinson, John 64, 78
Robinson, Thomas 78
Rupert, Prince 44
Rutland, Duke of 148
Ryder, Douglas 157–8

Sacheverell, Dr Henry 141–2, 147,
  158

Swift, Dr 144
Swynnerton, 56
Symcocke, John 34
Symcockes, Samuel 48

Tabley Hall 89
Talbot family (Earls of Shrewsbury)
    22, 23
Talbot, George, 4th Earl of
Shrewsbury 23
Talbot, John 19, 22–6
Tamworth 156
Tanat, Mr (Thomas?) 63
Taylor, Benjamin 64, 67, 88
Terrick House 77
Test Acts 89, 101, 110, 141
Testimony 48
Tettenhall 148
theological disputes 39–40
Thomas, Zechariah 62, 66
Tilstock 69, 78, 88, 149, 150, 152
    chapels at 27, 56, 61, 66, 162
tithes 30, 135–6
Toleration Act (1689) 108–10, 111,
    137, 139
Tories
    in reign of Anne 140–1, 143, 148
    in reign of Charles II 90
    in reign of George I 156, 157–8
    in reign of William and Mary 108
Trentham 96, 97
Trentham Hall 147
Trychay, Christopher 28
Tunstall, Bishop 18
Turner, Adam 127–8, 130, 144
Tyndale, William 9, 10, 12, 13
Tyrconnel, Earl of 101

Underdown, David 28
Unitarians 162
Utrecht, Treaty of 141

Vane, Gilbert 98
Vaughan, Sir William 44
venereal disease 119, 122, 125–6,
    131, 133
Vernon, George 9–10, 19–22
Vestrie men 37

Wallasey races 94, 96
Walter, Lucy 92
Warrington 154
Warwickshire, riots in 156–7
Watson, William 149
weavers 51
Wellington 34
Welsh, Thomas 48
Wem
    in Civil War 42
    Exercise in 57
    Loyal Address 102
    riot damage repair 158
Wergs, The 148
Wesley, John 162, 164
Weston 91
Whigs
    in reign of Anne 140, 141, 142,
        158
    in reign of Charles II 90
    in reign of George I 156, 157–8
    in reign of James II 92, 94, 104
    in reign of William and Mary 108
Whitchurch
    population 8
    riot 137, 139, 157
    riot damage repair 160
Whitchurch Free Grammar School
    24–6, 52–3, 69, 164
Whitehall, John 143
Whitehall, Rowland 53
Whitewell 63, 73, 137
Whitfield, Richard 16
Whittingham, George 52–3
Whixall 85, 91, 131, 132, 138–9,
    155
Wickstead, Edward 122–3, 127,
    130, 131, 134
Wickstead, Sarah 122, 144
Wickstead, Thomas 122–3, 124,
    131
Wickstead's apothecary's shop 116
William III, King (William of Orange)
    99, 106–8, 140
Wirksworth 138
Wittar, Joseph 55, 75
Wittenburg 11
Witter, Joshua 46–7
Wolverhampton 156, 157
Worcester 101, 102
Worthenbury 56, 60, 61, 63, 81
Wrenbury Wood 99

Notes

Notes